POCKET
BOOKS

It
Takes a Village

*and other lessons
children teach us*

Hillary Rodham Clinton

POCKET
BOOKS

LONDON • SYDNEY • NEW YORK • TORONTO

This edition first published in Great Britain by Pocket Books, 2007
An imprint of Simon & Schuster UK Ltd
A CBS COMPANY

5 7 9 10 8 6 4

Simon & Schuster UK Ltd
Africa House
64-78 Kingsway
London WC2B 6AH

www.simonsays.co.uk

Simon & Schuster Australia
Sydney

A CIP catalogue record for this book is
available from the British Library

ISBN 978-1-84739-056-1

Printed and bound in Great Britain by
CPI Books (UK) Ltd, Croydon, CR0 4YY

MIX
Paper from
responsible sources
FSC
www.fsc.org
FSC® C020471

Contents

———

CONTENTS

For the family that raised me,

the family I joined,

and the family we made.

Of course we need children! Adults need children in their lives to listen to and care for, to keep their imagination fresh and their hearts young and to make the future a reality for which they are willing to work.

MARGARET MEAD

Introduction

When I wrote *It Takes a Village* ten years ago, I was living in the White House, three years into Bill's first term, doing my best to navigate the role of First Lady while continuing my life-long advocacy for women and children. Bill was preparing to run for a second term as president, and our daughter Chelsea, a lively teenager, was engaged with school, church, ballet, and friends. Now Chelsea is a woman with a career and a life of her own, and Bill is a private citizen who, through his foundation and the Clinton Global Initiative, is tackling some of the world's most urgent challenges. And I am a senator from New York, still working to improve the lives and opportunities of children, including efforts to strengthen national security and ensure economic growth, also crucial to raising a new generation.

Even though our lives have changed, we still rely on each other as a family. I once thought we couldn't possibly be any more time-challenged than when we lived in the White House—but I was wrong. Luckily, Chelsea lives and works in New York, so we all get to see each other frequently. My eighty-seven-year-old mother is still going strong and living with us. Bill and I make time on week-ends and holidays to see as many movies as possible, to take long walks, and continue the conversation we started thirty-five years ago. We all love eating together as much as ever, even if our kitchen table is often a booth at one of our favorite restaurants.

Now that Chelsea is grown up, I look back and see more clearly than ever how much we benefited from the village every step of the way—and how much better off she is for having not just two parents, but other caring adults in her corner. And I have yet to meet a parent who didn't feel the same way.

The African proverb "It takes a village to raise a child" summed up for me the commonsense conclusion that, like it or not, we are living in an interdependent world where what our children hear, see, feel, and learn will affect how they grow up and who they turn out to be. The five years since 9/11 have reinforced one of my main points: How children are raised anywhere can impact our lives and our children's futures.

At the core of this book is my own experience as a mother and my conviction that parents are the most important influences on the lives of their children. But decades of work on behalf of children have taught me that no family exists in a vacuum, many parents need support to become the best parents they can be, and sadly, not every child has a parent as a champion.

In this book and my autobiography, *Living History*, I wrote about my own mother's difficult childhood. Abandoned by her teenage parents, mistreated by her grandparents, she was forced to go to work as a mother's helper when she was thirteen years old. Caring for another family's younger children while attending high school may sound harsh, but the experience of living in a strong, loving family gave my mother the tools she would need later when caring for her own home and children.

Learning about my mother's childhood sparked my strong conviction that every child deserves a chance to live up to her God-given potential and that we should never quit on any child.

We all depend on other adults whom we know—from teachers to

doctors to neighbors to pastors—and on those whom we may not—from police to firefighters to employers to media producers to political leaders—to help us inform, support, or protect our children. In the last ten years, science has proven how resilient children can be despite great obstacles. And that's where other adults may step in, to help nurture children and to provide positive role models.

THIS SMALL BOOK with the bright, whimsical jacket provided endless opportunities for headline writers, who have come up with such variations as "It Takes a Village to Have a Parade!," "It Takes a Village to Build a Zero Waste Community," and, my all-time favorite, "It Takes a Village to Raise a Pig." More significantly, the book helped initiate conversations about how parents and the greater community—the village—all shape the lives of children. People took its message to heart. During my travels as First Lady, several people told me that their PTA had adopted "It takes a village" as a slogan to encourage more community involvement. At a children's hospital, I saw staff wearing buttons that said: "This is the village that takes care of children." I got off a plane in Asmara, Eritrea, on an official trip to Africa and was greeted by a large group of women with a colorful painted sign: YES, IT REALLY DOES TAKE A VILLAGE.

Today's electronic village has certainly complicated the always difficult challenge of parenting and raising the next generation. When *It Takes a Village* was published, the Internet was largely the province of scientists; no one owned an iPod or a PSP; and cell phones weighed as much as bricks. Innovations are now coming at an exponentially faster pace, and media saturates our kids' lives as never before. Many of these changes are for the good: when I was in college, a phone call home was rare and a flight home, a once-a-year luxury. Now I know traveling parents who see and speak to their kids every day by computer and video hookups, and I think how much

Bill would have loved that while he was campaigning, or how much joy that kind of contact would have given my parents, who didn't live nearby when Chelsea was born. But knowing that one-third of kids under six have televisions in their rooms, that the fashion industry is marketing its latest styles to preteen girls, and that predators stalk our children through the World Wide Web makes me thankful to have raised Chelsea in a less media-saturated time.

Young children as well as teenagers have phones, computers, and televisions in their rooms, and cell phones and iPods in their backpacks. These new technologies make it more difficult for parents to monitor what their children are watching or hearing, unless they're prepared to supervise every minute of computer time or listen to every song in the iPod. A decade of new research confirms that heavy exposure to violent and sexually explicit media triggers unhealthy responses from boys and girls alike, but we don't yet know the full effects of all this technology on our kids. CAMRA, the Children and Media Research Advancement Act, which I introduced in the Senate, would coordinate and fund new research into the effects of viewing and using electronic media, including television, computers, video games, and the Internet on children's cognitive, social, physical, and psychological development.

In the last decade, we've also learned much more about our children's earliest development. Scientists now say that the foundation for intelligence—and emotional development—comes very early on and above all from the steady, dependable love and attention of one or two key people. They confirm that at least some of the capacity to learn grows out of the capacity for emotional attachment. Our genes interact with the environment to make us who we are; nature and nurture work hand in hand in children's development.

We know that, across the board, parents want to spend more time with their kids: mothers are spending less time on themselves so they can be with their children more, and an increasing number of fathers say their families come first. Men under forty are more likely to say they would give up pay to spend time with their families. What's more, according to new research, the time married fathers spend caring for their children has doubled since 1965. This is a great change for the better.

Yet economic and time pressures throw up new obstacles to putting our families first. As family incomes stagnate, parents work longer hours to pay for the material things their kids need and to keep up with the rising cost of health care, education, housing, and other basic services. It is harder and harder for one parent to stay home during the early years—even for those who desperately want to. And as we learn more about the kind of intensive child care that gives our kids the best start, parents worry that their kids' care doesn't measure up. Our tax policies do not reflect the costs of raising children, which is why we should expand the child tax credit for the first year of a child's life to help parents stay home and give lower-income parents who receive government support for child care the option to use the subsidies to cover the costs of staying home and caring for their own children. And I want to see the Family and Medical Leave Act expanded so that all families who need it can use it without fear of losing their jobs. It is past time for our national politics to do more than just talk about family values. We need to value families by helping them raise resilient, productive children. Not just for their own sakes, but for all of us.

Two stark threats intrude on our children's daily lives much more than they did ten years ago. Even very young children today live with the fear of terrorism and the knowledge of war. I met with many of the families who were victims of 9/11, and their lives and the lives of millions were changed by the events of that day and what has followed. My generation—which grew up with the Cold War and Viet Nam—had hoped we would never face those fears again. When we think about what kind of world we're leaving our children, we need to consider actions that stop the spread of terror not only by strengthening our military and safeguarding our homeland, but also by leading with our values and developing our alliances with other countries and cultures.

Even more than adults, children are aware of the threats posed by global climate change, catastrophic environmental events, and the spread of deadly diseases that know no national boundaries. We can sustain our kids' future by investing in alternative energy: reducing the pollution that causes climate change, cleaning up the environment, creating new American jobs. But our ability to address these and other challenges is imperiled by a federal debt that has grown by $3 trillion in the last five years, placing a birth tax of $28,000 on the tiny shoulders of each child born today.

"It takes a village" has never had more meaning as a concept than it does today. Beyond assembling the local support team it takes to raise a child well, we need to come together globally to create conditions that provide all children everywhere hope and opportunity.

We have a lot on our plate. I'm asked all the time whether I get discouraged by what's been done to reverse much of the progress our country enjoyed at home and abroad during my husband's administrations. I say, sure, but not defeated. What is remarkable about kids—their resilience—is also remarkable about our country. I believe we can come back and provide the next generation with a future that is brighter and better still.

I have been in the Senate for nearly six years now, and I have learned a lot on the job, sometimes the hard way. I've come to understand that one of the most useful questions I can ask when I consider a Senate vote is this: Is it good for our children? We lawmakers can sometimes disagree about what is good for our children, but the question is still the best bipartisan litmus test there is. My alliances in the Senate on issues relating to children are some of my strongest and most surprising. But I also believe that if lawmakers and citizens asked that question more frequently when they voted, our children's futures would be safer and brighter.

WHEN I NEED inspiration, I still look to young people like Ruben Rafaelov from Queens, who, in the space of just a few months, raised more than a thousand dollars for tsunami relief and collected four hundred student signatures on a petition requesting more U.S. support for the fight against HIV/AIDS. Jelani Freeman, a former intern in my Senate office, lived in six different foster homes between the ages of eight and eighteen, but went on to get a master's degree and now works to bring opportunity to another generation of kids at risk. And there's Nicole Apollo, a model of tenacity and spirit in a very tough situation. Nicole's parents asked my Senate office to help them fight their insurance company to get Nicole the bone marrow transplant that might save her life. It was a successful battle, and when Nicole was in remission, her mother wrote to me: "It takes a village to cure a child of cancer."

One of my favorite chapters of *It Takes a Village* is the one titled "The Best Tool You Can Give a Child Is a Shovel." It is about giving our children the skills they need to overcome adversity and to "shovel their way out from under whatever life piles on." It's my father's metaphor. Whenever I got stuck, he would say, "Hillary, how are you going to dig yourself out of this one?" In the past five years, life has piled some serious challenges on this country, and we've also dug ourselves into some very big holes. Every citizen, regardless of political party, must become part of a renewed commitment to our children and to a brighter future for them. I believe Americans across the political spectrum want to do better, and I believe the idea of the village and its shared responsibility for our children is even more essential today than it was in 1996. There's no question in my mind that we can respond to these challenges and raise a generation that is strong, smart, and secure—in our own communities and internationally. In many ways, our kids already are leading us beyond our national borders into a more interconnected world, with their online access to everything and everybody, their rising interest in studying abroad and learning languages, and their natural curiosity.

For this anniversary edition of *It Takes a Village*, I have added a section of Notes (see p. 299) to update some studies and observations in the original text and have started a Web site to continue the conversation (www.ittakesavillagebook.com). New research in childhood development establishes that a child's environment affects everything from IQ to future behavior patterns. These studies confirm the importance of breast-feeding infants, of setting aside time for family meals, and of empowering parents to shield their children from predatory marketing and the violent and sexually explicit media that contribute to aggressive behavior, early sexual experimentation, obesity, and depression. The case for quality early childhood education and programs like Head Start is stronger than ever, and we should be expanding them. According to a study conducted by Federal Reserve economist Rob Grunewald and Nobel laureate economist James Heckman, high-quality preschool programs are among the most cost-effective public investments we make, lowering dependency and raising lifetime earnings.

The simple message of *It Takes a Village* is as relevant as ever: We are all in this together. As long as we face our challenges and never give up on our children, we can rebuild a world where justice and hope and peace can overcome the forces of terror and fear. We can restore our children's stake in the American Dream, and the promise that if you work hard and play by the rules, you can succeed in this country. But there is much work to do, and it will take every member of the village to get it done.

It Takes a Village

It Takes a Village

We cannot live for ourselves alone. Our lives are connected by a thousand invisible threads, and along these sympathetic fibers, our actions run as causes and return to us as results.

HERMAN MELVILLE

Children are not rugged individualists. They depend on the adults they know and on thousands more who make decisions every day that affect their well-being. All of us, whether we acknowledge it or not, are responsible for deciding whether our children are raised in a nation that doesn't just espouse family values but values families and children.

I have spent much of the past twenty-five years working to improve the lives of children. My work has taught me that they need more of our time, energy, and resources. But no experience brought home the lesson as vividly as becoming a mother myself.

When Chelsea Victoria Clinton lay in my arms for the first time, I was overwhelmed by the love and responsibility I felt for her. Despite all the books I had read, all the children I had studied and advocated for, nothing had prepared me for the sheer miracle of her being. For the first time, I understood the words of the writer Elizabeth Stone: "Making the decision to have a child—it's wondrous. It is to decide forever to have your heart go walking around outside your body."

Bill and I had wanted to start a family immediately after we married, in 1975, but we were not having much luck. In 1979, we scheduled an appointment to visit a fertility clinic right after a long-awaited vacation. Lo and behold, I got pregnant during that vacation. (I have often remarked to my husband that we might have had more children if we had taken more vacations!)

Bill was then governor of Arkansas, and my pregnancy was so widely discussed I thought the entire state might show up for the delivery. A lot of folks did, although, as far as I know, no one took pictures, or I'm sure you would have seen them by now. Friends gave us helpful hints about how they had handled pregnancy and parenting. One of my favorites, from a burly ex–football player, was: "Think of a baby like a football, and hold it tight." We read the advice books and asked endless questions of doctors, mid-wives, and nurses.

I persuaded Bill to attend Lamaze classes, where he and the other first-time fathers-to-be sat silently, arms crossed defensively over their chests, trying to look as if they were somewhere else. Our instructor asked how many of them had ever baby-sat or held an infant or, heaven forbid, bathed or changed one. A few mumbled, but hardly any hands went up. Then the teacher asked how many were scared to death of being responsible for a baby. Nervous laughter erupted, and many arms flagged in the air. After that you couldn't keep them quiet!

Despite all our preparation, when I went into labor, three weeks early, I wasn't ready. Governor Bill Clinton, Lamaze list in hand, rushed about trying to help me pack. One of the items on the list was a small plastic bag to be filled with ice for me to suck during labor. As I hobbled to the car, I saw someone loading a huge sack of ice into the trunk, and I remembered what a woman reportedly said as she was helped over the railing of the *Titanic:* "I rang for ice, but this is ridiculous!"

CHELSEA'S BIRTH transformed our lives, bringing us the greatest gift of joy—and humility—any parent could hope for. Like every child, Chelsea was her own person from the beginning. She arrived with a look of determination on her face that conveyed a focus and intensity we would come to know well. I prayed that I would be a good enough mother for her.

Every uncertainty and doubt I had was mixed with wonder and astonishment. I was beginning to discover for myself a timeless truth: Parenthood has the power to redefine every aspect of life— marriage, work, relationships with family and friends. Those helpless bundles of power and promise that come into our world show us our true selves—who we are, who we are not, who we wish we could be.

From the time I was a child myself, I loved being around children, looking into their faces or listening to the stories they told. Like many firstborn children, I learned to care for children by baby-sitting my two younger brothers. As a teenager, I baby-sat for other children too, and at thirteen I got my first "real" job, supervising children at a park on summer mornings. Through my church, I helped care for the children of migrant farmworkers while their parents labored in the fruit orchards and vegetable fields near my home.

In college, I tutored children, and later, in law school, I got permission to add an extra year to the regular curriculum to study child development. I wondered about children I passed on the streets, and I worried about their journeys to adulthood. As a law professor and a staff attorney at the Children's Defense Fund, as well as in my private practice, I saw firsthand the results of our failure to invest in children at the most critical stages of their lives.

Too often, the best interests of children seemed not to be a priority on either individual or national agendas. The consequences are there for any of us to see: children's potential lost to spirit-crushing poverty, children's health lost to unaffordable care, children's hearts lost in divorce and custody fights, children's futures lost in an overburdened foster care system, children's lives lost to abuse and violence, our society lost to itself as we fail our children.

And then I had a child of my own to love, wonder at, and worry about. Like most mothers, I am the designated worrier in our family. When Chelsea arrived, I went from worrying only five days a week to worrying on weekends too. My biggest challenge was to quell my longing to protect my daughter from everybody and everything that might hurt or disappoint her. As any parent knows, that is mission impossible. Life is unpredictable—and a child's impulse toward independence ultimately too powerful.

At four, my daughter refused my request to wear a sweater on what seemed to me an unusually chilly summer day. "I don't feel cold, Mommy," she said. "Maybe you do, but I have a different thermometer." Chelsea speaks up when she thinks I have exceeded the acceptable maternal worry quotient. But, like many parents, I feel there is much to worry about when it comes to raising children in America today.

Everywhere we look, children are under assault: from violence and neglect, from the breakup of families, from the temptations of alcohol, tobacco, sex, and drug abuse, from greed, materialism, and spiritual emptiness. These problems are not new, but in our time they have skyrocketed. Against this bleak backdrop, the struggle to raise strong children and to support families, emotionally as well as practically, has become more fierce. It is a struggle that has captured my heart, my mind, my life.

Parents bear the first and primary responsibility for their sons and daughters—to feed them, to sing them to sleep, to teach them to ride a bike, to encourage their talents, to help them develop spiritual lives, to make countless daily decisions that determine whom they have the potential to become. I was blessed with a hardworking father who put his family first and a mother who was devoted to me and my two younger brothers. But I was also blessed with caring neighbors, attentive doctors, challenging public schools, safe streets, and an economy that supported my father's job. Much of my family's good fortune was beyond my parents' direct control, but not beyond the control of other adults whose actions affected my life.

Children exist in the world as well as in the family. From the moment they are born, they depend on a host of other "grown-ups"—grandparents, neighbors, teachers, ministers, employers, political leaders, and untold others who touch their lives directly and indirectly. Adults police their streets, monitor the quality of their food, air, and water, produce the programs that appear on their televisions, run the businesses that employ their parents, and write the laws that protect them. Each of us plays a part in every child's life: It takes a village to raise a child.

I chose that old African proverb to title this book because it offers a timeless reminder that children will thrive only if their families thrive and if the whole of society cares enough to provide for them. Soon after I began writing, a friend sent me the cartoon on this page, which I think about every time I hear someone say that children are not the responsibility of anyone outside their family.

The sage who first offered that proverb would undoubtedly be bewildered by what constitutes the modern village. In earlier times and places—and until recently in our own culture—the "village" meant an actual geographic place where individuals and families lived and worked together. To many people the word still conjures up a road sign that reads, "Hometown U.S.A., pop. 5,340," followed by emblems of the local churches and civic clubs.

For most of us, though, the village doesn't look like that anymore. In fact, it's difficult to paint a picture of the modern village, so frantic and fragmented has much of our culture become. Extended families rarely live in the same town, let alone the same house. In many communities, crime and fear keep us behind locked doors. Where we used to chat with neighbors on stoops and porches, now we watch videos in our darkened living rooms. Instead of strolling down Main Street, we spend hours in automobiles and at anonymous shopping malls. We don't join civic associations, churches, unions, political parties, or even bowling leagues the way we used to.

The horizons of the contemporary village extend well beyond the town line. From the moment we are born, we are exposed to vast numbers of other people and influences through radio, television, newspapers, books, movies, computers, compact discs, cellular phones, and fax machines. Technology connects us to the impersonal global village it has created.

To many, this brave new world seems dehumanizing and inhospitable. It is not surprising, then, that there is a yearning for the "good old days" as a refuge from the problems of the present. But by turning away, we blind ourselves to the continuing, evolving presence of the village in our lives, and its critical importance for

Reprinted with special permission of King Features Syndicate.

how we live together. The village can no longer be defined as a place on a map, or a list of people or organizations, but its essence remains the same: it is the network of values and relationships that support and affect our lives.

One of the honors of being First Lady is the opportunity I have to go out into the world and to see what individuals and communities are doing to help themselves and their children. I have had the privilege of talking with mothers, fathers, grandparents, civic clubs, Scout troops, PTAs, and church groups. From these many conversations, I know Americans everywhere are searching for—and often finding—new ways to support one another.

Around the country, for example, neighborhoods organize to close down crack houses and protect children as they walk to school. Businesses adopt family-friendly policies, open child care centers, offer parent education and marriage counseling. Churches, synagogues, and other religious institutions expand their traditional activities to include everything from aerobics classes and recovery groups to intergenerational day care centers. Parent-teacher associations, once lagging in attendance, find new life in some school districts as the baby boomer generation flocks to back-to-school nights and volunteers time in the classroom. Even our technology offers us new ways of coming together, through radio talk shows, E-mail, and the Internet.

The networks of relationships we form and depend on are our modern-day villages, but they reach well beyond city limits. Many of them necessarily involve the whole nation. They are the basis for our "civil society," a term social scientists use to describe the way we work together for common purposes. Whether we harness their potential for the greater good or allow ourselves to drift into alienation and divisiveness depends on the choices we make now.

We cannot move forward by looking to the past for easy solutions. Even if a golden age had existed, we could not simply graft it onto today's busier, more impersonal and complicated world. Instead, our challenge is to arrive at a consensus of values and a common vision of what we can do today, individually and collectively, to build strong families and communities. Creating that consensus in a democracy depends on seriously considering other points of view, resisting the lure of extremist rhetoric, and balancing individual rights and freedoms with personal responsibility and mutual obligations.

The true test of the consensus we build is how well we care for our children. For a child, the village must remain personal. Talking to a baby while changing a diaper, playing airplane to entice a toddler to accept a spoonful of food, tossing a ball back and forth with a teenager, are tasks that cannot be carried out in cyberspace. They require the presence of caring adults who are dedicated to children's growth, nurturing, and well-being. What we do to participate in and support that network—from the way we care for our own children to the jobs we do, the causes we join, and the kinds of legislation we support—is mirrored every day in the experiences of America's children. We can read our national character most plainly in the result.

How well we care for our own and other people's children isn't only a question of morality; our self-interest is at stake too. No family is immune to the influences of the larger society. No matter what my husband and I do to protect and prepare Chelsea, her future will be affected by how other children are being raised. I don't want her to grow up in an America sharply divided by income, race, or religion. I'd like to minimize the odds of her suffering at the hands of someone who didn't have enough love or discipline, opportunity or responsibility, as a child. I want her to believe, as her father and I did, that the American Dream is within reach of anyone willing to work hard and take responsibility. I want her to live in an America that is still strong and promising to its own citizens and lives up to its image throughout the world as a land of hope and opportunity.

I do not pretend to know how to nurture and protect every American child so that each one fully reaches his or her God-given potential. But I do know that we are not doing enough of what works. As of this writing, one in five children in America live in poverty; ten million children do not have private or public health care coverage; homicide and suicide kill almost seven thousand children every year; one in four of all children are born to unmarried mothers, many of whom are children themselves; and 135,000 children bring guns to school each day. Children in every social stratum suffer from abuse, neglect, and preventable emotional problems.

Even though our national rhetoric proclaims that children are our most important resource, we squander these precious lives as though they do not matter. Children's issues are seen as "soft," the province of softhearted people (usually women) at the margins of the larger economic and social problems confronting our country. These issues are not soft. They are hard—the hardest issues we face. They are intimately connected to the very essence of who we are and who we will become. Whether or not you are a parent, what happens to America's children affects your present and your future.

I WRITE these words looking out through the windows in the White House at the city of Washington in all its beauty and squalor, promise and despair. In the shadow of great power, so many feel powerless. These contradictions color my feelings when I think about my own child and all our children. My worry for these children has increased, but remarkably, so has my hope for their future.

We know much more now than we did even a few years ago about how the human brain develops and what children need from their environments to develop character, empathy, and intelligence. When we put this knowledge into practice, the results are astonishing. Also, because when I read, travel, and talk with people around the world, it is increasingly clear to me that nearly every problem children face today has been solved somewhere, by someone. And finally, because I sense a new willingness on the part of many parents and citizens to turn down the decibel level on our political conflicts and start paying attention to what works.

There's an old saying I love: You can't roll up your sleeves and get to work if you're still wringing your hands. So if you, like me, are worrying about our kids; if you, like me, have wondered how we can match our actions to our words, I'd like to share with you some of the convictions I've developed over a lifetime—not only as an advocate and a citizen but as a mother, daughter, sister, and wife—about what our children need from us and what we owe to them.

This book is not a memoir; thankfully, that will have to wait. Nor is it a textbook or an encyclopedia; it is not meant to be. It is a statement of my personal views, a reflection of my continuing meditation on children. Whether or not you agree with me, I hope it promotes an honest conversation among us.

This, then, is an invitation to a journey we can take together, as parents and as citizens of this country, united in the belief that children are what matter—more than the size of our bank accounts or the kinds of cars we drive. As Jackie Kennedy Onassis said, "If you bungle raising your children, I don't think whatever else you do matters very much." That goes for each of us, whether or not we are parents—and for all of us, as a nation.

In the pages that follow, we will consider some of the implications of what is known about the emotional and cognitive development of children. We will explore both big and bite-sized ideas we can put to work in our homes, schools, hospitals, businesses, media, churches, and governments to do a better job raising our own children, even when the odds seem weighted against us. Above all, we will learn ways to come together as a village to support and strengthen one another's families and our own. Most of these lessons are simple, and some may seem self-evident. But it's apparent that many of us have yet to learn them or to apply them in our families and communities.

These lessons come from family, friends, and neighbors; from dedicated volunteers and professionals; and from the many men and women whose passion is to see the promise of children fulfilled. I wish I had the space to introduce more than a few of the many people whose determination to help children has touched me and to describe more than a fraction of the innovative ways in which our villages are working right now to improve the lives and futures of my child and all our children.

Some lessons come from countries I have had the opportunity to visit. The sight of baby carriages left unattended outside stores on the streets of Copenhagen said more to me about the safety of Danish babies than any research study could, and it made me long to know what the Danes and other cultures might teach us. As Eleanor Roosevelt said, "There is not one civilization, from the oldest to the very newest, from which we cannot learn."

Perhaps most important are the lessons I have learned from my daughter and her friends and from children all over the world. Children have many lessons to share with us—lessons about what they need, what makes them happy, how they view the world. If we listen, we'll be able to hear them. This book is about the first and best lesson they have taught me: "It takes a village to raise a child."

No Family Is an Island

Snowflakes are one of nature's most fragile things,
but just look what they can do when they stick together.

VERNA M. KELLY

I WANT YOU to know a little about my family, because my experiences, like everyone's, have informed my views. Whether or not we are parents, we were all once children, and that alone gives us opinions on the subject of raising them.

I grew up in a family that looked like it was straight out of the 1950s television sitcom *Father Knows Best*. Hugh Ellsworth Rodham, my father, was a self-sufficient, tough-minded small-businessman who ran a plant that screen-printed and sold drapery fabrics. He was the only employee, except when he enlisted my mother or us children or hired day labor. He worked hard and never encountered a serious financial setback. But like many who came of age during the Great Depression, he constantly worried that he might. "Do you want us to end up in the poorhouse?" was a familiar refrain.

He grew up in Scranton, Pennsylvania, as the middle of three boys, surrounded by a multitude of kinfolk on both sides of his

13

family. He attended Penn State, where he was a loyal member of the Delta Upsilon fraternity. He graduated with a degree in education in 1935. His first job after college was back home in Scranton, selling lace curtains, but he moved to Chicago when he was offered a better job, selling textiles throughout the Midwest.

One of our favorite pastimes as children was listening to him tell stories of his life "before you were born." We loved hearing how, as a boy, he would go down into the local coal mines to find mules who were blind from spending their lives underground and would lead them out into the sun. He also hopped freight trains and then jumped off as they rolled slowly along the countryside. One time, however, a train took off so quickly he wound up riding all the way to Binghamton, New York. A boy doing any of that today would be called "delinquent."

Another time, after he had hitched a ride on the back of an ice truck, he was rammed from behind, and his lower legs and feet were badly broken. He was taken to the hospital, where the doctors wanted to amputate both feet. His mother, a formidable woman, barricaded herself in his room, refusing to let anyone in until her brother-in-law, a country doctor, arrived. Then she ordered him to "save my sonny's legs." He did, and my father went on to have an active childhood and sports career, lettering in football in high school and college. Sometimes Mother knows best too!

After Pearl Harbor, my father joined the navy, became a chief petty officer, and trained recruits at Great Lakes Naval Base, north of Chicago. He and my mother, Dorothy Howell, were married in 1942 and lived first in apartments in Chicago, where I was born in 1947. After they had saved up enough cash, they bought a house in the city of Park Ridge. My father didn't believe in mortgages or credit, then or later.

By upbringing and conviction, my father was a devout

Methodist, who prayed kneeling by the side of his bed every night. He also was an old-fashioned Republican, who, until he met Bill Clinton, eagerly pulled the "R" lever in every voting booth he entered.

I saw my father as the emissary from our home to the outside world, a place he perceived as very competitive. He was determined to give me and my two younger brothers, Hugh and Tony, the life tools we needed to survive and thrive. That meant, among other things, paying higher property taxes to live in a suburb that supported the schools his children attended. It meant periodic object lessons like driving us down to skid row to see what became of people who, as he saw it, lacked the self-discipline and motivation to keep their lives on track. It also meant having high expectations and pushing us to meet them.

When I brought home straight A's from junior high, my father's only comment was, "Well, Hillary, that must be an easy school you go to." By raising the bar, he encouraged me to study even harder, and in fact, comments like that spurred me on. I realized later that this well-meaning motivational ploy could have had the opposite effect on a child of a different temperament than mine, who might have decided she could never live up to the expectations that had been set for her.

As it happened, my father's parenting tactics were harder on my brothers than on me, perhaps because they were boys. They idolized him, and he saw them as appropriate subjects for the training methods he had applied in the navy to prepare young men for combat. He was less certain of how to treat a daughter, beyond broadly encouraging me to do whatever I did as well as I could. He often told us, "When you work, work hard. When you play, play hard. And don't confuse the two."

My father was devoted to his own family and took us to visit them every August at Lake Winola, outside Scranton. We stayed at

15

my grandfather's cottage, which had neither hot water nor an indoor bath or shower. We kids didn't mind. We loved exploring the mountain in back of the cottage, fishing in the Susquehanna River, and swimming every day "to stay clean."

The whole clan, along with friends and neighbors who dropped by regularly, sat for hours on the front porch of the cottage, chatting and playing pinochle. Part of what I loved about those vacations was spending time with my grandfather, who had come to America from Durham County, England, as a young boy and had started working in the lace mills at eleven. He was proud of the high school diploma he had earned through correspondence courses, and of the gold watch he had received after working in the same place for fifty years. My grandmother died when I was quite young, but my grandfather, along with my great-aunts and great-uncles, steeped us in stories of the family's life in England and Wales. Those vacations were a big part of my childhood, not least because they provided some of the best times I ever had with my dad.

My father constantly reminded us how many advantages we had compared to his generation and to most people in the world. "You will never know how lucky you are" was a phrase I heard more times than I can count. He and the fathers of most of my friends were men who had paid their dues and then devoted their energies to giving their families the financial security they themselves had missed. If my friends and I were foolish enough to ask for extra pocket money or an advance on our allowance, we received the classic lecture about money not growing on trees or how they had walked miles to school through the snow. All of our fathers thought we had easy lives compared to theirs.

When the neighborhood fathers took us ice-skating on the Des Plaines River, they stood around the fire drinking hot toddies, trading stock market lore, and, yes, complaining about politicians. We may have rolled our eyes, but we learned a lot from watching and listening to them, even when they were not interacting with us directly. None of them could have explained what "quality time" was. They were just there for us—at dinner, on weekends, during holidays, as part of our daily lives. They were fulfilling the traditional paternal role, supporting the family financially, guiding us into the uncharted terrain of adulthood by toughening us up, scouting out dangers ahead, and preparing the way.

My mother assumed an equally traditional role, providing the unlimited affection and encouragement that smoothed our path and balanced the pressures my father imposed. She organized our daily lives and fed us with her devotion, imagination, and great spirit. She attended every school and sports event and cheered for us whether we scored or struck out. She taught Sunday school, helped out at our public school, and was there when we came home for lunch. She entertained our friends, took us to the library, and made sure we did our chores.

My mother loved learning and spent hours discussing our school projects and typing our papers. She had not had the money to attend college, although she later took college courses for credit. But during the hours I spent with her, I learned some of the most important lessons of my life—above all, what it means to have unconditional love and support.

My family, like every family I know of, was far from perfect. But however imperfect we were, as individuals and as a unit, we were bound together by a sense of commitment and security. My mother and father did what parents do best: They dedicated their time, energy, and money to their children and made sacrifices to give us a better life.

IN 1994, the Carnegie Corporation issued a comprehensive report, *Starting Points*, which details the conditions that are undermining the development of America's youngest citizens—its infants and toddlers. In the report, child development expert Dr. David Hamburg, the Carnegie Corporation's president, describes the ideal landscape in which to plant a child: an "intact, cohesive, nuclear family dependable under stress." That description calls to mind the family in which I grew up.

My parents also had a lot of help from the village in raising my brothers and me. Our community was a visible extension of our family. We were in and out of our friends' yards and houses constantly. We played softball, curb ball, and a form of tag called chase-and-run, and we staged elaborate team contests modeled on the Olympics, all under the watchful eyes of parents.

On summer nights, our parents sat together in one another's yards or on porches, chatting while we kids played. Sometimes a few of the fathers dressed up in sheets and told us ghost stories. We marched with our Scout troops or school groups or rode bikes in holiday parades through our town's small downtown, to a park where all the kids were given Popsicles.

Our relatives were a visible, daily part of the village as well. Grandparents, aunts, uncles, and cousins all pitched in if illness or some other misfortune strained the family. When my brother Tony had rheumatic fever at nine, he had to stay in bed for months, recuperating. Our grandfather came from Scranton and sat for hours at Tony's bedside, playing card games and reading aloud until he lost his voice.

There were plenty of other caring, responsible adults who did their best to see that all the children in the community were getting the attention they needed. From librarians to crossing guards to Scout leaders, adults looked out for us, made sure we had enough to do and a place to do it.

There was a consensus among adults that they needed to present a united front when dealing with children. Adult authority gave us both a structure to our lives and a target to rebel against. We knew what the rules were, even if we sometimes broke them.

Community resources were managed for the benefit of children. The land surrounding each school served as a park and playing field for kids all year round. The schools were open summer mornings for sports and arts-and-crafts programs run by teenagers.

The church was an important presence in our lives. My brothers and I went faithfully to Sunday school and were usually back at church at least once more during the week for youth group meetings, athletic competitions, potluck suppers, or play rehearsals.

Our church exposed us to the world beyond our all-white middle-class suburb. Sunday school teachers taught us that prejudice was wrong in the sight of God and explained that the reason God made so many different kinds of people was to enjoy their diverse beauties and gifts, like a garden's various fruits and flowers. Those simple but powerful lessons were reinforced by our youth minister, who took us to meet black and Hispanic teenagers in downtown Chicago for service and worship exchanges. He also arranged for a group of us to meet Dr. Martin Luther King, Jr., when he came to Chicago to speak.

Because my village was so secure, I had a hard time imagining what life was like for those in less fortunate circumstances. My church gave me concrete experiences that forced me to confront the reality of inequity and injustice. Without my knowing it at the time, my village was starting to expand. The stability of family life that I knew growing up was not limited to my privileged little pocket of the world, of course.

I've talked with my friend Marian Wright Edelman, president of the Children's Defense Fund, about her childhood in segregated Bennettsville, South Carolina, during the 1940s and 1950s. In her books *The Measure of Our Success* and *Guide My Feet*, she describes the web of relationships that her family sustained and was sustained by. Her father and mother not only raised five children and ran a church; they also took in foster children, tended the sick and elderly, and were leaders in the black community. Marian and her family encountered brutal instances of racism, but they had something much stronger to lean on: their religious faith and their commitment to one another. They were a strong family anchored in a village that supported them against the evil and injustice of the larger society.

For good or ill, our families and the environments in which we live are the backdrop against which we play out our entire lives. Families shape our futures; our early family experiences heavily influence, and to a degree determine, how we forever after think and behave. At the same time, our families are shaped by the forces at work in the larger society—and by the village, whether it is a suburb or a ghetto, in which the family lives. That is why it is important for us to try to understand the personal and social forces that formed our own families, and how they shaped—and continue to shape—both our lives and the village around us.

THOSE WHO urge a return to the values of the 1950s are yearning for the kind of family and neighborhood I grew up in and for the feelings of togetherness they engendered. The nostalgia merchants sell an appealing Norman Rockwell–like picture of American life half a century ago, one in which every household was made up of stable parents, two kids, a dog, and a cat who all lived in a house with a manicured lawn and a station wagon in the driveway. Life seemed simpler then, and our common values clearer.

I understand that nostalgia. I feel it myself when the world seems too much to take. There were many good things about our way of life back then. But in reality, our past was not so picture-perfect. Ask African-American children who grew up in a segregated society, or immigrants who struggled to survive in sweatshops and tenements, or women whose life choices were circumscribed and whose work was underpaid. Ask those who grew up in the picture-perfect houses about the secrets and desperation they sometimes concealed.

The longing we feel for "the way things used to be" obscures not only the reality of earlier times but the larger settings in which the family finds itself today, as it struggles with the effects of broken homes, discrimination, economic downturns, urbanization, consumerism, and technology. Whenever someone bemoans the loss of "family values," I think about the changes that began when I was a child in the 1950s which have dramatically altered the way we live, much as the automobile reshaped the lives of an earlier generation.

Nobody predicted the magnitude of the changes, good and bad, that the technological revolution would bring. The advent of television is the most obvious instance. We got our first set in 1951. It was a fascinating novelty, and my father complained that we would watch television all day, starting with 6:00 A.M. mass for shut-ins, if he would let us. But television was not nearly the presence in families' lives or the influence on their values that it has become.

Another big innovation was fast-food restaurants. We lived near the very first McDonald's franchise in America, in Des Plaines, Illinois. I can remember how the sign announcing the number of hamburgers sold was changed from week to week. But most of us still ate dinner at home, at the same time every night, facing each other at the table and "minding our manners." Going out to eat— even for a hamburger—was a special, memorable occasion. Today I know adults so busy with their jobs that they cannot tell you the last time they had a family meal that included their kids—and excluded the television set.

Starting in the 1950s, we also began to move around more.

When President Eisenhower championed the country's massive federal highway system and airport-building program for national defense reasons, few people imagined how those roads and airports would come to influence family life. I took my first plane ride when I was in high school; my nephews flew across the country as infants.

New roads permitted more people to commute to work in cities from suburbs like mine and to settle even farther away. The construction of highways broke up some existing neighborhoods and sapped the economic life of others. Daily visits with cousins and grandparents became rarer as businesses began transferring workers all over the country. We were among the lucky who could choose to sink roots and stay in one place.

Advances in telecommunications were just starting then too. The houses in my neighborhood typically had one phone downstairs and one upstairs, with only one line. Children had to limit their time on the phone and use it in a public part of the house. We were not slaves to our phones; if someone called and we were out, they would call back if it was important. No one had an answering machine. And there were no cellular phones to interrupt what we were doing or to distract us from those around us.

In many ways, families like mine had the best of both worlds—the prosperity generated by new technology and mass production, without the conflicts and anxiety these developments inflicted on households and individuals within a few decades. We could attain a comfortable standard of living on a single income, typically the father's. Even with a limited education, people could find work and expect to keep it until retirement, without worrying about being rendered obsolete by automation or information technology. A third of the work force belonged to unions, and the gap between what workers and their managers were paid seemed like a fordable stream.

Most of all, we felt that we were part of the same enterprise. It may have been the cold war that brought us together, but together was how we felt. When President Eisenhower urged us to study more math and science after the Soviet Sputnik was launched, we believed that our President and our country needed us to do that. President Kennedy's call to public service inspired many of us too. We were not subjected to a daily diet of second-guessing and cynicism about the motives and actions of every leader and institution.

It is difficult, for those of us who grew up in an era that appeared to embody so many ideals people yearn for now, to acknowledge that it unwittingly set in motion the very forces that sometimes make us feel isolated within our own households and communities today. So alienated do we feel from the larger society at times that we cannot imagine the village existing in any form anymore. But each era gives birth to the village of the next generation.

Like our families, the culture we inherit is a product largely of events and decisions we had little hand in choosing. Not that the culture is our destiny, any more than the family is: families have thrived in the harshest conditions, and individuals have survived in the harshest families. But the society is our context; we do not exist in a vacuum. Even now, in ways we cannot yet feel or recognize, the village in which our children will raise their children is taking shape. It is up to us to think carefully about what kind of legacy we want to leave them.

Every Child
Needs a Champion

---

*If I could say just one thing to parents, it would be simply
that a child needs someone who believes in him
no matter what he does.*

ALICE KELIHER

MOST OF the people I knew growing up had families remarkably like mine. I did not have a single close friend, from kindergarten through high school, whose parents were divorced. But there was someone I knew very well who was the child of divorce: my mother.

My mother was born in Chicago in 1919, when her mother was only fifteen and her father just seventeen. A sister followed five years later, but both parents were too young for the responsibilities of raising children, and they decided they no longer wished to be married. When my mother was only eight years old and her sister barely three, her father sent them alone by train to Los Angeles to live with his parents, who were immigrants from England.

When my mother first told me how she cared for her sister during the three-day journey, I was incredulous. After I became a mother myself, I was furious that any child, even in the safer 1920s, would be treated like that.

To this day, my mother paints a vivid picture of living in southern California seventy years ago. She describes the smells of the orange groves she walked through on the way to school and the excitement of taking a streetcar to the beach. But these carefree memories were shrouded in harshness. Her grandmother was a severe and arbitrary disciplinarian who berated her constantly, and her grandfather all but ignored her. Her father was an infrequent visitor, and her mother vanished from her life for ten years.

Yet my mother was not without allies and a "village" to support her. A kind teacher noticed that she was often without milk money and bought an extra carton of milk every day, which she gave my mother, claiming she herself was too full to drink it. A great-aunt, Belle, gave my mother gifts and from time to time intervened to protect her from her grandmother's ridicule and rigidities.

When she was fourteen, my mother moved out of her grandparents' home and went to work taking care of a family's children in exchange for room and board. The position enabled her to attend high school, but not to participate in after-school activities. Every morning, she was up very early to prepare breakfast for the children, and every night she stayed up long after they had gone to sleep, to do her homework. The family appreciated her way with children, saw her true worth, and encouraged her to finish high school. The mother, a college graduate, gave her books to read, challenged her mind, and emphasized how important it was to get a good education. She also provided a role model of what a wife, mother, and homemaker could be.

How I wish I could have met Aunt Belle and the woman who employed my mother. I would tell them of my gratitude for the nurturance and encouragement that helped my mother overcome the distrust and disappointment she met with in her own family.

They healed her of what could have been lifelong wounds. And yet, to a great extent, my mother's character took shape in response to the hardships she experienced in her early years. From those challenges came her strong sense of social justice and her respect for all people, regardless of status or background. From them, too, came her passion for learning, and for the joy that knowledge brings.

After high school, my mother moved back to Chicago and took a series of secretarial jobs. At one of them, she met and began dating my father. While my father was in the navy, my mother continued working. When the war ended, my father started his own business. My mother helped him with his work and raised the three of us.

I found myself thinking about my mother's story when I first met my husband at law school, in 1971. Like her, Bill had grown up in circumstances that were less than ideal. His mother, the late Virginia Kelley, one of the great originals of our time, grew up in Hope, Arkansas, as an only child. After high school, she studied nursing, and during the war she met Bill's father, William Blythe of Texas. They were married in September 1943, just before he left for the battlefields of Europe.

When he got back, in 1945, he and Virginia moved to Chicago. I've often wondered whether Virginia Kelley and my mother might have crossed paths there, perhaps while standing in line at Marshall Field's big department store downtown.

Virginia became pregnant and went back to Hope to be among family and friends for her baby's birth. Her husband planned to join her as soon as he got their new apartment ready. He left Chicago to drive to Arkansas, and on the dark, rainy night of May 17, 1946, he had a fatal car crash outside Sikeston, Missouri.

Virginia, although devastated by the loss of her husband, was determined to do her best to provide for her baby. William Jefferson Blythe arrived three months later, on August 19, the birthday of

Virginia's father, James Eldridge Cassidy. Virginia and he went home from the hospital to live with her parents, who shared responsibility for raising him during his first six years. Despite their differences, Virginia and her strong-willed mother, Edith Valeria Grisham Cassidy, were united in one thing—their devotion to Bill.

Wanting to provide a better life for her child, Virginia left Hope to attend a program in New Orleans that would grant her a nurse-anesthetist's degree. That meant leaving Bill in the care of her parents for a year. Virginia often said that being away from her son almost killed her. One of Bill's earliest memories was taking the train with his grandmother to visit Virginia for the weekend. As they were leaving on Sunday, he remembers seeing his mother drop to her knees, crying, by the side of the tracks.

Bill's family were people of modest means, but they understood how important a child's early years were for his development—intellectually, socially, and emotionally. His grandmother, who had earned a degree in nursing by taking correspondence courses, quizzed him on his numbers, using playing cards taped around his high chair. She read aloud to him every day and encouraged him to learn to read before he started kindergarten.

His grandfather, who had only finished grade school, spent lots of time with Bill, taking him along on errands and to the little grocery store he ran, always stopping to visit with friends along the way. Bill surely owes much of his gregarious nature to those early days of chatting his way through town.

Although I never met Bill's grandparents, I know that their profound and engaging love for him helped to fill the hole left by the father he never knew and to protect against the pain he would later face.

Bill's life changed dramatically when he was four. Virginia married Roger Clinton, a local car dealer, and they moved into their own small house in Hope. Almost from the beginning, the marriage was anything but hopeful. Roger had a tendency to drink too much, becoming a mean and bullying drunk. The story of the abuse and violence Virginia suffered at his hands is told in her warm and funny autobiography, *Leading with My Heart*.

I asked Virginia once why she stayed married to Roger. She explained that she was raised to believe marriage was for life and divorce was wrong. And, she added, most of the time—when he wasn't drunk—Roger could be sweet and a lot of fun. Even so, she did divorce him in 1962, when his alcoholic rages became too much for her to bear. But three months later, feeling sorry for him and believing his promises to change his ways, she remarried him, against Bill's advice. Bill, now larger than his stepfather, warned Roger in no uncertain terms never to hit or threaten his mother again.

Roger and Virginia had moved to the larger town of Hot Springs, Arkansas, when Bill was seven. Although Virginia could no longer call on her parents for daily help and felt uncomfortable relying on Roger, there was a clan of Clinton uncles, aunts, and cousins who provided family support for Bill through the years. Virginia also hired a neighbor, Mrs. Walters, to help care for Bill and, later, his brother, Roger, while she was at work. Even with a full-time job and the ongoing tensions in her marriage, Virginia saw to it that their home became a haven for neighborhood kids, who gathered after school to shoot baskets, play music or cards, or just talk. When she got home from work, she joined right in.

Because Bill was old enough to distance himself, physically and emotionally, from his stepfather's behavior, he was able to weather the tensions of his home life. He also developed relationships with other adults. Some doctors his mother worked with took a special interest in him and spent time counseling him. The teachers and band directors he studied under encouraged his academic and musical talents. And no matter how hard times were, his mother got up every morning to do her job and set an example of self-discipline and resilience that spoke louder than words.

The human family assumes many forms and always has. The Clinton household didn't fit the conventional model. But it would be presumptuous of anyone to say it was not a legitimate family or that it lacked "family values." Bill never doubted that his mother and the other adults in his life supported him with all their hearts. His family had its problems. So did mine, and, I imagine, yours. But as psychologist Urie Bronfenbrenner reminds us, "The one most important thing kids need to help them survive in this world is someone who's crazy about them." Bill and I were both fortunate to have that.

That kind of love can make up for a lot, but it can't remedy everything. Virginia loved her second son, Roger junior, who was born in 1957, every bit as deeply as she loved Bill. But as much as she loved him, she could not shield him from the worsening effects of his father's chronic alcoholism. The problems he experienced growing up were typical of the difficulties children undergo when the structure of the family is unstable, either within a two-parent family or because of divorce.

There is no set formula for parenting success. Many single-parent, stepparent, and "blended" families do a fine job raising children. But in general their task is harder. And these days parents are less likely to have readily available support from extended family or a close-knit community. There are fewer Aunt Belles, grandparents, and other relatives close by, and many of us no longer feel free to ask a neighbor to lend a hand or an ear.

The instability of American households poses great risks to the healthy development of children. The divorce rate has been falling slowly, but for a high proportion of marriages, "till death do us part" means "until the going gets rough." And there has been an explosion in the number of children born out of wedlock, from one in twenty in 1960 to one in four today.

More than anyone else, children bear the brunt of such massive social transitions. The confusion and turmoil that divorce and out-of-wedlock births cause in children's lives is well documented. The results of the National Survey of Children, which followed the lives of a group of seven- to eleven-year-olds for more than a decade, and other recent studies demonstrate convincingly that while many adults claim to have benefited from divorce and single parenthood, most children have not.

Children living with one parent or in stepfamilies are two to three times as likely to have emotional and behavioral problems as children living in two-parent families. Children of single-parent families are more likely to drop out of high school, become pregnant as teenagers, abuse drugs, behave violently, become entangled with the law. A parent's remarriage often does not seem to better the odds.

Further, the rise in divorce and out-of-wedlock births has contributed heavily to the tragic increase in the number of American children in poverty, currently one in five. And while divorce often improves the economic condition of men, who are rarely awarded custody, it nearly always results in a decline in the standard of living for the custodial parent—generally the mother—and the children.

The disappearance of fathers from children's daily lives, because of out-of-wedlock births and divorce, has other, less tangible consequences. Girls are more likely to respond with depression and inhibited behavior, whereas boys are more likely to drop out of school and to have academic or behavioral problems. As Senator Daniel Patrick Moynihan warned more than thirty years ago, the absence of fathers in the lives of children—especially boys—leads to increased rates of violence and aggressiveness, as well as a general loss of the civilizing influence marriage and responsible parenthood historically provide any society.

A child's prayer is used as the logo for the Children's Defense Fund: "Dear Lord, be good to me. The sea is so wide and my boat is so small." Children without fathers, or whose parents float in and out of their lives after divorce, are the most precarious little boats in the most turbulent seas.

Many who protest loudly against welfare, gay rights, and other perceived threats to "family values" have been uncharacteristically silent about divorce. One does not have to agree with all the remarks of former Secretary of Education William Bennett to welcome his acknowledgment before the Christian Coalition that divorce is hard on children: "In terms of damage to the children of America, you cannot compare what the homosexual movement . . . has done to what divorce has done to this society. In terms of the consequences to children, it is not even close."

Perhaps the most compelling evidence comes from the mouths of children themselves. I recently received a letter from a fifteen-year-old boy in Louisiana whose parents had divorced. "I've come to distrust you adults and the legal system in this country," he wrote. "It seems to me that you adults do a lot of talking and nothing more." He went on to describe what the breakup is doing to his family, as a unit and as individuals. "I try hard not to become an angry, bitter young man towards my father and the system," he told me. "But it is not fair to me or my mom that she has to be both mother and father to me and my little brother. It makes no sense to me." It should make no sense to any of us.

MY PERSONAL wish, that every child have an intact, dependable family, will likely remain a wish. But there is much we can do to encourage and strengthen marriages and to provide adequate support for children of divorced and single parents. Here are a few examples of what is already happening.

After years of casual attitudes about divorce in this country, heartening efforts are under way to help more couples preserve their marriages. Grassroots campaigns that urge men to take more responsibility for family well-being are cropping up around the country. Diverse (and sometimes controversial) as they and their leaders are, the popular response they have elicited reflects a broad public concern with the question of personal accountability. Promise Keepers, a nondenominational ministry, has filled football stadiums with men seeking guidance and encouragement to live more ethical lives. The Million Man March on October 16, 1995, filled the Capitol Mall with men who, in a genuine spirit of atonement and reconciliation, expressed their determination to take responsibility for themselves, their families, and their communities.

Seminars in marital reconciliation are thriving in educational and religious organizations throughout the country. In his State of the Union address in 1995, the President recognized the work of the Reverends John and Diana Cherry, two AME Zion ministers from Maryland. Through their sermons and their premarital and marital counseling courses, they have dedicated much of their ministry to helping couples stay together or get back together. Their church has an unusually high male membership because of this direct appeal to men to accept and enjoy family responsibility.

The American Bar Association has initiated a pilot project, the First Year Anniversary Course, which assists new couples in identifying problems most likely to emerge early in a marriage. The course allows couples in crisis to participate in communication and negotiation sessions with lawyers and human relations experts.

The Partners Project, created by Lynne Gold-Bikin, a former chair of the association's section on family law, is a practical video course designed to teach communicating and negotiating skills to high school students, long before they marry. Each session focuses on a different topic—sharing family income, for example, or domestic violence. Students take turns role-playing in scenarios that dramatize common domestic conflicts: who cooks if both partners are tired, say, or who decides how money is spent. Instructors ask students to identify the problem in each scenario, then to consider alternative approaches. If the staged conflict results in one partner's considering divorce, a visit with an attorney is enacted, and the teens are introduced to the harsh realities that accompany marital breakup.

My strong feelings about divorce and its effects on children have caused me to bite my tongue more than a few times during my own marriage and to think instead about what I could do to be a better wife and partner. My husband has done the same. Bill and I have worked hard at our marriage with a great deal of mutual respect and deepening love for each other. That we are blessed with Chelsea enhances our commitment.

I am not saying that there are not reasons for divorce. The abuse and violence Virginia Kelley experienced is something no parent or child should endure. But with divorce as easy as it is, and its consequences so hard, people with children need to ask themselves whether they have given a marriage their best shot and what more they can do to make it work before they call it quits.

For this reason, I am ambivalent about no-fault divorce with no waiting period when children are involved. We should consider returning to mandatory "cooling off" periods, with education and counseling for partners.

One of the many difficulties with divorce is that it becomes a public matter. It goes to court. Painful child custody decisions must be made. Regardless of individual feelings, everyone involved in the process, especially a parent, has an obligation to temper the pain children will inevitably experience.

Anyone who has raised children knows how attached they are to the security of routine. Long after divorce, they usually harbor hopes that their parents will reconcile. The anxieties that come with divorce require that parents do whatever they can to avoid creating additional uncertainty. Parents need to remember that little things often matter most—maintaining mealtimes, helping with homework, telling bedtime stories, taking weekend excursions, praying together. Children's needs must come first.

In deference to their children's feelings of shock, abandonment, and insecurity, adults have to control their own feelings, whether they are relieved and pleased at leaving a marriage, or angry and resentful at being left. This requires a degree of awareness and self-control that can be hard to muster in the midst of so traumatic an event.

Simple acts of decency and civility may be most important: Refusing to criticize the other parent to a child. Providing a decent level of child support, because your child deserves to be taken care of financially, regardless of your feelings about your former spouse. Honoring the times you promise to spend with your child. Using that time to become involved with your child's life, whether by attending sports events, volunteering at school, or simply sitting together talking. Making the effort to celebrate birthdays and holidays and attend school performances. Sparing your child adult disagreements.

As a lawyer, I handled my share of divorce cases and tried my hardest to keep the parties out of court by working to help them solve their disagreements. Time and again I saw otherwise rational adults, twisted by revenge, jealousy, or greed, attempting to use their children as bargaining chips. Watching one parent browbeat the other over child support or property division by threatening to fight for custody or withhold visitation, I often wished I could call in King Solomon to arbitrate.

That wise king, faced with two women who both claimed to be the mother of a child, ordered that the child be cut in two, so each could receive half the body. The woman who cried out that Solomon should give the child to the other, rather than kill him, revealed herself as the real mother by placing the child's welfare above the contest over his custody. How I wish that all modern-day parents, divorce lawyers, and judges would put so high a priority on determining a child's best interests.

There are signs of hope, however. Some courts now require that divorcing parents attend classes to learn about the potential effects of divorce on their children. They are given training in ways of keeping their children out of marital conflict, opening up lines of communication, and arranging for parenting to continue in a loving and supportive manner.

I admire the way the Parent Education Program in Columbus, Ohio, treats divorce as a public health issue, "because it constitutes a major life stress for 40 percent of American children and can put many of these children at risk for long-lasting difficulties that can derail their development." Twenty-three states have already established voluntary child custody mediation programs, and four more require mediation through statewide programs.

In Michigan, the Friend of the Court system investigates and makes recommendations on custody, visitation, and support in all domestic relations matters, including divorce. The total population of Michigan is only about 4 percent of the nation's, yet that one state repeatedly collects more child support than any other—10 percent of the nation's total in 1993. At the same time, the state strictly enforces visitation rights, in line with its philosophy of treating "the non-custodial parents as more than simply a billfold."

It is incumbent on the village—friends, teachers, mediators, counselors, and ministers, among others—to advocate for children during and after divorce, especially when parents cannot or will not be there for them. Adults beyond the immediate family reached out

to my mother, giving her enough support to make it through a difficult childhood. Similarly, the Louisiana teenager who wrote to me
found a male role model in a friend of the family.

A long-term study of children in Hawaii examined why some
children from poor and broken homes were resilient in the face of
adversity while others were not. The study found that resilience
depended on many factors, key among them the dependability of
the adults in the child's life and the social supports available to the
family.

Although children's relationships with parents, particularly
their mothers, were found to be especially important, relationships
with siblings, grandparents, other adult caregivers, teachers, ministers, and neighbors were significant too. The study reported that
positive changes in behavior and attitudes were possible even after
early childhood, "if the older child or adolescent encounters new
experiences and people who give meaning to one's life, and a reason for commitment and caring."

Anyone can provide that reason for commitment and caring, as
long as he or she is stable and devoted to the best interests of the
child. When a parent needs help, individuals in the village can pull
a child into their embrace and provide guidance and support,
informally or through organizations like Big Brothers/Big Sisters or
Boy and Girl Scouts.

In the terrible times when no adequate parenting is available
and the village itself must act in place of parents, it accepts those
responsibilities in all our names through the authority we vest in
government. That means our city, county, and state social welfare
services are not only the province of their employees. They inter-
vene in families to protect children on our behalf. And by any fair
assessment of our foster care and adoption system, we are not
doing a good job taking care of our children.

Approximately 450,000 children are in our foster care system at any given time, and close to 100,000 of them will not be reunited with their families. Too many children are in limbo for far too long. There are not enough qualified foster parents to go around, and those who are available are frequently discouraged from forming warm attachments with children whose futures are still uncertain. Caseworkers are overwhelmed by the numbers of children for whom they are responsible and by the severity of the emotional and physical damage many have suffered.

Loving adults are eager to offer permanent homes to many of these children. But the American adoption process can be a nightmare of complex regulations, outdated assumptions, and institutional inertia. Public adoptions can take years, and private adoptions may be too costly for many to afford. One woman wrote to tell me how she and her husband, both musicians, had spent thousands of dollars adopting a little boy who is "the joy of our life." When her cousin's teenage daughter recently became pregnant and could not afford to keep her child, the same couple volunteered to adopt again. As simple as this case should have been—the parents and baby being members of the same extended family and all parties agreeing to the adoption—it still cost upward of $4,000 because of legal fees and paperwork.

For others, there is the shadow of fear cast by uncommon but highly publicized cases in which birth parents sue to reverse an adoption. A forty-year-old newscaster I met in New Mexico wanted to adopt but was discouraged by notorious cases like that of Baby Richard, in which a child lived happily with his adoptive parents until his birth father won custody of him a few years later. However rare they are, such cases undermine people's faith in our adoption system and encourage them to look to other countries for children, while so many of our own country's children go without proper care or love. At an event in the East Room of the White House promoting National Adoption Month, thirteen-year-old

Deanna Moppin spoke eloquently about the longings of these children: "I would have a place that I would call home. I would have a room that I would call my room. I would have a family that I could love and would love me back."

Adoption in America is also made more difficult because of a historical bias against interracial adoptions, which can mean interminable waiting until children are matched with parents of the same race. Although many adopting parents would prefer to bring up children who share their own cultural and racial identity, many others do not have a preference and would gladly take a child of a different background. Today, despite heroic efforts by groups like One Church, One Child, there are far more minority children needing homes than there are same-race homes for them. To prevent these children from languishing in foster care, my husband signed legislation and ordered that new guidelines be put in place to prohibit federally funded agencies from using race as the sole deciding factor in placing children.

The village can take it further. We could set a goal of reducing our foster care and adoption rolls by 100,000 children each year for the next five years by moving children either back home or into adoptive families, whichever is in their best interests. We could be willing to terminate parental rights more quickly whenever physical or sexual abuse is involved. We could recruit qualified citizens to share with overworked social workers, lawyers, and judges the burden of moving children's cases through the courts. We could make decisions by birth parents to give up children for adoption more difficult to overturn, especially when a child has already become strongly attached to an adoptive family. We could ensure that government continues to cover some of the costs associated with adoption. We could enlist more businesses to follow the leadership of Wendy's president Dave Thomas, who has been vocal about businesses subsidizing adoption costs as well. In these and other ways, we can see to it that considerations like regulations, money, skin color, and even parental rights and adult prerogatives take a back seat to the love and security children so deeply need.

Discussions of modern families often miss the point. Although the nuclear family, consisting of an adult mother and father and the children to whom they are biologically related, has proved to be the most durable and effective means of meeting children's needs over time, it is not the only form that has worked in the past or the present. I know many successful adults, like my mother and my husband, who were raised in families that did not fit the conventional mold. Others I know thrived in the care of biological and adoptive surrogates, and even in foster care or institutions. What a family looks like to outsiders is not as important as whether adults know what children need to develop positively, and work to fulfill their responsibilities to each other and to their children.

In addition, however, every society requires a critical mass of families that fit the traditional ideal, both to meet the needs of most children and to serve as a model for other adults who are raising children in difficult settings. We are at risk of losing that critical mass in America today. Parenting has never been easy, but today, when most adults consciously choose to become mothers and fathers, we owe an even higher degree of love and respect to the children we bring into this world.

Whatever the strengths and weaknesses of the families we grew up in, we get a second chance at domestic happiness when we create a family of our own. Bill and I have watched with joy as Roger and his wife, Molly, and my brother Tony and his wife, Nicole, have joined us in parenthood. We've been impressed with the willingness our brothers have shown to participate in the daily tasks of child care, and particularly with Roger, who learned by negative example the importance of a father's influence on a son's life. Every parent makes mistakes, sometimes serious ones. But if we find mediating influences along the way, as Roger found in his mother, brother, extended family, and wife, we can learn even from the painful lessons our upbringing has to teach us.

Those of us who work hard enough—and are lucky enough—to create a flourishing family life have a bounty of joy and security to share with others less fortunate. By extending our good fortune, we create a village that acknowledges children as our first allegiance and strives to ensure that every child has at least one champion.

The Bell Curve
Is a Curve Ball

---

*There is no defense or security for any of us
except in the highest intelligence and development of all.*

BOOKER T. WASHINGTON

My brother Hugh once told me about a professional football coach who stands before his players at the first session of spring training, holds up a football, and says, "Gentlemen, this is a football."

I am particularly fond of this story because it is a reminder that most of us could use a little coaching to do our best, even at long-accustomed tasks. That is at least as true of parenting as it is of football.

Recent discoveries in neuroscience, molecular biology, and psychology have given researchers a whole new understanding of when and how the human brain develops. Their findings are a crucial kind of coaching that can show parents and other caregivers how to elicit a child's full potential. The rest of the village can, if we listen in, pick up information and ideas that will help us to steer our communities' efforts and our nation's policies in a more productive direction for children. Above all, this new information makes clear that a child's character and potential are not already determined at birth.

THE BELIEFS we hold about why children think, feel, and behave in certain ways have a tremendous impact on how we treat them. When those beliefs are inaccurate, the consequences can be dire.

During law school, I worked with the staff of the Yale–New Haven Hospital in Connecticut to help draft guidelines for the treatment of abused children. Sometimes these children were brought into the emergency room by parents who themselves had inflicted the injuries. Often the parents denied what they had done, but sometimes they tried to justify it. One father who brought in his badly injured three-year-old claimed that he had beaten the boy to "get the devil out of him." Behind his horrifying actions lurked the belief that babies are born either good or bad. If their fundamental nature is "bad," as evidenced by behavior like persistent crying, this crazy logic goes, they must be punished, beaten if necessary. (Never mind that the "remedy" generally has the perverse effect of encouraging "bad" children to live up to their label.)

That same year, I also studied children at the Yale Child Study Center. One of the people I was privileged to work with was the late Dr. Sally Provence, a pioneer in the field of infant behavior. I remember watching her work with a mother who had brought in her seven-month-old son because he was having trouble eating and sleeping. The mother was at her wits' end and feared she might hurt her baby. She didn't understand what was wrong with him, but instead of writing him off as a "bad" child, she'd had the wisdom to seek help.

Under Dr. Provence's gentle questioning, the woman revealed that her first pregnancy, which resulted in the birth of a girl, had been a joyous experience, and her daughter was an "easy" child. But her second pregnancy had been strained by marital and other tensions in her life, which had persisted. Dr. Provence helped the woman to see that even though her son had a different and more difficult temperament than her daughter, the problems she was having with him stemmed mostly from his keen awareness of her feelings of distress when she was around him. The two of them were caught in a cycle, and as the months went by, the baby's prospects for healthy development were spiraling downward.

With Dr. Provence's guidance, the mother learned to change the way she behaved around her son. She learned how to soothe him when he became fussy by holding him snugly. She talked to him more, in a gentler voice. Her new way with him allowed him to relax and become more manageable, which in turn softened her attitude toward him and restored her confidence in her abilities as a parent.

It is not only parents who need expert "coaching" in children's development. The rest of the village does too. In my years of work with children's organizations—the Carnegie Council on Children, the Children's Defense Fund, and the Arkansas Advocates for Children and Families, for example—I saw many dedicated souls trying to see that current knowledge guided practical decisions about children's welfare.

Once, about fifteen years ago, I represented an Arkansas couple who wanted to adopt a four-year-old boy who had been in their foster care for three years. The boy had been badly neglected as a baby by his biological mother, who was overwhelmed by psychological problems. When he was less than a year old, she turned him over to the local social service agency so she could follow her boyfriend to another state. At that point, the baby showed all the symptoms of severe mistreatment: he had gained little weight since birth, he was unresponsive, and he shied away from human contact.

In his foster family, however, the boy began to thrive. He put on weight and began to allow people to touch him. He learned to walk and began talking. His foster parents fell in love with him and decided they wanted to adopt him, even though they had signed the customary contract with the state, which at that time prohibited foster parents from trying to adopt children in their care. The state adoption agency, reluctant to break precedent, had refused their request. At the same time, however, the agency decided not to return the boy to his birth mother, who had filed suit to get him back, claiming she had overcome her psychological problems and was fit to care for him. Instead, the state planned to take him from the security of the family he knew and turn him over to strangers whose names were on the adoption lists.

I argued on behalf of the boy's foster parents that the best interests of the child should take precedence over both the birth mother's claims of her biological rights and the state's claims to its contractual agreement. I asked the judge to allow testimony from a child psychologist about the boy's progress while he had been in the care of his foster parents, and about the possible consequences to his physical, intellectual, and emotional development if he was now separated from them. The judge, who had children and grand-children of his own, did not think that he had much to learn about child development, but he agreed to hear the testimony.

The psychologist explained how disrupting warm and secure attachments like those the boy had formed with his foster family could irreversibly damage his emotional development. He described the symptoms and stages of grief that would typically accompany so great a loss at this age: anger and hostility, renewed withdrawal from human contact, depression and emotional detachment. At his stage of psychological development, the boy would also be inclined to believe he had been deliberately rejected by the foster parents he had come to trust and love. The testimony of the child psychologist riveted the entire courtroom, and it weighed heavily in the judge's determination that allowing the foster parents to adopt the boy served his best interests.

The years since I had these experiences have been light-years in terms of the progress researchers have made in understanding children's emotional and cognitive development. Unfortunately, much of this information is not yet known to enough people. At the risk of grossly oversimplifying the research, I want to summarize what is known, with the hope of reaching people whose attitudes toward and treatment of children might benefit from it.

Some of the most significant headway has been made in the field of biology, where researchers have begun to grasp how the brain develops.

At birth, an infant's brain is far from fully formed. In the days and weeks that follow, vital connections begin to form among the brain cells. These connections, called synapses, create the brain's physical "maps," the pathways along which learning will take place, allowing the brain to perform increasingly complicated tasks. A newborn's brain is like an orchestra just before the curtain goes up, the billions of instruments it will need to express itself in language, thought, and impulse furiously tuning up.

The first three years of life are crucial in establishing the brain cell connections. But they don't form in a vacuum. Babies need food for their brains as well as their bodies, not only good physical nourishment but loving, responsive caregiving from their parents and the other adults who tend to them. They need to see light and movement, to hear loving voices, and, above all, to be touched and held.

As science writer Ronald Kotulak explained in a series of Pulitzer Prize–winning articles in the *Chicago Tribune*, "The outside world is indeed the brain's real food . . . [which it] gobbles up . . . in bits and chunks through its sensory system: vision, hearing, smell, touch, and taste." He quotes psychiatrist Felton Earls of Harvard University's School of Public Health, who elaborates, "Just as the digestive system can adapt to many types of diets, the brain adapts to many types of experiences."

Kotulak uses an analogy from cyberspace to make the process clearer. If we conceive of the brain as the most powerful and sophisticated computer imaginable, the child's surroundings act like a keyboard, inputting experience. The computer comes with so much memory capacity that for the first three years it can store more information than an army of humans could possibly input. By the end of three or four years, however, the pace of learning slows. The computer will continue to accept new information, but at a decreasing rate. The process continues to slow as we mature, and as we age our brain cells and synapses begin to wither away.

What sets the brain apart from any computer in existence, however, is its fragile and ongoing relationship to the world around it. The brain is an organ, not a machine, and its "hardware" is still being wired at birth, and for a long time afterward. With proper stimulation, brain synapses will form at a rapid pace, reaching adult levels by the age of two and far surpassing them in the next several years. The quality of the nutrition, caregiving, and stimulation the child receives determines not only the eventual number of these synapses but also how they are "wired" for both cognitive and emotional intelligence. Synapses that are not used are destroyed.

As neuroscientist Bob Jacobs says, the bottom line is: "You have to use it or you lose it." If we think of the brain as our most important muscle, we can appreciate that it requires activity in order to develop. Just as babies need to flex their arms and legs, they also need regular, varied stimulation to exercise all the parts of their brains.

When parents talk to their babies, for example, they are feeding the brain cells that process sound and helping to create the connections necessary for language development. A University of Chicago study showed that by the age of two, children whose mothers had talked to them frequently since infancy had bigger vocabularies than children from the same socioeconomic backgrounds whose mothers had been less talkative.

What I am passing along to you is a bare-bones description of what scientists believe happens within the developing brain; the processes are more complex than I can do justice to, and they are not yet fully understood. But it is clear that by the time most children begin preschool, the architecture of the brain has essentially been constructed. From that time until adolescence, the brain remains a relatively eager learner with occasional "growth spurts," but it will never again attain the incredible pace of learning that occurs in the first few years.

Nevertheless, as long as our brain stays healthy, we will have plenty of synapses left for learning. Even late in life, and even after a long diet of mental "junk food," the brain retains the capacity to respond to good nourishment and proper stimulation. But neurologically speaking, playing catch-up is vastly more difficult and costly, in terms of personal sacrifice and social resources, than getting children's brains off to a good start in the first place.

THE PICTURE of the brain as a developing organ that has begun to emerge from biological research dovetails with some key findings from the world of psychology. Nowhere is this more welcome than in the study of what constitutes intelligence, an area of inquiry that has been clouded by controversy, misinformation, and misinterpretation.

It has become fashionable in some quarters to assert that intelligence is fixed at birth, part of our genetic makeup that is invulnerable to change, a claim promoted by Charles Murray and the late Richard Herrnstein in their 1994 book, *The Bell Curve*. This view is politically convenient: if nothing can alter intellectual potential, nothing need be offered to those who begin life with fewer resources or in less favorable environments. But research provides us with plenty of evidence that this perspective is not only unscientific but insidious. It is increasingly apparent that the nature-nurture question is not an "either/or" debate so much as a "both/and" proposition.

Dr. Frederick Goodwin, former director of the National Institute of Mental Health, cites studies in which children who could be described as being "at risk" for developmental problems were exposed at an early age to stimulating environments. The result: The children's IQ scores increased by as much as 20 points. A similar study, best known as the Abecedarian Project, examined this same process in a long and intensive research effort begun under the leadership of psychologist and educator Craig Ramey at the University of North Carolina in the early 1970s.

Ramey gathered together a group of more than a hundred newborns, most of them African-Americans. Their parents, most of whom had not graduated from high school, had an average IQ of 85. The majority of the families were living on welfare.

At the age of four months, half of the children were placed in a preschool with a very high ratio of adult staff to children. But it wasn't only the attention these children were given that was special. When adults spoke to them, they used words that were descriptive and that were suited to the child's stage of learning. They were doing precisely what responsive parents do when they communicate with their young sons and daughters.

The children in this group were given good nutrition, educational toys, and plenty of other stimulation, as well as the encouragement to explore their surroundings. A "home-school resource teacher" met with each family every other week to coach the parents on how to help their children with school-related lessons and activities.

By the time the children were three years old, those in the experimental group of children averaged 17 points higher on IQ tests than the other half of the original group, 101 versus 84. Even more significant than these impressive gains is their durability: the differences in IQ persisted a decade later, when the children were attending a variety of other schools. Dr. Ramey is continuing to follow the children to see what their further development brings.

Bear this research in mind when you listen to those who argue that our nation cannot afford to implement comprehensive early education programs for disadvantaged children and their families. If we as a village decide not to help families develop their children's brains, then at least let us admit that we are acting not on the evidence but according to a different agenda. And let us acknowledge that we are not using all the tools at our disposal to better the lives of our children.

ANY DISCUSSION of how the brain's processes affect cognitive intelligence tells only half the story about the first blossoming of intelligence. The other half is how we behave in our relations with other people—what is now being called our "emotional intelligence."

One unusual aspect of living in the Arkansas governor's mansion was getting to know prison inmates who were assigned to work in the house and the yard. When we moved in, I was told that using prison labor at the governor's mansion was a long-standing tradition, which kept down costs, and I was assured that the inmates were carefully screened. I was also told that onetime murderers were by far the preferred security risks. The crimes of the convicted murderers who worked at the governor's mansion usually involved a disagreement with someone they knew, often another young man in their neighborhood, or they had been with companions who had killed someone in the course of committing another crime.

I had defended several clients in criminal cases, but visiting them in jail or sitting next to them in court was not the same as encountering a convicted murderer in the kitchen every morning. I was apprehensive, but I agreed to abide by tradition until I had a chance to see for myself how the inmates behaved around me and my family.

I saw and learned a lot as I got to know them better. We enforced rules strictly and sent back to prison any inmate who broke a rule. I discovered, as I had been told I would, that we had far fewer disciplinary problems with inmates who were in for murder than with those who had committed property crimes. In fact, over the years we lived there, we became friendly with a few of them, African-American men in their thirties who had already served twelve to eighteen years of their sentences.

I found myself wondering what kind of experiences and character traits had led them to participate in the violent and self-destructive acts that landed them in prison. The longer and better I came to know them, the more convinced I became that their crimes were not the result of inferior IQs or an inability to apply moral reasoning. Although they had not finished high school, they seemed to have active and inquisitive minds. Some had whimsy as well as street smarts. They showed sound judgment in solving problems in their work, and they plainly knew the difference between right and wrong. What, I wondered, had caused them to commit a crime that resulted in the loss of another's life?

Now that I have read Daniel Goleman's *Emotional Intelligence*, I am better able to understand what back then I could only wonder about.

Goleman brings to our attention new breakthroughs in psychology and neuroscience that shed light on how our "two minds"—the rational and the emotional—operate together to determine human behavior. Both forms of intelligence are essential to human interaction, and as any parent or teacher can tell you, both are constantly at work. If rational intelligence is unchecked by feeling for others, it can be used to orchestrate a holocaust, run a drug cartel, or carry out serial murders.

The power of emotion is equally dangerous if it is not harnessed to reason. People who cannot control their emotions are often prone to impulsive overreaction. They may be quick to perceive threats and slights even when none are intended, and to respond with violence. They are, in Goleman's phrase, "emotional illiterates." Many of the gang members interviewed as part of a recent study released by Attorney General Janet Reno to investigate the extent of illegal use of firearms fit this profile. More than one in three said they believe it is acceptable to shoot someone who "disses" them—shows them disrespect.

As with cognitive intelligence, the development of emotional intelligence appears to hinge on the interplay between biology and early experience. Early experience—especially how infants are held, touched, fed, spoken to, and gazed at—seems to be key in laying down the brain's mechanisms that will govern feelings and behavior. Some experts speculate that the brains of emotional illiterates are hard-wired early on by stressful experiences that inhibit these mechanisms and leave people prey to emotional "hijacking" ever after.

Most of us don't habitually react with impulsive violence, but all of us "blow our tops," give in to irrational fears, or otherwise feel overwhelmed—hijacked—by our emotions from time to time. Why do we, as thoughtful human beings, allow emotional impulse to override rational thinking?

As Goleman explains, the temporary "hijackings" are ordered

by the amygdala, a structure in the oldest, most primitive part of the brain, which is thought to be the physical seat of our emotions. This brain structure acts like a "home security system," scanning incoming signals from the senses for any hint of experience that the primitive mind might perceive as frightening or hurtful.

Whenever the amygdala picks up such stimuli, it reacts instantaneously, sending out an emergency alarm to every major part of the brain. This alarm triggers a chain of self-protective reactions. The body begins to secrete hormones that signal an urgent need for "fight or flight" and put a person's senses on highest alert. The cardiovascular system, the muscles, and the gut go into overdrive. Heart rate and blood pressure jump dramatically, breathing slows. Even the memory system switches into a faster gear as it scans its archives for any knowledge relevant to the emergency at hand.

The amygdala acts as a storehouse of emotional memories. And the memories it stores are especially vivid because they arrive in the amygdala with the neurochemical and hormonal imprint that accompanies stress, anxiety, or other intense excitement. "This means that, in effect, the brain has two memory systems, one for ordinary facts and one for emotionally charged ones," Goleman notes. And he adds, "A special system for emotional memories makes excellent sense in evolution, of course, ensuring that animals would have particularly vivid memories of what threatens or pleases them. But emotional memories can be faulty guides to the present."

Problems arise because the amygdala often sends a false alarm, when the sense of panic it triggers is related to memories of experiences that are no longer relevant to our circumstances. For example, traumatic episodes from as far back as infancy, when reason and language were barely developed, can continue to trigger extreme emotional responses well into adulthood.

The neocortex—the thoughtful, analytical part of the brain that evolved from the primitive brain—acts as a "damper switch for the amygdala's surges." Most of the time the neocortex is in control of our emotional responses. But it takes the neocortex longer to process information. This gives the instantaneous, extreme responses triggered by the amygdala a chance to kick in before the neocortex is even aware of what has happened. When this occurs, the brain's built-in regulatory process can be short-circuited.

Most people learn how to avoid emotional hijackings from the time they are infants. If they have supportive and caring adults around them, they pick up the social cues that enable them to develop self-discipline and empathy. According to Dr. Geraldine Dawson of the University of Washington, the prime period for emotional development appears to be between eight and eighteen months, when babies are forming their first strong attachments. As with cognitive development, the window of change extends to adolescence and beyond, although it narrows over time. But children who have stockpiled painful experiences, through abuse, neglect, or exposure to violence, may have difficulty enlisting the rational brain to override the pressure to display destructive and antisocial reactions later in life.

The answer to Goleman's essential question—"How can we bring intelligence to our emotions—and civility to our streets and caring to our communal life?"—appears to be that, difficult as it may be, it is never too late to teach the elements of emotional intelligence. The structure imposed by the responsibilities of work and the enlightened assistance of concerned people in the prison system and at the governor's mansion helped those onetime murderers I knew in Arkansas to achieve a greater understanding of and control over their feelings and behavior.

A number of schools around the country are incorporating the teaching of empathy and self-discipline—what social theorist Amitai Etzioni calls "character education"—into their curricula. In New

Haven, Connecticut, a social development approach is integrated into every public school child's daily routine. Children learn techniques for developing and enhancing social skills, identifying and managing emotions like anger, and solving problems creatively. The program appears to raise achievement scores and grades as well as to improve behavior.

WE ARE beginning to act—albeit slowly—on the evidence biology and psychology provide to us. But practice lags far behind research findings. As Dr. Craig Ramey notes, "If we had a comparable level of knowledge with respect to a particular form of cancer or hypertension or some other illness that affected adults, you can be sure we would be acting with great vigor."

If, in scientific terms, the twentieth century has been the century of physics, then the twenty-first will surely be the century of biology. Not only are scientists mapping our genetic makeup, but new technologies are letting them peer into living organisms and view our brains in action. The question we must all think about is whether we will put to good use this accumulating knowledge. Can we find ways to communicate it to all parents, so that it can help them to raise their children and to seek out coaching if they need it? Will we give working mothers and fathers enough time to spend feeding their babies' brains? Will we have the foresight and the political will to provide more and better early education programs for preschoolers, especially those from homes without adequate "brain food"? Will we challenge elementary school students with foreign languages, math, and music to reinforce brain connections early in a child's life? Given the increasing level of violence and family breakdown we see around us, why wouldn't we?

IN THE next few chapters I will explore what happens in families during the first few years of children's lives—the period that we now know is so vital in giving them a solid start. Researchers may differ over how particular experiences influence a child's development, but no research study I have ever read has disputed that the quality of life within the family constellation strongly affects how well infants and young children will adapt to the circumstances that confront them throughout their lives. On the contrary, the research underscores the critical importance of constructive stimulation during a child's earliest years.

But if family life is chaotic, if parents are depressed and unexpressive, or if caregivers change constantly, so that children can rely on no one, their ability to perform the essential tasks of early childhood will be impaired. The next time you hear someone using the word "investment" to describe what we need to do for our younger, more vulnerable family members, think about the investments the village has the power to make in children's first few weeks, months, and years. They will reap us all extraordinary dividends as children travel through the crucial stages of cognitive and emotional development to come.

Kids
Don't Come
with Instructions

We learn the rope of life by untying its knots.

JEAN TOOMER

There I was, lying in my hospital bed, trying desperately to figure out how to breast-feed. I had been trained to study everything forward, backward, and upside down before reaching a conclusion. It seemed to me I ought to be able to figure this out. As I looked on in horror, Chelsea started to foam at the nose. I thought she was strangling or having convulsions. Frantically, I pushed every buzzer there was to push.

A nurse appeared promptly. She assessed the situation calmly, then, suppressing a smile, said, "It would help if you held her head up a bit, like this." Chelsea was taking in my milk, but because of the awkward way I held her, she was breathing it out of her nose!

Like many women, I had read books when I was pregnant—wonderful books filled with dos and don'ts about what babies need in the first months and years to ensure the proper development of their bodies, brains, and characters. But as every parent soon discovers, grasping concepts in the abstract and knowing what to do with the baby in your hands are two radically different things. Babies don't come with handy sets of instructions.

How well I remember Chelsea crying her heart out one night soon after Bill and I brought her home from the hospital. Nothing we could do would quiet her wailing—and we tried everything. Finally, as I held her in my arms, I looked down into her little bunched-up face. "Chelsea," I said, "this is new for both of us. I've never been a mother before, and you've never been a baby. We're just going to have to help each other do the best we can."

In her classic book *Coming of Age in Samoa*, Margaret Mead observed that a Samoan mother was expected to give birth in her mother's village, even if she had moved to her husband's village upon marriage. The father's mother or sister had to attend the birth as well, to care for the newborn while the mother was being cared for by her relatives. With their collective experience as parents, they helped ease the transition into parenthood by showing how it was done.

In our own American experience, families used to live closer together, making it easier for relatives to pitch in during pregnancy and the first months of a newborn's life. Women worked primarily in the home and were more available to lend a hand to new mothers and to help them get accustomed to motherhood. Families were larger, and older children were expected to aid in caring for younger siblings, a role that prepared them for their own future parenting roles.

These days, there is no shortage of advice, equipment, and professional expertise available to those who can pay for it. If breast-feeding is a problem, for example, there are lactation specialists, state-of-the-art breast pumps, and more books on the subject than you can count. But nothing replaces simple hands-on instruction, as I can attest. People and programs to help fledgling parents are few and far between, even though such help costs surprisingly little. We are not giving enough attention to what ought to be our highest priority: educating and empowering people to be the best parents possible.

Education and empowerment start with giving parents the means and the encouragement to plan pregnancy itself, so that they have the physical, financial, and emotional resources to support their children. Some of the best models for doing this come from abroad. I'm reminded in particular of a clinic I visited in a rural part of Indonesia.

Every month, tables are set up under the trees in a clearing, and doctors and nurses hold the clinic there. Women come to have their babies examined, to get medical advice, and to exchange information. A large poster-board chart notes the method of birth control each family is using, so that the women can compare problems and results.

This clinic and thousands like it around that country provide guidance that has led mothers to devote more time and energy to the children they already have before having more. The fathers, I was told, have also been affected by the presence of the clinic. They are more likely to judge their paternal role by the quality of life they can provide to each child than by the number of children they father.

This community clinic program, which is funded by the government and supported by the country's women's organizations and by Muslim leaders, is a wonderful example of how the village—both the immediate community and the larger society—can use basic resources to help families. The honest, open, matter-of-fact manner of dealing with family planning issues that I observed in Indonesia provided me with a point of comparison to the approaches I have observed in many other places.

The openness about sexuality and availability of contraception in most Western European countries are credited with lowering rates of unintended pregnancy and abortion among adolescent and adult women. By contrast, more than one hundred million women around the world still cannot obtain or are not using family planning services because they are poor or uneducated, or lack access to care. Twenty million women seek unsafe abortions each year.

In October 1995, I saw a striking example of the consequences when I visited the Tsyilla Balbina Maternity Hospital in Salvador da Bahia, Brazil. I learned that half the admissions there were women giving birth, while the other half were women suffering from the effects of self-induced abortions. I met with the governor and the minister of health for the state, who have launched a campaign to make family planning available to poor women. As the minister pointed out to me, rich women have always had access to such services.

We may think that our country is far from this end of the spectrum, but the statistics tell a different story. Two in five American teenage girls become pregnant by the age of twenty, and one and a half million abortions are performed in America each year. It is a national shame that many Americans are more thoughtful about planning their weekend entertainment than they are about planning their families. And it is tragic that our country does not do more to promote research into family planning and wider access to contraceptive methods because of the highly charged politics of abortion. The irony is that sensible family planning here and around the world would decrease the demand for legal and illegal abortions, saving maternal and infant lives.

As usual, the children pay. When too-young parents have children, or when families expand without the means to support their growth, children are affected by the burdens and anxieties of parents who cannot meet their obligations. Family planning, more than just limiting the number of children parents have, protects the welfare of existing and future children.

The Cairo Document, drafted at the International Conference on Population and Development in 1994, reaffirms that "in no case should abortion be promoted as a method of family planning." And it recognizes "the basic right of all couples and individuals to decide freely and responsibly the number, spacing, and timing of their children and to have the information and means to do so." Women and men should have the right to make this most intimate of all decisions free of discrimination or coercion.

Once a pregnancy occurs, however, we all have a stake in working to ensure that it turns out well.

THERE IS no experience more moving than to walk through a neonatal intensive care unit crowded with babies born too early—the whir of the ventilating machines, the rushing about, the smell of newborns mixed with the smells of hospital halls, the tangle of tubes inserted into wrinkled little bodies. I have walked through many such units in my lifetime, in Washington, Chicago, Little Rock, Boston, Oakland, Miami. The scenes are all the same—babies no bigger than my hand fighting for a life they've barely tasted.

In a 1992 study by the World Health Organization, the United States ranked twenty-fourth among nations in infant mortality. That means twenty-three countries, led by Japan, do a better job than we do of ensuring that their babies live until their first birthday. Seventeen countries, led by Italy, have better maternal health than we do. We shouldn't be surprised at these results, since nearly one quarter of all pregnant women in America, many of whom are teenagers, receive little or no prenatal care.

We know that women who receive prenatal care, especially in the first trimester, are more likely to deliver healthy, full-term, normal-weight babies, while women who do not receive adequate prenatal care are more than twice as likely to give birth to babies weighing less than five and a half pounds, the definition of "low birth weight." And women who do not receive complete prenatal advice on alcohol and drug use, smoking, and proper nutrition are also more likely to give birth to low-birth-weight babies. In 1991, such babies represented only 7 percent of all births but about 60 percent of all infant deaths, for they were twenty-one times as likely to die before their first birthday as babies born weighing more. Inadequate prenatal care also results in higher rates of preventable problems, including congenital anomalies, early respiratory tract infections, and learning difficulties.

We spend billions of dollars on high-tech medical care to save and treat tiny babies. In 1988, a child born at low birth weight cost $15,000 more in the first year of life than a child born at normal birth weight. It is a modern miracle that we are able to save thousands of babies who would have died if they had been born a few years ago and that we can help thousands more to develop normally. In many cases, however, good prenatal care and emergency obstetric services could have averted the need for medical heroics altogether.

FOR many pregnant women in America, prenatal care is not accessible or affordable. They live in isolated rural areas or in urban centers. Their employers do not offer insurance, and their families do not make enough money to buy it on their own. Even families who have insurance sometimes find that health care is out of their reach. A couple I met told me their story: Having limited resources, they decided to insure their children and the breadwinning father, but not the homemaker mother. When the mother unexpectedly became pregnant, they saved their money to pay the hospital bills and decided to forgo the expense of prenatal care and anesthesia during delivery. This purely economic decision put both mother and baby at risk.

Many pregnant women are not even aware that they should be seeking prenatal care. They may be teenagers in denial about their pregnancy or trying desperately to hide their situation from their families. They may be women who do not have husbands, family, friends, or others concerned and informed enough to encourage them to seek medical attention or, at the very least, to stop smoking, drinking, or taking drugs during the pregnancy. In general, women whose already chaotic lives have been further complicated by pregnancy tend to be reluctant to seek services until the last possible moment, leaving their babies vulnerable to much greater health risks.

Ultimately, we women must take responsibility for ourselves and our health, but many of us will need assistance and support from the village. Peer pressure can work. We all know instances where family and friends have consistently and firmly reminded an expectant mother to forgo an alcoholic drink or a cigarette. But such informal means of monitoring care are no substitutes for formal systems that have as their primary mission good health for all women and babies.

Examples of the village at work can be found in countries where national health care systems ensure access to pre- and post-natal care for mothers and babies. Some European countries, such as Austria and France, tie a mother's eligibility for monetary benefits to her obtaining regular medical checkups.

While it is doubtful that our country will anytime soon develop a formal means of offering or monitoring prenatal care, there are things we can do now that will lower medical costs for all of us and prepare children for a lifetime of good health, starting before birth.

Some states, health care plans, community groups, and businesses have created their own systems of incentives to encourage women to obtain prenatal care. In Arkansas, we enlisted the services of local merchants to create a book of coupons that could be distributed to pregnant women. This "Happy Birthday Baby Book" contains coupons for each of the nine months of pregnancy and the first six months of a child's life. After every month's pre- or postnatal exam, the attending health care provider validates a coupon, which can be redeemed for free or reduced-priced goods such as milk or diapers.

The Arkansas Department of Health, which has run television and radio ads with a toll-free number to obtain the book, estimates that nearly seven out of every ten pregnant women in the state have received the coupon book. Preliminary reports indicate that women who have participated in the coupon program have had fewer low-birth-weight babies.

Businesses have also begun to recognize that preventive care saves health care costs in the long run. Many have begun to provide incentives to encourage their employees to seek prenatal care. Haggar Apparel Company in Dallas, Texas, for example, offers to pay 100 percent of employees' medical expenses during pregnancy if they seek prenatal care during the first trimester of pregnancy. Levi Strauss in San Francisco offers pregnant employees a $100 cash incentive to call a toll-free "health line," which provides information and advice to callers and screens them to identify those at risk for early delivery.

Insurance companies, particularly those offering managed care plans, are underwriting classes on healthy lifestyles for pregnant women and providing incentives like car seats and diaper services to encourage women to participate in baby-care training. Other insurance companies are offering one-on-one help, making nurse midwives or nurse practitioners available to pregnant women by phone around the clock.

Projects that team pregnant mothers with knowledgeable counterparts on the phone or in person have been greeted with much enthusiasm. People want to learn to be good parents.

In South Carolina, the Resource Mothers program has been linking pregnant teenagers with experienced mothers who live nearby since the early 1980s. The older women meet with the younger women before and after the baby is born, to teach them basic skills like bathing, changing, and feeding, and also to demonstrate constructive ways of interacting verbally and nonverbally with young children. The teens also receive counseling about the effects of substance abuse during pregnancy and information about child safety and development.

Resource Mothers has already had an impact both in improving the health of babies and in reducing the incidence of child abuse, which is often triggered by parents' not knowing how to cope with the demands of child rearing. The program is supported by state and federal funds for maternal and child health care and by Medicaid.

In San Antonio, Texas, a program called Avance began teaching basic parenting skills to fifty mothers in 1973. By 1994, the program was serving five thousand individuals in the Mexican-American communities in San Antonio, Houston, and the Rio Grande Valley. Operating in public housing projects, elementary schools, and through its own family service centers, Avance not only enlists project graduates to pass on the basic skills they have learned but offers classes in child development, English-language tutoring, and employment training programs as well.

Avance places a special emphasis on helping young fathers connect to and stay involved with their children. It uses home visits to monitor the progress of young families, keeping open the lines of communication as infants move into early childhood. The success of the program has been measured in the positive attitudes of the young parents it reaches, who learn that their responsibility as parents includes creating a more nurturing and stimulating environment for children. Avance recently received a state grant to build centers in Dallas, Corpus Christi, El Paso, and Laredo over the next few years.

While programs like Resource Mothers and Avance contribute greatly to the success and good health of parents and their babies, there is much that hospitals can do to ensure that parents go home better equipped to cope with the demands of parenthood in the first place.

On a trip to the Philippines, I visited the Dr. José Fabella Memorial Hospital, in one of the poorest sections of Manila. Over the past decade, the hospital has kept newborns with their mothers, not in a separate nursery. In the maternity ward, dozens of new mothers lie in beds facing their babies. Mothers and their tiny ones learn each other's touch, becoming comfortable together and starting to build a special intimacy.

The doctors and nurses at the hospital spend time at each bedside, patiently teaching mothers how to breast-feed. To my astonishment, I also saw one- and two-day-old infants, mouths pursed, sipping from cups. I learned that the hospital began training mothers who could not breast-feed to use cups once they discovered how difficult it was for poor mothers living in unsanitary conditions to sterilize and clean bottles and nipples. It was much easier and simpler for them to keep a baby's drinking cup clean. With the money saved from closing the nursery, the hospital hired additional staff to teach basic parenting skills.

American hospitals have also instituted changes in recent decades that encourage both parents to begin caring for their babies in the hospital. Hospitals provide birthing rooms for both labor and delivery. Fathers are allowed to room in and are urged to be present at the birth. Most hospitals that provide delivery services offer basic classes in parenting and child care for new parents.

Hospitals, as the primary point of contact with parents of newborns, have a natural opportunity and a responsibility to help babies and parents get off to a good start. No mother should leave the hospital without being given the opportunity to ask every question she has about proper baby care. A wallet-sized card listing the immunizations a baby needs, when and where to get them, and how much they cost is a useful item hospitals could provide. They could also make available lists of affordable pediatricians in the area.

Perhaps most important, hospitals should evaluate the parent-child relationship to determine whether additional advice and help will be needed. This is critical for teenage mothers. Hawaii has pioneered such a program, Healthy Start, which currently screens more than half of the sixteen thousand babies born in the state each year.

Healthy Start's workers ask to visit new parents while they are still in the hospital. Most consent to the visit and are grateful that someone cares enough to talk to them. The workers ask them about their family histories and their current situation, noting potential problems. "We look for parents who were abused or neglected as children," explains Gail Breakey, one of Healthy Start's founders and the director of the Hawaii Family Stress Center. "We know from research there is an intergenerational pattern."

If the family is considered to be at risk, Healthy Start offers a follow-up home visitor. The home visitor helps the parents learn about their child's developmental needs and acts as a liaison with other agencies to make sure that the family's needs are attended to—from marriage counseling to employment training to drug abuse treatment. Healthy Start has been successful in reducing child abuse to less than 1 percent among the more than three thousand families who have accepted follow-up help over the last five years—far below the national child abuse rate of 4.7 percent. Healthy Start projects now operate in communities in more than twenty-five states.

While Healthy Start operates on a consensual basis, states might also consider making public welfare or medical benefits contingent on agreement to allow home visits or to participate in other forms of parent education.

Despite its proven success, funding for Hawaii's Healthy Start is not secure. As the federal budget is cut and states are forced to pick up more costs, investments in prevention-oriented programs are likely to take a back seat to prisons, emergency medical care, or other programs with a political constituency.

It is interesting to note that all Western European countries provide some form of home health visitors. England has a long history of providing home visits through its national health service. After mother and newborn child come home from the hospital, a qualified nurse-midwife from the local hospital visits each day for a minimum of ten days. A "family health visitor," a fully qualified nurse who is usually associated with the local clinic, is also available for phone consultation or home visits upon request from birth until the child goes to school at age five.

An American friend of mine who was living in England during her pregnancy quickly came to appreciate home visits. Before having her baby, she was sure that all the books she was reading would explain everything she needed to know. In any case, she reasoned, her mother planned to arrive by the time the baby did. But her mother became too sick to travel, and my friend found herself home alone with her new baby. Like me, she found that the reading she had done, interesting as it was, left her with lots of unanswered questions. When the nurse came knocking at the door, my friend pulled the startled woman inside and began babbling at her: "Why won't she sleep for more than an hour? Will she ever open her eyes? Do you think she can hear me?"

I cannot say enough in support of home visits, whether the visitor is a social worker or nurse from a program or an aunt who rides the bus on Saturday to see how her niece and the newborn are doing. Beginner parents need people to talk to and people to call on for help and encouragement.

THE ELECTRONIC village can play a role in assisting rookie parents as well. Radio and television stations could broadcast child care tips between programs, songs, and talk show diatribes. Imagine hearing this kind of "news you can use" sandwiched in the middle of the Top Ten countdown: "So you've got a new baby in the house? Don't let her cry herself red in the face. Just think how you'd feel if you were hungry, wet, or just plain out of sorts and nobody paid any attention to you. Well, don't do that to a little kid. She just got here. Give her a break. And give her some attention now!"

Videos with scenes of commonsense baby care—how to burp an infant, what to do when soap gets in his eyes, how to make a baby with an earache comfortable—could be running continuously in doctors' offices, clinics, hospitals, motor vehicle offices, or any place where people gather and have to wait.

I saw another promising innovation in action in the South Bronx in New York City, when I visited Highbridge Communicare Center, which provides basic medical services to the poor residents of the area. Highbridge offers parents a card with a twenty-four-hour toll-free number that connects them to a doctor or nurse who can give them immediate medical advice and help in determining whether a medical problem is serious enough to require either emergency care or an appointment at the clinic. In just a few months of operation, the hot line decreased substantially the number of visits to the local hospital's emergency room.

Can you imagine a hot line in every community? Local hospitals could pool their resources to sponsor one. Many hours of anxiety and millions of dollars in costs could be avoided if mothers and fathers had someone to call to talk through a baby's problem instead of showing up at the only place they can think of to find help—the hospital emergency room.

NO MATTER how much advice and information is available to a new mother, she and her baby need adequate time to recover from childbirth before she can put it to use. Yet increasingly, American insurance practices are forcing hospitals to discharge mothers and newborns as quickly as possible. As insurance companies look for more ways to cut costs, new mothers are often rushed out of the hospital only twenty-four hours after an uncomplicated birth and three days after a cesarean. For many women, that just is not enough time to emerge from exhaustion, let alone to learn how to breast-feed properly or adjust to a new sleeping schedule and the other changes that arrive along with the baby.

I was hardly able to get around for the first three days after my cesarean. Fortunately, Bill roomed in at the hospital to care for both me and Chelsea. But almost as soon as I got home, five days after delivery, I had to turn around and go back to the doctor, with a high fever and acute pain from an infection.

A friend of mine who was pregnant with twins began hemorrhaging during labor and had to undergo an emergency cesarean under full anesthesia. After the delivery, she was severely anemic and was placed in intensive care. Even so, her insurance company, basing its decision on a "checklist" of medical factors, said it would not pay for more than three days in the hospital. In the end, the company did cover a longer stay, but only because her doctor spent hours on the phone arguing that it was medically unsafe to send her home. Some doctors won't take on such battles, because they fear being dropped by the managed care companies with which they do business.

Another friend's wife was covered for seven days in the hospital after a complicated childbirth. But the insurance company insisted on considering the baby independently of his mother. When my friend was told that meant the child would have to leave after three days, he asked, "Do you expect the baby to walk down to the parking lot and drive himself home?"

Insurance companies claim that limiting a baby's time in the hospital not only is a money-saver but also reduces exposure to hospital germs. On the other hand, most experts agree that a minimum of forty-eight hours is required to assess the medical risks for mothers and newborns. Generally, new mothers and babies who are discharged in the first twenty-four hours do not develop medical complications. But what happens if the baby develops an infection or other problem—like jaundice, which can cause permanent brain damage or death if it is not treated—that becomes apparent on only the second or third day after birth? What if the new mother has difficulty learning to breast-feed properly, which could result in dehydration or other serious problems for her baby?

In 1992, the American College of Obstetricians and Gynecologists and the American Academy of Pediatrics released a set of Guidelines for Perinatal Care, which recommended that discharge decisions take into account the medical stability of the mother and infant and whether the mother has learned to feed her baby adequately, been instructed in other basic care, and been informed about the availability of appropriate follow-up supports and services. All of these factors are dependent on the evaluations of doctors and nurses who care for mothers and babies, not of the accountants who pay bills or the patients themselves. (In the dizzying aftermath of childbirth, some mothers may decide they are ready to leave prematurely; others might choose to stay for weeks if permitted.)

Insurance companies point out that most new mothers are entitled to home visits by a nurse, who can help spot problems after they leave the hospital. But the reality is that many insurance companies cover only one home visit per patient; others simply provide for a phone consultation with a nurse in the days after childbirth. And cases have been reported in which the nurse or home visitor simply didn't show up.

A retired transit worker in New Jersey, Dominick A. Ruggiero, Jr., told this story to the New Jersey legislature earlier this year: His niece had an uneventful pregnancy and childbirth and was discharged after twenty-eight hours. At home, however, her baby, Michelina, suddenly took a turn for the worse. A nurse was supposed to visit the home on the second day, but she never came. When the family called, they were told the visiting nurse wasn't aware the baby had been born. Several times, the family called the pediatrician, who said the baby had a mild case of jaundice and did not need to be examined. The baby died from a treatable infection when she was two days old.

Thanks in part to Ruggiero's testimony, New Jersey now has a law that will make sure that insurance covers mothers for a minimum of forty-eight hours in the hospital after uncomplicated deliveries and ninety-six hours following cesarean deliveries. Maryland passed similar legislation last spring, and Congress is now considering a bill that would enforce such provisions nationwide. This is not a partisan issue. Maryland had a Democratic governor and legislature when it acted, and New Jersey's bill was passed by a Republican legislature and signed by a Republican governor. Pending congressional legislation has sponsors from both parties. Although some have suggested that such laws are another example of unwarranted government intrusion, it is difficult to dispute that the health of new mothers and infants is important enough to be safeguarded by the government.

THE WONDER, worry, and work of parenting does not end with concern about a baby's physical health. Emotional health and development demand equal attention. The mother-infant ward I visited in Manila took special interest in promoting bonding, the initial contact between parents and child immediately following birth. Watching the mothers and babies there, I remembered how minutes after her birth, Chelsea was cleaned up and handed to me and her father to hold. This initial contact began our lifelong commitment to our child.

My mother, like most American women giving birth in hospitals during the 1940s and '50s, was under general anesthesia for each delivery. She didn't breast-feed, because at the time breast-feeding was not encouraged, and she doesn't remember even seeing me until she was able to walk to the nursery, the day after I was born. She is understandably skeptical about the significance of immediate bonding, but she subscribes wholeheartedly to the importance of establishing in a child's first year what psychologists call a "secure attachment." Secure attachment is the foundation of the love and trust children develop in response to warm, dependable, sensitive caregiving. It develops over the first weeks and months of a child's life, not in the first few minutes.

Our country's favorite pediatrician, Dr. T. Berry Brazelton, describes how, in the islands of Japan's Goto archipelago, a new mother stays in bed for a month after delivery, wrapped in a quilt, warmly snuggled with her baby. During that time she has but one responsibility—to feed and hold her newborn. All her female relatives attend her. She herself is considered a child during this time and is spoken to in a sort of baby talk.

Personally, I could do without the baby talk, and a month strikes me as too long to be wrapped in a quilt, but I do admire the way this ritual celebrates and supports a new mother's most important task: helping her child establish a secure attachment with at least one adult. The secure attachments babies form in the first year give them the security and confidence they will need to explore the world and to develop caring relationships with others.

The smallest attentions to infants' needs—picking them up when they cry, feeding them when they are hungry, cuddling and holding them—promote the kind of positive stimuli their brains and bodies crave. A psychologist at the University of Miami recently studied two groups of premature babies. Both groups of infants were given state-of-the-art medical care and proper nutrition, but one group also received gentle, loving stroking for forty-five minutes each day. The babies who were touched warmly every day gained weight and developed so rapidly that they were ready to go home six days earlier than babies in the other group. (This simple human contact, resulting in early hospital release of these infants, also saved medical costs of $3,000 a day.)

Gentle, intimate, consistent contact that establishes attachment takes time, and as much freedom as possible from outside stress. The more rushed and harried new parents are, the less patience they will have for the considerable demands of newborns. Infants, of course, have no way of knowing the causes of their parents' stress, whether it be marital conflict, depression, or financial worries. But we know that babies sense the stress itself, and it may create feelings of helplessness that lead to later developmental problems.

Researchers at the University of Minnesota, one of the premier centers for the study of attachment, have followed almost two hundred people from birth into their twenties. Their findings echo the conclusion reached by scientists conducting research in the area of emotional intelligence: there is a connection between aggression and the lack of secure attachment. "To really understand violence in children," explains psychologist Allan Sroufe, "you have to also understand why most children and people aren't violent, and that has to do with a sense of connection or empathy with other people . . . that is based very strongly in the early relationships of the child and maybe most strongly in the earliest years of life."

Like other aspects of parenting, establishing a secure attachment with an infant may not come naturally, except in the sense that we are likely to do to our children what was done to us, unless someone or some experience gives us a different model. However, with an open mind and informed guidance, most parents can learn to relate better to their children, regardless of temperament.

Dr. Sally Provence, the child development expert I observed at the Yale Child Study Center, had a gift for reading the subtle signs of babies' discomfort in the way they reacted to being fed or held, and for teaching parents to do the same so that they could adjust their own behavior accordingly.

I remember standing behind a one-way glass, watching her work with a mother whose baby kept crying and arching his body away from her. The child looked as if he was trying to propel himself into space. I observed how Dr. Provence soothed the baby, speaking to him the same way she touched him, gently but firmly.

She translated what she did into simple instructions, for instance showing the mother how to hold the baby less stiffly by using her whole hand instead of just her fingertips. If that kind of hands-on instruction were readily available to more parents, many behavioral and emotional problems could be prevented.

THE VILLAGE can do much to give parents the time they need to establish their children's well-being in the first weeks and months of life. The Family and Medical Leave Act, the first bill my husband signed into law as President, on February 5, 1993, enables people who work at companies with fifty employees or more to take up to twelve weeks' leave in order to care for a new child, a sick family member, or their own serious health condition, without losing their health benefits or their jobs. Although the leave is unpaid, and employees at smaller firms are not covered at all, this is a major step toward a national commitment to allowing good workers to be good family members—not only after the birth or adoption of a child but when a child, parent, or spouse is in need.

My husband and I have heard from hundreds of Americans whose lives have already been helped by this historic legislation. One father pushing his daughter in a wheelchair on a tour through the White House saw the President and asked to speak with him. He thanked my husband for making it possible for him to spend time with his little girl, who was dying of leukemia, without fear of losing his job. This is real "family values" legislation.

WE CAN GO much further to allow and encourage parents to be there when children need them, most critically in the earliest weeks and months of life. Children do not arrive with instructions, but they do confer the immense and immediate responsibility of figuring out how best to care for them. Parenting does not all "come naturally," but ready or not, it comes. The village as a whole owes expectant and new mothers and fathers its accumulated experience and wisdom, and the resources they will need to tackle the important and exciting task ahead.

The World
Is in a Hurry,
Children Are Not

Many things we need can wait. The child cannot.
Now is the time his bones are being formed;
his blood is being made; his mind is being developed.
To him we cannot say tomorrow. His name is today.

GABRIELA MISTRAL

One Mother's Day, when Chelsea was about four years old, we were at church in Little Rock. During the children's sermon, the minister brought all the kids up to the front of the church and asked each of them, "If you could give your mommy anything in the world today, what would it be?" When it was Chelsea's turn, she answered without hesitation, "Life insurance." That broke up the congregation, and after the sermon a life insurance agent came up and offered to sell me a policy.

Later I asked Chelsea what she had meant. It turned out she had heard someone talking about life insurance, and she thought it meant that you could live forever. It was one of those "Kids say the darndest things" episodes, but to me it was the best Mother's

Day gift I could have received. This tiny child wanted me to live forever. Isn't that what being alive is all about—being loved like that?

Of course, children can't hang on to us forever, nor can we to them. Long before they lose us entirely, we relinquish them to their independence, in a series of surrenders that begins with our surrendering them to the world beyond the womb. Down the road, we surrender them to caregivers, teachers, employers, spouses—to the village, for good and ill.

We are right to think that with each step they take out into the world, they take a step away from us. As children develop, their sense of self unfolds. They learn to respond to their names, recognize their reflections in the mirror, and find their designated places at the dinner table. Learning to walk, kick a ball, or wave bye-bye allows them to explore the boundaries of the self, to discover where they stop and the rest of the world begins.

Initially, they tend to attribute godlike powers to adults, who, after all, provide everything that sustains them. A toddler watching a squirrel run across the yard turns delightedly to a parent and requests, "More?" And every parent knows the helpless feeling of hearing a sick child's plea to make an earache or a sore throat disappear or kiss away a scrape.

Given the powers they vest in us, it is tempting for us to see our children as extensions of ourselves. Too often, we try to correct our own flaws through them, even to right the wrongs done to us in the past. If you bite your nails, your child had better not bite his. If you are poor at math, you want her to be an Einstein. If you have a wicked temper, you pray that he will be blessed with the patience of Job. This impulse is understandable; we're only human. But parenthood is not a second childhood, and children are not miniature versions of ourselves. From the beginning, they are individuals who must be respected for who they are and are meant to become.

As children continue to grow and to learn, they develop a sense of their own power. The process of individuation is fascinating for parents to watch, but it can be painful too. What parent hasn't felt a pang the first time a toddler learning to walk bumps his head or the day a five-year-old starts school? It is difficult not to interpret a daughter's emerging independence as rejection, not to take a son's distinctly different tastes as a comment on our own.

It surprised us to discover that Chelsea did not like hot dogs or hamburgers—when we went to McDonald's, it was strictly Chicken McNuggets for her. That was easy to laugh about, but differences that go beyond fast-food preferences can be disconcerting. Bill, who loves nearly every kind of sporting event, relished watching Chelsea play soccer and softball. When she decided in high school to concentrate on ballet instead of continuing with team sports, he was disappointed, but her mind was made up.

Does inevitable independence mean that children need us less as they grow up? Exactly the opposite. They need us every step of the way. Paradoxically, in order to become their own autonomous selves, kids need us to talk with them, to listen to them, to read to them, to play with them, to teach them, simply to spend time with them.

The moments when a child arrives at some astounding new insight or makes a major leap in development, like forming his first letter or riding her first bike, are hugely pleasurable and never to be forgotten, but they are also far less frequent than many television commercials would have you believe. "Significant" moments arise out of long stretches of togetherness that may look uneventful to us but are crucial to helping children develop, both emotionally and intellectually.

•　　•　　•

ONE SATURDAY afternoon when Chelsea was about two, Bill was carrying her around and trying to talk to her, but their conversation kept being interrupted by the ringing of the phone. Finally, as Bill reached one more time to answer it, Chelsea, determined to get his attention, bit him on the nose.

Needless to say, he got her message. Kids need our time, and lots of it. In fact, child development experts believe "unhurried time" with a few loving adults is as important to children as good health and a safe environment.

For adults, time has many dimensions. We reflect on the past, worry about the future, and, increasingly, lament how the present flies by. Work spills over into time that used to be reserved for family, leisure, and other pursuits. This is partly because businesses downsizing and other economic stresses have "upsized" workloads, increased commutes and overtime, and wreaked havoc with our daily routines. These changes take an emotional and spiritual toll too. The growing sense that little is stable or permanent in our lives—families, neighborhoods, jobs, or values—clouds our priorities. So many of us have become part of what Secretary of Labor Robert Reich has called "the anxious class," for whom worrying is a way of life.

We also allow modern technology, with all its "labor-saving" inventions, to render our private time captive to beepers, buzzers, and bells. Instead of working less, now we can conduct business from our bathtubs or our cars. And rather than be ashamed of this, some of us boast, "Boy, I nearly killed myself last week. I worked eighty hours. . . . " Even our nonworking life has become less leisurely and more like work. We can, if we choose, shop or surf the Internet twenty-four hours a day.

American mothers, both those who stay at home and those who work outside it, spend less than half an hour a day, on average, talking with or reading to their children, and fathers spend

less than fifteen minutes. Most parents know that this is insufficient. In a 1993 study of working parents, two thirds said they didn't
spend enough time with their children. Another study found that a
good portion of the time parents and children are together is likely
to be spent watching television, when they relate not to each other
but to the set. Mothers who stayed home spent more time watching television with children than those who did not. And for all
mothers, time away from the TV was spent not talking but doing
household chores.

If we only stopped to listen to them for a few minutes, kids
could tell us that we move too fast, for their good and ours. Watch
the serenity of a baby taking in everything that happens around
her, absorbing the messages of her new environment. Every
moment has significance to her.

The present is very present to children, especially young children. They do not recognize, let alone comprehend, demands on
parents' time other than their own. And inconvenient as it is to
admit, they don't need or appreciate "quality time" so much as
"quantity time." That does not mean they require our every waking
moment. But there are limits to what we can expect of others who
care for them, and there is no substitute for regular, undivided
attention from parents.

THE FIRST years of life are not just important; they are more crucial
to shaping children than any other time. Even before they can
speak, children are extremely sensitive to the messages adults send
them. From the way we touch them and our tone of voice when we
bathe or change them, they sense whether we enjoy their company,
whether we are paying attention or are just going through the
motions, whether we are listening.

I remember vividly a little boy who was being observed and
treated at the Yale Child Study Center because he was having diffi-

culty relating to people. The psychiatrist treating him was convinced that he had trouble distinguishing between fantasy and reality, a perception the boy's parents came to share. One day the boy's father took him out in a rowboat off the coast of Maine. Suddenly the boy began to scream, "Look, there's a whale, there's a whale!" "Right, right," said his father, without even bothering to look. But it turned out there *was* a whale.

The point of this story, which I refer to as "The Boy Who Cried Whale," is an obvious one, but it bears repeating. If we bring preconceptions to our relationships with children, we will be unable to hear what they are trying to tell us. If we listened to them more—and more attentively—we would have far fewer angry, aimless, ill-defined adults. And chances are we would be more mindful of how we talk to them.

At any playground, for example, you will find parents hovering around the sandbox, comparing notes on their kids' progress in walking, feeding themselves, speaking, and toilet training. Children not only develop at their own paces; they have different gifts. A friend of mine with two-year-old twins notices that her little girl can recite the words to simple songs and talk up a storm, while her son, though less verbal, can build towers with blocks and shoot a ball through a three-foot-high basket.

Children who are subjected to constant comparisons may lose heart in their pursuit of a developmental task or abandon it altogether. Instead of quietly celebrating children's special ways of unfolding, we often make their uniqueness occasions for criticism and comment. Practically from the time children have learned the words to "Itsy Bitsy Spider," we are already ranking them: "She sings well." "He's tone-deaf." Why not encourage them all? Eventually the ones destined to be great singers will emerge from the pack. In the meantime, other children—even tone-deaf ones like me—may enjoy singing for the mere pleasure and sense of belonging it brings. (When I tried out for *Bye Bye Birdie* in high school, I was given a part in the chorus on condition that I dance but not sing. I didn't mind lip-synching; I just loved being part of the show.)

ON A HOT summer day in 1982, Bill and I were campaigning, together with Chelsea, on behalf of his candidacy for governor of Arkansas. We were walking up and down the streets of a small town, visiting with people about the election. Chelsea was holding my hand when I approached a group of women and children and introduced myself. I said to one mother, who was holding an infant, "I bet you're having fun, playing with her and talking to her all the time." The woman looked at me in amazement and said, "Why would I talk to her? She can't talk back."

Betty Hart and Todd Risley, two researchers who have dedicated their lives to learning how kids learn, have much to tell us about the importance of talking to children. In their book, *Meaningful Differences*, they tell how they recruited forty-two couples of varying socioeconomic and educational backgrounds, who allowed their babies' everyday interactions to be recorded one hour per month over the course of two and a half years.

While the families differed in income and educational background, all were stable and functioned well. The poorer parents and less educated parents were just as devoted to their children as more affluent parents, the researchers found. Yet they interacted with their children less, and the families as a whole were more isolated. For example, they did not venture out to places like the zoo or museums as frequently.

The biggest difference among the various households, though, was in the sheer amount of talking that occurred. The more money and education parents had, the more they talked to their children, and the more effectively from the point of view of vocabulary development. At the rate they were going, by age three, the children of the best-educated, most affluent parents would have heard more than thirty million words, three times as many as the children in the least-privileged families.

There were also significant differences in the ways parents talked to their children. On average, the parents with the most income and education tended to speak more affirmatively, conveying frequent and explicit approval with statements like "That's good," "That's right," "I love you." Working-class parents generally praised their children, but less frequently, and they more often voiced statements of disapproval, such as "That's bad," "You're wrong," "Stop," "Quit," "Shut up." Poor parents praised their children even less often and criticized them even more frequently.

Children's linguistic accomplishments appear to have less to do with the economic and educational advantages of their families than with the ways in which their parents communicate with them. Regardless of material advantages, children whose parents spoke frequently and affirmatively with them had larger vocabularies, as measured at age three. Follow-up testing in the third grade confirmed that the benefits of early language exposure persist, and do not seem to be caused by other factors, such as race or schooling.

This finding has great significance in a society such as ours, where children who start off learning verbal and analytic skills are more likely to be hired for the best-paying jobs later in life. It should give us hope that all parents, whatever their income or education, can offer their children a good intellectual start in life by learning a few simple rules about how to talk to them. Talking not only more but more constructively—painting "word pictures," telling and reading stories, and making the effort to speak positively—is something every parent can do.

Even in casual daily interactions with children, parents are teachers, and home is a child's first and most important classroom. For most of human history, in fact, home provided the only schooling children received in survival skills, job training, parenting, and becoming citizens of the larger world. Since the industrial revolution, in most advanced societies the lion's share of the task of instilling academic skills and knowledge has been delegated to formal education. But parents still play a crucial role.

As always, though, coaching parents is the first step. As less affluent and educated parents become aware that their own children can benefit from the kinds of experiences more privileged children get, Hart and Risley observe, they are more likely to give their children the advantages that are within their reach and to demand help with the "immense responsibilities a technological society has so casually assigned them."

MOST EARLY teaching and learning takes place in an unstructured fashion. "Play is the learning of childhood," says Dr. T. Berry Brazelton. But that does not mean the process will flourish without thought or planning. Kids need activities that engage them, physically, emotionally, intellectually, and sensually, not hours spent passively in front of the television set. Young children thrive on play that is spontaneous and responsive rather than goal-driven. Small kids appreciate small things. They don't need expensive or elaborate toys. Often a cupboard of pots and pans or plastic containers or a sock turned into a hand puppet is enough to fascinate them for hours.

My own mother was terrific at thinking up simple, imaginative activities to do with us. I remember how one time she took a cardboard box, filled it with sand, and spent the afternoon helping me to create a miniature world in it. We put a tiny mirror on the sand to make a lake, stuck in some evergreen twigs to make a little forest, and imagined adventures there for my dolls. Sometimes my mother and I would spend hours having picnics in our backyard and pointing out the shapes we saw in clouds.

The simple activities I shared with her became favorites of mine with Chelsea. We often spent hours in the backyard at the governor's mansion, stretched out on a quilt and looking at birds and clouds. We also used to lie on our backs in the front hallway when no one was around, watching the dancing rainbows the sun made as it struck the crystal chandelier.

Play continues to provide intellectual stimulation as children grow up. The marathon games of cards, Monopoly, and Clue that absorbed my brothers and me and our friends for long, rainy hours drilled us in basic concepts of math and logic.

An interest in science can be nurtured early and easily too. As every parent knows, children are fascinated with living things. Planting a garden with your child or taking care of a pet teaches valuable lessons and provides equally valuable time together. Dinosaurs are a surefire way of luring every preschooler I've ever met to the local natural history museum. Hanging a thermometer and barometer on the back porch can be an introduction to learning about the weather.

What adults consider work can often be made child's play. Many children find "real" activities just as engaging as toys, and they're also educational. Setting the table, for example, provides an opportunity to practice counting skills. Waiting for the cookies to come out of the oven is great motivation for learning to read the clock. Reading recipes aloud, step by step, gives older children practice with comprehension, and measuring spoons and cups give their fractions a workout.

One of my pet theories is that learning to tie shoelaces is a good way of developing hand-to-eye coordination in small children. Every adult around Chelsea spent time watching her struggle with her shoes. Her grandmother Virginia thought my theory led to wasting a lot of time that could have been spent playing, and she bought Chelsea a pair of shoes with Velcro fasteners; but I refused to let Chelsea wear them until she mastered the laces. It may sound silly now, but I loved the look of accomplishment on her face when she showed us all what she could do for herself.

To encourage these earliest discoveries is to help children develop not only specific skills but, just as important, the personality traits that are essential to later learning: confidence, motivation, effort, responsibility, initiative, perseverance, caring, teamwork, common sense, and problem solving. These "megaskills," as Dorothy Rich, founder of the Home and School Institute, calls them, are also the foundation of self-respect and the moral, ethical, and spiritual codes that guide us through life.

Children should be encouraged to learn in all sorts of ways, not just scholastic ones. They have a natural sense of curiosity and a love of discovery that needs to be nurtured to sustain itself. Applaud and encourage learning for learning's sake, whether it's cloud-watching or understanding what keeps a kite in the sky or mixing paints to make new colors. Helping kids to identify and explore their passions will prepare them to get the most out of not only school but life.

This is especially important for teenagers. Developing mutual interests with older children is an important way of keeping lines of communication open as well as establishing an ongoing influence on their intellectual and moral growth. Too often parents fail to understand that while teenagers need some space, they also need to know that adults are available and interested in the things that are important to them.

Young kids love repetition and the comfort of recurring patterns. I can't count the number of times that I read *Goodnight Moon* to Chelsea or watched *The Sound of Music* with her, in a nearly catatonic state. Whenever Julie Andrews got ready to launch into "Doe, a deer, a female deer," Chelsea's eyes would light up and she would say, "Here it comes, Mommy, my favorite song!"

Knowing what to expect next gives children a sense of security. Familiar stories, music, toys, and routines are the everyday landmarks that make them feel they belong. And repetition is one of the most important tools they use to learn.

Still, for many parents the repetition can be a little trying at times. I found that it was better to acknowledge the tedium than to feel guilty about it. I tried to bear in mind my own mother's admonition that what might seem trivial and repetitious to me could be the highlight of a child's day.

Routine—structured, ritualized time—is as essential to kids as unstructured play time. Dr. Brazelton describes a simple routine that works wonders. He recommends that when parents get home from work, they take some time to focus on their children right away. That may sound like a tall order if you feel the way I do at the end of a workday. But if you walked in the door and discovered you had unexpected adult company, you would probably pull up a chair and make conversation. And if you needed fifteen minutes at work to finish an important task, chances are you would make time for that too. Why should we consider spending time with adults and on work (even when they bore or annoy us) more crucial than spending time with our own children?

Family meals are a time-honored and important ritual of daily life, one that is, sadly, disappearing from the American landscape, a casualty of television, fast food, microwaves, and overtime. But it is precisely because our lives are so hectic that Bill, Chelsea, and I try to sit down to at least one meal a day together, usually dinner. After grace, which we take turns saying, there is no better time to catch up on what we have been doing all day, what we are excited about, and what troubles us. This evening, for instance, Bill talked about the budget debate in Congress and Chelsea talked about her history paper. Together, we talked about plans for Thanksgiving.

We're lucky that we "live above the store," the way a lot of families used to. On the other hand, we have had to give up the easy mobility and daily activities we used to take for granted. When Chelsea was small, I took her to ballet class every Saturday. On the way home, I took her to lunch or on errands, which gave us a chance to talk and be together. Now we have to work harder to find that kind of informal time. We make a point of taking breaks from our respective homework in the evening for a chat or a quick game of three-handed pinochle.

I admire the way Mormons set aside one night a week for family activities. When Chelsea was small, Bill and I adopted this idea. We took turns deciding what we would do. We went miniature golfing (guess who picked that?), rented movies, took long walks, played in parks, and did other simple activities.

One memorable night, Chelsea wanted us to go buy a coconut. She had never tasted one, but they were featured frequently in the Curious George stories she loved. We walked to our neighborhood store, brought the coconut home, and tried to open it, even pounding on it with a hammer, to no avail. Finally we went out to the parking lot of the governor's mansion, where we took turns throwing it on the ground until it cracked. The guards could not figure out what we were up to, and we laughed for hours afterward.

MOST CHILDREN have bedtime rituals, and Chelsea was no exception. From the time she was a baby, Bill and I took turns reading to her and praying with her. We promised ourselves that we would not skip this routine, no matter how tired we were. There were nights when one of us had to wake the other for "your turn."

But I don't think we fully appreciated the importance of this ritual to Chelsea until she was in first grade. Bill and I, concerned that she seemed reluctant to read to us at home, mentioned it during a conference with her teacher, a sensitive and insightful woman. She, too, had noticed that Chelsea was not enthusiastic about reading. Something seemed to be holding her back. The teacher urged us not to pressure Chelsea but to wait for her to decide on her own that she was ready to read.

Worried as we were, we took her advice. Eventually we realized that Chelsea herself was worried. She feared that we would stop reading aloud to her if she learned to read all by herself. When we assured her we would keep reading to her as long as she wanted us to, she relaxed and started to enjoy her own increasing skill.

Reading together is a wonderful pastime for parents and children, at any time. Just think: If you spend only twenty minutes reading to your child, that is more uninterrupted time than most fathers spend talking with their children each day. (Getting older siblings to read to younger children gives them valuable practice too.)

The village can encourage this all-important activity. The American Library Association is currently administering a three-year national demonstration project whose goal is to help low-income parents and those with poor literacy skills to raise children who are "born to read." The program works with adults to improve their own reading skills and emphasizes the importance of reading to children. The Association of Booksellers for Children is promoting a program called The Most Important Twenty Minutes of Your Day . . . Read with a Child. One aspect of the project has been getting pediatricians to "prescribe" reading aloud for parents, and for children as well when they reach reading age.

In addition to being read to, children love to be told stories. Storytelling has the advantage of convenience. You can do it in the car, in the doctor's office, in the bathtub, waiting in line. The stories don't have to be elaborate or even very good to engross a child. Bill made up episodes for Chelsea featuring characters from her life who performed heroic feats. A sailboat she saw when we visited the beach became "George the Sailboat," who had adventures all over the world. I told her stories whose heroines were brave little girls who rescued unicorns or slew dragons. Bill and I often paused to ask her what she thought happened next, drawing her into the storytelling role.

Children learn how to treat others from how they are treated themselves. If we want them to grow into attentive, affectionate, generous, and respectful adults, our treatment of them must embody those qualities. And if we also want our children to become inquisitive, independent thinkers who will find creative and productive outlets for their unique characters and talents, we would be wise to demonstrate those qualities in our earliest dealings with them.

Parents discover that this modeling of behavior is a two-way street. How many times have you watched a child playing and thought: If only I could bottle that energy? Children throw themselves with gusto into whatever they do. Not only are their bodies flexible and unwearied, but in some ways their lives are better integrated than ours. Because they are more attuned to the present than the future, the process than the product, they are not afraid to fail or to make fools of themselves, until we teach them otherwise. Spending time with children elevates our perceptions and energizes us.

As we get older, many of us abandon the activities we enjoy. The teacher who secretly writes fiction gives up after several magazines reject her work. The weekend artist puts away his watercolors. The former competitive swimmer can't tolerate the natural deterioration of her body and stops doing laps. Somehow we convince ourselves that to spend time doing these things, which don't pay the electric bill or look impressive on our résumés, is childish.

It is. Children teach us to see things in their most elemental forms. They teach us about uncluttered joy. Natural clowns, they remind us that life is full of comic moments. Whether they are making sand castles or dreaming up new kinds of people and animals, they are always looking at novel ways of putting things together. In all these ways, they remind us what is really important, and in so doing, they renew our spirit.

Not long ago, on a trip to Arkansas, I ran into a man whom Bill and I had known some years earlier. He had never graduated from high school but was a hard worker who made a living cooking, catering, painting, and doing odd jobs. He had recently become a father, and I asked him if he was enjoying talking to his baby daughter. He reminded me that he was quiet and shy by nature, not one to converse much with anybody, let alone an infant. "I'd feel like a fool talking to someone who wouldn't understand a word I was saying," he said. "Anyway, I wouldn't know what to talk about."

I suggested that he and his wife tell their daughter about their experiences during the day, or what they were watching on television, or even the trees, flowers, cars, and buses they could see as they walked down the street.

He looked a little uncertain, but he promised to try.

I could understand his uncertainty. Much as he loves her, his baby will not consciously remember the details of his earliest attentions to her. Even older children remember selectively; the details we treasure are not always those that made the greatest impression on them. But the time we spend with children—and what we do with it—is more than an indulgence for parents. It is an investment in children's future—an investment we can't make up later. As psychiatrist and writer Robert Coles has said, "Children who go unheeded are children who are going to turn on the world that neglected them." But children who get the early attention they need, from the family and the village, will repay our efforts a thousandfold, in the strong bodies, minds, and characters they carry into the future.

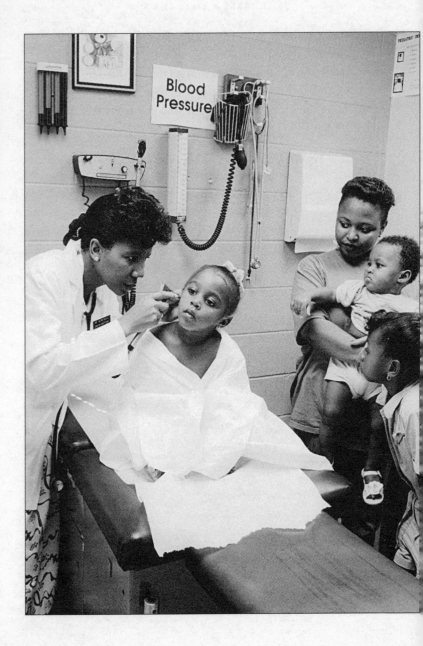

An Ounce of Prevention
Is Worth a Pound of
Intensive Care

Health is number one. You can't have a good offense, a good defense,
good education, or anything if you don't have good health.

SARAH MCCLENDON

D r. Betty Lowe, the medical director at Arkansas Children's
Hospital, who has been president of the American Academy
of Pediatrics and, most important, one of Chelsea's doctors, taught
me many lessons during the past two decades. Her medical expertise and down-to-earth manner reassured me, and her common
sense about preventive health care changed how I thought.

Years ago, we were both speaking to the Little Rock Junior
League about children's needs. After our speeches, a woman in the
audience asked Dr. Lowe what she would do to improve the
health of children. Without hesitating, she replied that she would
guarantee them clean water and good sanitation; nutritious food,
vaccinations, and exercise; and access to a doctor when they
needed one.

Dr. Lowe explained that the vast majority of children she saw in the hospital ended up there because of adults' failures to take care of them: the town that failed to clean up the sewage ditch behind some houses; the parents who failed to immunize a baby or to feed a toddler properly; the doctors who failed to accept Medicaid or treat the uninsured; the welfare worker who failed to protect a child from abuse or neglect; the landlord who failed to provide the heat promised in winter or to haul away garbage in summer; the teacher who failed to refer the belligerent or depressed teenager for help.

There's probably no area of our lives that better illustrates the connection between the village and the individual and between mutual and personal responsibility than health care. Every one of us knows we should take care of our bodies and our children's bodies if our goal is good health, and many of us try to do that. We also know, though, that we are dependent on others for the health of our environment and for medical care if we or our children become ill or injured. Knowing these things, however, does not always lead either individuals or societies to take action.

The effort to immunize children against preventable childhood diseases is a good illustration of the challenges before us. The American Academy of Pediatrics recommends that babies be taken for preventive checkups and receive appropriate immunizations when they are one, two, four, six, nine, twelve, and eighteen months old, then again at two, three, and four years. We've come a long way toward these goals from where we were a few years ago. Our national rate of immunization is higher than it has ever been, and as a result, we are at or near the lowest incidence ever recorded for every vaccine-preventable disease.

Some of this improvement may be due to the increased funding for immunizations and the outreach and education campaigns we have embarked on since my husband took office. We know that when funding for immunization decreased in the past, the incidence of serious disease increased. After the federal government's immunization funding was cut in the 1980s, a measles epidemic between 1989 and 1991 struck 55,000 people and killed 130 of them, many of them children. Medical costs of the epidemic exceeded $150 million, more than was "saved" by the cutbacks.

Providing funding for the inoculations themselves is key, because the vaccines are expensive and getting more so. In 1983, the private cost for a full series of immunizations was $27. Today the cost is ten times that much for just the shots themselves, and nearly as much again in administrative fees. Although nearly all managed care policies cover immunization costs, about half of conventional health insurance policies do not.

I will never forget the woman from Vermont whom I met at a health care forum in Boston. She ran a dairy farm with her husband, which meant that she was required by law to immunize her cattle against disease. But she could not afford to get her preschoolers inoculated as well. "The cattle on my dairy farm right now," she said, "are receiving better health care than my children."

Convenience is also a factor. Until recently, private doctors referred patients without adequate cash or insurance to the public health clinic, the only place families could take their children for free inoculations. But that doesn't mean the families went. Faced with a hodgepodge of providers, clinics' inconvenient hours and locations, and long waits, many parents delayed having their kids immunized.

In 1993, as part of a larger initiative to improve immunization rates, Congress adopted the Vaccines for Children program, which provides free vaccines to needy children through private doctors as well as clinics. The initiative also includes state funding to improve outreach and education, lengthen clinic hours, hire additional staff, and expand services. But these advances are already under grave threat from budget cuts.

We have a lot of ground to cover as it is. In immunization rates, we still trail behind a number of other advanced countries and even some less developed ones. And although three out of four of today's two-year-olds have the proper immunizations (up from about one in four in 1991), that leaves almost 1.4 million toddlers who have not received all the vaccinations they need.

Most parents are aware that immunizations are required for a child to enter school, but many of them, and even some health care providers, don't know that 80 percent of the required vaccinations should be given by the age of two. That is why the village needs a town crier—and a town prodder.

Kiwanis International, the community service organization, has been both, working to promote the needs of children from prenatal development to age five through an international project called Young Children: Priority One. Among other efforts, the project has launched a national public education campaign, which features my husband on billboards and in public service announcements calling for "all their shots, while they're tots."

Two women I greatly admire have campaigned for more than two decades to make sure that children get the vaccinations they need, on time. Rosalynn Carter, a distinguished predecessor of mine who is compassion in action, and Betty Bumpers, the wife of the senior U.S. senator from Arkansas and an energetic advocate for children, have worked with spirit and dedication to persuade Americans to invest the money and energy necessary to ensure that all children receive their immunizations on time. When the measles epidemic began in 1989, they started a nonprofit immunization education program, called Every Child by Two, working with community leaders, health providers, and elected officials at the local, state, and national levels to spread the word about timely immunizations and to establish and expand immunization programs around the country.

We know that requiring children to show proof of immunization before they enter school guarantees that children get their shots by five or six. States and cities looking for similar ways to ensure compliance for toddlers are linking immunization efforts to social service programs. A program in Maryland requires families on welfare to show proof of immunization in order to receive benefits, a requirement I have long advocated. Recent studies in Chicago, New York, and Dallas show that coordinating immunization services with the Special Supplemental Nutrition Program for Women, Infants and Children (WIC) significantly improves immunization rates.

If we can see to it that cows get their shots, we can see that kids do too—before the cows come home.

Of course, cows don't cry at the sight of hypodermic needles. It takes more than a village to persuade children that the sting of a shot is really in their interest. It helps to explain to the child in advance what the shots do, perhaps by illustrating it with her favorite dolls and stuffed animals. I know parents who take a favorite teddy bear to the doctor's office to have its "shots" as well. That allows the child to commiserate with the bear when the needle is applied, and the bear to sympathize with the child when her turn comes.

PEDIATRICIANS recommend that children continue to get checkups at five, six, eight, and ten years. From the age of eleven on, the most explosive period of growth after infancy, they should be examined yearly. Between checkups, there are steps each of us can take to keep children healthy. From basic hygiene habits like frequent hand washing to healthier eating and exercise, prevention works.

Let's talk first about food, as we love to do. This country dreams of food, thinks about it constantly—lemon tarts shimmering under meringue, ribs drenched in barbecue sauce, golden-brown fried chicken, mashed potatoes swimming in butter, and mile-high chocolate pies, beckoning us to indulge, indulge, indulge.

Our passion for food is a national obsession, and so is our guilt over it. Pick up a magazine or listen to the punch lines of talk show comedians, and you are left with the notion that America's conscience is concerned chiefly with diet and weight. And with some reason: One in three adults is overweight, up from one in four during the 1970s. And one in five teenagers—up from fewer than one in seven—is overweight or close to becoming overweight, according to a survey conducted by the Centers for Disease Control between 1988 and 1991.

At the same time, it is estimated that one in twelve American children suffers from hunger. So while we will focus here on avoiding the health problems brought on by eating too much and exercising too little, let's not forget those among us who have too little on the table to begin with. It is critical that we continue to give nutritional assistance, especially to pregnant women, infants, toddlers, and schoolchildren, through government programs like WIC, food stamps, and school lunches.

I GREW UP in the "clean plate" era. Today I look back at my family table, circa 1959—the pot roast and potatoes piled high and spilling over the edges of our plates—and see a catastrophe of calories, whose consequences my brothers and I avoided during childhood by walking or biking back and forth to school and around town and playing hours and hours of sports. We were expected to eat all of whatever we were served: If we balked, we heard, like a broken record, stories about starving children in faraway lands who would gladly eat what we scorned. My brother Hugh became a champion cheek-stuffer. Tony offered to mail his food to any country my father named. In the end, we ate whatever we had to in order to be "excused" from the table.

As with so many other aspects of family life in recent decades, the pendulum has swung to the other extreme—in this case, from the "clean plate" theory of nutrition to the "no plate" one. Many families rarely sit down to even one daily meal together at a table in their home. It's easier to grab a doughnut on the run in the morning, a burger and fries at lunch, and then for dinner to graze on takeout, with one eye on the TV.

The majority of adults and teenagers, who do not drink excessively or smoke, can go a long way toward safeguarding their long-term health through diet and physical activity. As Dr. C. Everett Koop, the former surgeon general, has said, "If we could motivate the public to focus on achievable and maintainable weight, we would have taken a very significant step toward preventing one of the most common causes of death and disability in the United States today."

It is far easier to begin good nutrition in childhood, when parents largely determine their children's diet and the eating habits of a lifetime are established. It's important, however, that diet not become a household mania. Every parent knows that children go through "eating phases," which they will outgrow and the rest of us must endure. When Chelsea was in preschool, there were a few weeks when she would not eat anything for lunch but green grapes and a grape jelly sandwich on white bread. After a few days of observing her class, a worker from the state's child care licensing division asked the head teacher why the parents of the curly-haired blond girl sent her to school every day with such an inadequate lunch. The teacher refrained, thankfully, from naming the parents and assured her that she would talk to them.

Most of us are more relaxed than our parents were about exactly what our kids eat and how much, but a greater leniency should not become an excuse for poor nutrition. Despite—or maybe because of—all the nutrition information bombarding people every day, there is a lot of confusion about what to feed ourselves, let alone our kids. Even in the face of good information, we may be resistant to change. Head Start teachers have told me that after they'd taught children about healthy foods, some parents complained that they couldn't afford the foods their kids requested or that they just didn't "eat that stuff" in their house.

Good nutrition does not have to be expensive. As part of the Shape Up America! program he started, Dr. Koop recommends making healthy eating a permanent part of a family's way of life, not an occasional "diet." There has been a revolution in the past decade when it comes to information about food, and many of us now grasp the basics: we should be eating more grains, beans, fish, fruits, and vegetables and less meat, fat, and sugar. We should encourage our families to fill their plates with a moderate amount of food—a sensible meat serving, for example, is about the size of a deck of cards—and to refrain from seconds. New nutrition labels help us choose lower-fat milk and cheese and select other products that are lower in fat as well as higher in fiber. Many restaurants offer healthier alternatives—lean or "spa" cuisine.

We need to teach children to take responsibility for their own weight, rather than passing the buck to genetics or a slow metabolism. Although diet is not an exact science, and we differ in the amounts and kinds of foods we can healthily consume, these physiological factors account for only a small number of overweight people. Most of us (including me) simply exercise too little and eat too much.

If your children need to lose weight, help them to set a reasonable goal and make a sensible plan for getting there. Parents of teenage girls, who often believe they are overweight even when they are not, should take particular care to prevent their daughters from dieting excessively or obsessing about their weight. As Richard Troiano, one of the epidemiologists who conducted the Centers for Disease Control survey, reminds us, "There is already too much of a culture of thinness leading to eating disorders in this age group." Their risk of nutritional deficiencies is serious.

I have read advice like Dr. Koop's a thousand times and know that I could do better in my own eating. Since moving into the White House, I have enlisted the ingenuity of chef Walter Scheib in concocting menus for official events and family meals that live up to nutritional guidelines as well as the expectations visitors have for presidential hospitality. For family meals, we moved a table into the second-floor serving kitchen, where we usually (but not always!) dine on vegetables, grains, fruits, lean meats, and fish.

Diet alone does not account for the dramatic increase in weight among Americans, however, especially among children and teenagers. The main culprit is a combination of poor food choices and too little exercise. In many American households, the juvenile couch potato whose only operating muscles appear to be in his jaws, chomping away hour after hour on high-calorie nonfoods, is a familiar sight. A study by the Centers for Disease Control confirmed this picture, showing that physical activity among children and teenagers has declined during the time average weight has gone up.

In a 1990 Youth Risk Behavior Study, only 37 percent of high school students reported getting at least twenty minutes of vigorous exercise three or more times a week, down from more than 60 percent in the 1970s. My home state of Illinois is the last to mandate daily physical education for all students, kindergarten through twelfth grade, although the Illinois legislature recently passed a law allowing local school districts to apply for waivers. In most states, requirements are already left up to local school districts, and the results are not encouraging. Only half of American teenagers are enrolled in physical education classes, and only one in five attend daily. More than one in three, however, report watching three or more hours of television or videos every school day.

I was not always happy to have to take physical education classes every day of my school life, especially when I had to rush to my next class, my hair still dripping from the heavily chlorinated old pool. But I am grateful in retrospect that I learned about different sports, developed some athletic skills, and, most important, exercised my body as well as my mind each day.

I regret the move away from organized physical education and the reduction of recess time for younger kids. All children, especially in today's stressful world, need the joyful release of free play as well as healthful exercise. *Mens sana in corpore sano*, the ancients advised, and it still holds true—a strong mind in a strong body.

How can we achieve that for our children? For starters, turn off the TV, VCR, and computer, get up, and get moving—and get your kids to do the same. Brisk walking, hiking, and bicycling are all good exercise and are great ways to spend time together as well. Put physical education and recess back into the school day. Thirty minutes a day of exercise is recommended for adults or children of average weight, forty-five minutes for overweight people, but it doesn't have to be all at once. You can build shorter periods into your and your kids' regular daily routines. Walk them to the park, school, or store instead of jumping in the car to go two blocks. Take the stairs instead of the elevator. Try to plan vacations and outings around exercise—nature walks, hiking trips, or camping and canoeing in our national parks.

The knowledge that poor nutrition and inactivity are clearly implicated in the high incidence of arthritis and such serious and often fatal illnesses as cancer, heart disease, and diabetes should be enough to get us and our children to shut the refrigerator door and open the front door.

The village can do its part to help. The U.S. Department of Agriculture, which oversees school lunch and breakfast programs, has started Team Nutrition, a partnership between the federal government, states, school districts, farmers, and businesses to promote healthy food choices in homes and schools and in the media. Among other projects, Team Nutrition has recruited volunteer chefs from leading restaurants to concoct recipes for nutritious cafeteria food—lemon chicken, vegetable lasagna, oranges and strawberries in tangerine juice—that kids actually will eat. I tried some rice pilaf with lentils, beans, and chick peas with a group of fifth and sixth graders, who not only ate what was served but said they liked it.

The President's Council on Physical Fitness and Sports is working hard to convince schools both to require physical education for all grades and to give younger students opportunities during the school day to play outside in safe, supervised settings. The goal is to get at least half of all schoolchildren participating in daily physical education. The council emphasizes that classes should include more activities that people can readily pursue over a lifetime, like swimming, bicycling, jogging, and racquet sports.

It also recommends that communities increase the availability and accessibility of facilities for these and other activities. Many churches, like my husband's, Immanuel Baptist in Little Rock, have built family centers that include athletic facilities for exercise classes, basketball games, and jogging or walking. But community recreation centers, especially for teenagers, are nonexistent in many neighborhoods where kids need them most. I can't understand the political opposition to programs like "midnight" basketball and other recreational activities. Providing funds to inner-city neighborhoods to give young people positive outlets for their energies under adult supervision sounds great to me, as a way not only to prevent health problems but to prevent kids from getting into trouble.

KEEPING CHILDREN healthy in body and mind is the family's and the village's first obligation. But we all know that no matter how conscientious a parent might be or how committed to preventive health a community might be, children will inevitably suffer from disease and injury. Then medical care is required.

Three tales of our era:

A Texas teenager suffered from high blood pressure and recurring stomach pain, but he was uninsured and his family could not afford the tests that would determine the cause of his problems. Then he developed difficulty raising his arms as well. When he needed immediate medical care, he went to the emergency room of the local hospital. His mother applied for Medicaid but was told that the family's income slightly exceeded the state's eligibility level.

A six-year-old Kansas girl developed a severe infection that required mastoid surgery. When she was released from the hospital, physicians prescribed antibiotics to be administered by IV at home, but the family's insurance policy refused to cover the cost. Without the antibiotics, she developed seizures and inflammation of the brain, and ultimately lost many fine motor and cognitive skills, including the ability to speak. She now requires complicated therapy and nursing care to manage her condition.

A Virginia woman was unable to afford health insurance for her son, who suffered from severe asthma. When he had an asthma attack, she would take him to the emergency room, where doctors would treat him and prescribe medication for him to continue at home. But his mother could not afford to have the prescriptions filled, and even when the doctors gave her a free dose to take home she held off giving it to him until the last possible minute, knowing she could not afford more.

I could tell you many other stories that end in the same question: Is this the kind of health care system our children deserve?

Today there are more than ten million children, most with working parents, who do not have health insurance; that number has been rising by about a half million a year. The rate will accelerate even more if Congress's proposed cutbacks in Medicaid, which provides government insurance for poor children, are enacted. That would channel even more children into overworked emergency rooms for basic care, where overworked staffs will eventually be forced to turn them away.

When I look into the eyes of parents whose children's illnesses are not only taking an emotional toll but exacting a cruel financial cost because they could not afford insurance, I think, There but for the grace of God go I and everyone I love. The number of Americans who will face these heartbreaks is growing.

Some families who can afford to pay for private insurance are unable to find coverage. In Cleveland, Ohio, I met a couple who have two daughters with cystic fibrosis and a healthy older son. The father, a self-employed professional, provided health insurance to his employees and their families. The family could afford private insurance for themselves and their son and would have bought it for their daughters but could find no one willing to sell them a policy because of the girls' conditions. They repeated to me the words of one insurance agent—words I will never forget as long as I live. "What you don't understand," the agent told them, "is that we don't insure burning houses."

I find this attitude deplorable. What kind of message does it send to hardworking people who love their children but cannot protect them? And if we are willing to write off these children, whose will be next? That is a question for all of us to ponder, because as research in genetics continues to advance, scientists will soon be able to tell us which of our genes predispose us to cancer or diabetes or many other serious diseases. Will those of us who carry such genes and the children we pass them on to eventually be denied insurance too?

When I met seven-year-old Ryan Moore of South Sioux City, Nebraska, I knew I had encountered a young person of heroic disposition. Ryan was born with a congenital syndrome that produces multiple birth defects. His father, Brian, was able to provide his family with good health insurance until Ryan was a year old, when the company Brian worked for went out of business. Brian searched for work but was unable to find a job because companies were wary of his son's health care needs. "It's like they looked right through me and only saw my son," said Brian. "I have a lot to contribute, and I couldn't even get work as a janitor."

Seven-year-old Ryan, however, did find work. He has become a local celebrity, mainly by being himself—hopeful, happy, and resilient in the midst of all his troubles. Ryan has been working with the Children's Miracle Network and raising money to support his high medical and travel costs. This brave little boy loves to quote Piglet from *Winnie-the-Pooh:* "It is hard to be brave when you are such a small animal."

Another small, brave soul I met was four-year-old Mike Bebout, who came to the White House for a children's health event. He has suffered all his life from short bowel syndrome, which prevents his body from absorbing the nutrients it needs. His parents could not get private insurance to cover his treatments. His older brother, another Ryan, told me that he thought every kid should get the health care he needs, and he had come up with an acronym for the cause—MIKE—Medical Insurance for Kids Everywhere.

The lack of adequate health care for many Americans forces us into an emergency situation on every level. People use emergency wards as clinics, overburdening hospitals' resources and often receiving, in turn, inadequate preventive or follow-up care. Infants and children end up with serious conditions requiring expensive care because we don't invest in prevention. Toddlers don't get their immunizations on time. School-age children don't get the nourishment or exercise they need to feed their growing minds and bodies.

Many people believe that we cannot guarantee health care to all because of cost. In fact, a sensible universal system would, as in other countries, end up costing us less. That's because most children who become ill or injured are eventually treated somewhere, even if they are given too little, too late, and at a greater cost than they—or we—would have paid if we had made sure their symptoms had been treated earlier. But until we are willing to take a long, hard look at our health care system and commit ourselves to making affordable care available to every American, the village will continue to burn, house by house.

You can already get a good look at the fallout from our procrastination by visiting the emergency room of any large urban hospital. On display are not just the medical crises for which an emergency room is designed but dozens of children, from infants to teenagers, who don't appear to have any serious ailment. Why are they there? They have fever, earaches, stomach upsets—the kinds of aches and pains that are better treated by a school nurse or at a doctor's office or clinic, or, better yet, warded off with good preventive care.

But most schools no longer have nurses, and doctors cost money—and even people with insurance find that many policies do not cover routine preventive services for children. Most public health clinics are not open at hours that are convenient for working parents. The for-profit clinics sprouting up in shopping malls keep longer hours but require cash or verifiable credit and are not always easily accessible.

If the number of uninsured Americans continues to rise and the influence of profit-driven medicine continues to grow, many nonprofit hospitals will be forced to close, and ultimately those who cannot afford the cost of expert care will be forced to fall back on low-tech, hands-on solutions. Ironically, less developed nations will be our best models for the home doctoring we will then need to master. If this scenario sounds farfetched, let me tell you that it is already happening. When I visited the International Center for Diarrheal Disease Research in Bangladesh, funded in part with American aid, I met a doctor from Louisiana who was there to learn about low-cost techniques he could use back home to treat some of his state's more than 240,000 uninsured children.

I started this chapter with Dr. Lowe's prescription, and like all the remedies she's ever prescribed for my child, I've found it sound: Commonsense prevention in our homes and schools. A reformed health care system that guarantees all children the medical care they need. Money would be saved from both these approaches instead of the billions of dollars we now spend to fix problems we could have avoided in the first place.

I'm not sure we will follow Dr. Lowe's prescription in the short run, but I know we will eventually. One of the reasons I worked so hard on health care reform was that I could not stand the fact that there are millions of children who do not have health insurance and millions more who are dependent on Medicaid, which may not be as available in the future if the current Congress gets its way. Our society will not be able to afford the moral or economic costs of intensively caring for children who should have been, in Dr. Lowe's words, "treated right in the first place."

Security Takes More
Than a Blanket

There's no place like home . . . there's no place like home.

DOROTHY

I must have been about eight years old when my mother's mother took me and my brother Hugh to see *The Wizard of Oz*. We went downtown to one of Chicago's grand old movie palaces on a Saturday afternoon. I'd never been in so majestic a theater before.

On our way there, my grandmother kept warning us that little children sometimes got kidnapped by strangers from city movie houses. When we reached our seats, she sat between us and looped her arms around my brother and me to protect us from harm, real and imagined.

The scenarios she conjured up were enough to give us goose bumps even before the movie started. By the time those weird-looking winged monkeys flew out of the witch's castle and Dorothy and Toto were grabbed and taken away, kids were screaming and my brother was trying to climb under his seat to hide. I grabbed hold of my grandmother's hand for comfort, only to discover that it was as clammy as mine. It was the first time I remember being thoroughly scared.

Finally the monkey scene ended and the witch melted away. Dorothy and her friends found their way back to the Emerald City. Kids around us stopped crying, and Hugh settled back in his seat. My grandmother even relaxed her grip a little. When Dorothy clicked the heels of her ruby-red slippers, I tapped my sneakered feet together under my seat and repeated along with her, "There's no place like home . . . there's no place like home."

When I got home, my mother asked us to tell her about the movie. Before I could open my mouth about the amazing girl who had the same name she did, Hugh was describing the monkeys flying at him and the scary music and the dark forest. My parents reassured us that the story was only make-believe and that they would never let something like that happen to us.

But it wasn't only the monkeys that had scared me. What disturbed me more deeply was the realization I'd had, sitting there in the dark, that all the people around me—even the adult who was in charge of me—were also scared. It was a profoundly disconcerting experience. In those days, for most people, it was also a rare experience.

In my town, kids rode their bikes everywhere—to the library, to the movie theater, to the shops, to restaurants. (My favorite was the Robin Hood, which had scenes of Sherwood Forest on the walls. For years, my friends and I thought we had invented the idea of putting ketchup on french fries there.)

My brother Hugh, a born adventurer, went off with his buddies on exploits for hours on end. When the neighborhood mothers couldn't find their boys, they'd call the local police. The first time that happened, the police found them playing among the foundations of the half-built homes in a new development. Hugh, remembering my mother's firm instructions, refused to get into the patrol car with a stranger, even if he was a policeman. So the police car followed him slowly all the way home, as the other kids sat in the back seat.

There were real dangers. A local murder or kidnapping made headlines from time to time. We encountered the occasional stranger who exposed himself to us in the parks or tried to get one of us to go for a ride or, as happened to my friends and me once, pulled out a butcher knife to scare us when we were exploring a building site. Perils existed, but they seemed manageable if we followed the basic rules of safety our parents taught us.

Once, while I was still in grade school, an older boy who was visiting in the area chased me, threw me to the ground, and kissed me until I kicked and hit him hard enough to extricate myself and scramble home. I ran to the kitchen sink and washed my face over and over again, while screaming to my mother about what had happened. She calmed me down and, after making sure that I was not hurt, talked with me about how I could avoid that boy and take better care of myself in the future.

With fewer guns around, a stranger's desperation or a family member's sudden burst of anger was less likely to have lethal consequences than today. Children's disagreements generally ended with no injury more serious than hurt feelings or, at worst, bruises from a fistfight. Friends of my generation who grew up in inner cities or isolated rural areas recall moments of fear or danger, but nothing like the pervasive anxiety about safety that has seeped into every corner of our country's psyche.

One warm spring afternoon when Chelsea was about nine years old, she and a friend, who had been riding their bikes around the fountain in front of the governor's mansion, came inside to ask if they could bike to the public library ten blocks away. I remembered all the trips I'd made to my local library at their age, unaccompanied and unafraid. Tears welled up in my eyes as I told her no. I put aside what I was doing and drove the girls to the library instead.

My reaction may have been disproportionate to the actual risk involved, but it was symptomatic of the general anxiety about children's safety that grips every parent I know. Jennifer Allen, a mother and writer who traveled around the country for *Life* magazine to talk with parents about the dangers facing children today, emphasizes that household accidents and unintentional injuries are more common threats to their well-being. Yet, she observes, "we can't stop worrying about the other things, the less dangerous, less likely things like strangers abducting our children."

There *is* no place like home in children's lives. Brain research teaches us that feeling "safe and protected" is essential to healthy neurological development. But home should provide an emotional as well as a physical haven. Children have an uncanny ability to detect adults' feelings of powerlessness. It is impossible for them to feel safe when they sense that we are uncertain we can protect them.

SECURITY DOESN'T end with the physical environment, but it begins there. Safety-minded parents keep household poisons, plastic bags, and matches out of reach. Landlords and public housing authorities install screens to prevent accidents, fix dripping hot-water faucets so children don't scald their hands, and repaint peeling walls so that children don't ingest lead, which can harm their developing brains.

Ann Brown, whom I like to think of as the Pied Piper of child safety—she chairs the Consumer Product Safety Commission—has pulled together a wealth of information on "childproofing" homes. Recently, she invited me to accompany her to the Mazique Parent-Child Center in Washington, D.C., as she teamed up with Gerber Products and the Food Marketing Institute to unveil the Baby Safety Shower How-To Kit. Brown suggested that baby showers with a safety theme are a great way to help new and expectant mothers childproof every room in their homes. I was so impressed by the shower idea that I gave safety items at a White House shower I hosted for a friend who had just adopted a baby.

I watched as Ann performed a test that all new parents should know about: If a can of soda held upright fits through the slats on the side of a baby's crib, the space between them is too wide and babies can get their heads caught. Baby mattresses should be firm and flat; mattresses that are too soft can smother babies as they sleep. Inexpensive plugs for electrical outlets and safety gates to block stairways can avoid other serious mishaps.

Three times as many children die each year from preventable household accidents as from murder. By definition, accidents are unpredictable. Beyond a certain extent, then, they cannot be avoided, but serious injuries from them most often can be. My mother remembers the time when, as a toddler, I spotted a Coke bottle that painters in our apartment building had filled with turpentine. I began drinking it before anyone knew what I was doing. The adults around me reacted quickly to prevent serious consequences. The experience cured me of ingesting anything I wasn't sure about (except for the fermented mare's milk I sampled as the honored guest of a nomadic family in Mongolia). But as I grew up, even with watchful adults hovering close by, I still had more than my share of accidents: an arm scalded with boiling water, gashed ankles, knees, and eyebrows; falling down stairs.

Parents should be willing to go toe-to-toe with their kids over taking certain precautions, like wearing helmets to bicycle, ride a motorcycle, skateboard, or Rollerblade. I remember once, on a trip to San Diego, telling Chelsea and a friend that they didn't need to wear helmets to accompany me on a short bike ride, and I didn't either. Imagine my horror when Chelsea's friend ran into the door of a truck that opened suddenly in her path. Thankfully, she was not hurt, and I got off with a good scare and deep embarrassment when articles about the incident ran in local newspapers. But wearing helmets could help protect some of the more than forty thousand children who receive head injuries each year. Car safety seats and seat belts, used properly, could help prevent another forty-nine thousand injuries in car accidents.

Among the most tragic accidents are those involving guns. Each year, about five thousand people under the age of twenty die because of firearms. One in ten of these deaths is said to be accidental, many of them caused by children who find loaded guns in their homes. Nearly half of all American households have guns, and often, instead of being locked up, they are just hidden or even left in a drawer, filled with ammunition. Accidental gun injuries have become so prevalent that the American Medical Association advises doctors to make a point of talking with patients who are gun owners about using safety locks on their guns and storing ammunition separately.

A safety lock is no substitute for the most essential form of child protection, however: the attentiveness of parents and other adults, and of the village at large.

Last summer, during one of the worst heat waves here in our nation's capital, four-year-old Iesha Elmore and her two-year-old brother, Clendon, wandered away from their house and climbed into an unlocked car in a nearby parking lot. A couple of hours later, both children were found dead of suffocation.

The headline on a follow-up story in the *Washington Post* read "No Place to Play." A neighbor of the children's family was quoted as cautioning those who don't live in the neighborhood not to judge the children's mother too harshly. Pointing past a blue plastic pool in the run-down housing project, which has no playground, she said, "What is there to do around here? Where is there to play?"

Stories like this sadden me for the senseless loss of young life. But they also anger me, because no one will take responsibility. Although the parents—both mother and apparently absent father—were primarily responsible for these children, it is too easy, as the neighbor suggests, to blame only them.

The residents are justified in pointing to the larger community's neglect. For years, they had tried in vain to get local authorities to install a playground and a speed bump that would slow down the cars careening through their streets. But the neighbors themselves deserve some of the blame. Why didn't they organize themselves to meet their children's needs or to demand that they be met? Why didn't they take turns watching the kids, pitch in to clean up the project's yard, chip in to buy a few outdoor toys that all the children could share?

Parents can't police kids twenty-four hours a day. They need to be able to rely on other adults for help, the way my mother and father could. In the neighborhood where I grew up, if a child fell from a tree or a fight broke out between kids, someone else's parent was likely to run out of the nearest house to help. Partly this was because more mothers were at home during the day, and other relatives frequently lived nearby. People also welcomed their neighbors' intervention, rather than seeing it as a criticism of their parenting.

A woman who is raising children of her own remembers that

when she was growing up, she had to be careful about what she did because her grandmother would find out about her behavior even before she got home. Her grandmother welcomed reports from neighbors, even when it was bad news, like the day she tried smoking for the first time.

Some communities are so besieged by issues of survival that children's needs get pushed aside. But here and there, neighborhoods are working to rebuild a sense of trust and mutual responsibility.

In Morningside Gardens, a racially mixed cooperative housing complex in Harlem that is home to almost a thousand families, neighbors make a point of getting to know one another. The complex includes a senior citizen center, a combination day care center and nursery school, a bank, and a grocery store. The complex has its own security patrol and a newspaper that spreads word of births, deaths, and other community news. Residents place a special emphasis on giving young people a stake in the life of the community. There are recreation and tutoring programs, and children and teens are recruited for cleanup projects and other neighborhood activities.

Residents attribute the health of their village to a strict resident selection process and their grassroots approach to problem solving. They also emphasize a third factor, which is increasingly on citizens' minds these days: public safety.

ONE EVENING during the 1992 presidential campaign, Bill and I were being escorted to a dinner through a hotel kitchen. A waiter reached out to shake Bill's hand. He said he had immigrated to this country from Greece and was now a citizen. "Governor," he said, "my boy is ten years old. He studies politics in school. He says you should be President. Since I trust my boy, I will vote for you." Bill smiled and said how honored he'd be to receive the vote.

"But I have something to ask you," the man continued. "Where I came from, we were poor, but at least we felt free. Here in America, my family is no longer free. When my boy cannot walk across the street to play in the park in our neighborhood unless I am with him, he is not free. If I do what my boy asks and vote for you, will you make him free?"

On April 29, 1994, James Darby, Jr., a boy just a year younger than that waiter's son, wrote to my husband from his home in New Orleans. "Dear Mr. Clinton," he began, "I want you to stop the killing in the city. People is dead and I think that somebody might kill me. So would you please stop the people from deading. I'm asking you nicely to stop it. I know you can do it. Do it. I know you could." He signed the note, "Your friend, James."

Reprinted with special permission of King Features Syndicate.

Nine days later, James Darby, Jr., was fatally shot in the head during a drive-by shooting in his neighborhood.

The freedom James and the waiter asked for is the kind Bill and I experienced when we were young. It existed because adults in our communities offered us both formal and informal means of protection when we ventured out. A number of efforts are under way to re-create that sense of freedom.

The first step is to take weapons off the streets and to put more police on them. The Brady Bill, which my husband signed into law in 1993, imposes a five-day waiting period for gun purchases, time enough for authorities to check out the buyer's record and for the buyer to cool down about any conflict he might have intended the gun to resolve. Since it was enacted, more than forty thousand people with criminal records have been prevented from buying guns. The 1994 Violent Crime Control and Law Enforcement Act banned nineteen types of military-style assault weapons whose only purpose is to kill people and it stopped the revolving door for career criminals with its "three strikes and you're out" provision. As part of a "zero tolerance" policy for weapons, drugs, and other threats to the safety of teachers and students, the President signed an executive order decreeing that any student who comes to school with a gun will be expelled and punished as a condition of federal aid.

Twenty-five thousand new police officers are being trained, with the goal of adding seventy-five thousand more by the end of the decade. Taking a cue from what's worked in the past, cities are deploying officers differently, getting them out from behind desks and putting them back on the sidewalks, where they can get to know the people who live and work on the streets they patrol. They will be doing what is called "community policing," where being a good police officer is as much about establishing good community relationships that help prevent crime as it is about responding to crime when it happens.

The other half of community policing, of course, is the community's role. Citizens have to be active participants in crime prevention. In Houston, nearly a thousand new officers added to the city's police force since 1991 have been joined by thousands of citizen patrollers observing and reporting suspicious or criminal behavior in an anticrime campaign spearheaded by Mayor Bob Lanier. In addition, Lanier, who understands that the entire ecology of a community affects crime, has supported soccer leagues and golf instruction for kids, built parks and playgrounds, started youth programs, and exhibited a respect for the diversity of the city that gives all citizens a stake in their city's future.

In the 1980s, residents of the Fairlawn neighborhood in Washington, D.C., fed up with the drugs on their streets, formed the Fairlawn Coalition. Every night, members of the coalition organize into groups, put on bright-orange hats to identify themselves, and patrol the streets in their neighborhood that are known to be centers of drug activity. The patrols do not confront drug dealers directly, but members carry notepads and sometimes video cameras to record information for the police. For their own safety, they carry walkie-talkies. The presence of the patrol serves as a deterrent to illegal activity. As one coalition member explains, "The dealers will deal drugs right in front of the police, but they won't do it in front of people who are from the community." Since the coalition went into action, neighborhood parents have become less fearful about letting their children play outside, and the entire community feels more secure.

Children know when adults are letting them down, and it angers them. A boy in Kansas City told members of the National Commission on Children what it was like for him to walk to school every day. What could have been a ten-minute walk took him double the time, because of the zigzagging course he took to avoid a house where he knew crack was being sold. "What I don't understand," the young man said to the commissioners, "is if the people who live on the street know what is going on in that house and the police drive by all the time as though they know something bad is going on in there, why don't adults do something about it?"

In another neighborhood in Kansas City, adults are doing something about it. After witnessing an escalation of crime in their neighborhood, a few concerned citizens started organizing to stop it. They formed the Wyandotte Countians Against Crime (WCAC), a citizens' group with more than 350 members. They closed one drug house by posting a sign in front announcing that drugs were being sold there. They managed to close down another by taking down the license number of every car that pulled up in front. They also organized a safe Halloween block party for kids in the neighborhood and are working toward creating a community center for teenagers.

The Community Anti-Drug Coalitions of America and the Center for Substance Abuse Prevention at the Department of Health and Human Services coordinate and help fund hundreds of such grassroots coalitions around the country. In addition to neighborhood patrols, these groups have initiated programs like after-school activities for young people and graffiti paint-outs, and have worked with local schools to establish drug-free, gun-free zones. These coalitions are living proof that we can take back our streets and communities and give back to our young people the security most of us took for granted when we were children.

In the meantime, we will have to take responsibility for the effects of exposing children to violence. Some youngsters have witnessed so much random bloodshed that they have begun to plan their own funerals. One little boy who had seen his mother murdered began to reenact her death repeatedly, falling down on the ground, lying still, and staring up at the ceiling with a dead look in his eyes. It was his way of remembering his mother and coping with his loss. Children who have been exposed to violence often have difficulty concentrating or sleeping. They may have violent flashbacks and difficulty forming relationships of trust. Some become paranoid or cynical about the future, which may lead them to take risks with alcohol and drugs. They need counselors and teachers who are trained to listen and to help them articulate what they have experienced, at just the time when many schools are paring back on such "extras."

In New Haven, where four out of every ten sixth, eighth, and tenth graders say they have witnessed a violent crime, police and mental health professionals have joined forces in the Child Development–Community Policing Program, designed to assist children caught in the crossfire of violence either at home or on the streets. Police officers are trained to deal with these vulnerable children, to recognize when they need additional counseling, and to see that they get it.

Children who witness continual violence in their homes may come to identify with the predominant behavior of the parent of their sex. Boys may take on a father's abusive behavior, while girls may find themselves in relationships in which they become victims as their mothers were. Equally troubling, boys and girls who are exposed to domestic violence may come to regard it as the chief way of resolving conflict and as the inevitable ingredient of any close relationship. Based on his own personal experience, the President gives high priority to the Violence Against Women Act, which treats intrafamily assaults as the serious crimes they are.

That same attitude ought to apply to the physical and sexual abuse of children. For most adults, the thought of an adult abusing a child is inconceivable. And yet, according to a 1995 report by the U.S. Advisory Board on Child Abuse and Neglect, two thousand children a year die from abuse or neglect. Homicide rates for children aged four and under have hit a forty-year high. Near-fatal abuse and neglect leaves eighteen thousand children permanently disabled each year, and tens of thousands of others will enter adulthood bearing the psychological scars. One out of three victims of abuse is a child under the age of one year. The report estimates that 141,700 infants and children were seriously injured or neglected in 1990 alone. It notes: "In the 33 years since Dr. C. Henry Kempe first described the Battered Child Syndrome, more children have died from child abuse and neglect than from urban gang wars, AIDS, polio, or measles; yet the contrast in public attention and commitment of resources is vast."

The sexual abuse of children is even harder for us to fathom, but the statistics are equally dire. In 1993 alone, nearly 140,000 children were reported as victims of sexual abuse. No one can calculate how many more cases of sexual abuse go unreported. Former Miss America Marilyn Van Derbur was among those who forced this ugly issue into the open when she spoke out bravely about the sexual abuse she was subjected to by her father.

Sexual abuse may not leave visible bruises or broken legs, but its injuries are profound and long-lasting. And it is often made worse by the conspiracy of silence among adults in the home who look the other way or refuse to believe or protect the child. Some experts also suggest that the loosening of sexual mores and the pervasive use of sex in advertising, including the exploitation of children in grown-up ads, have combined to sabotage the fundamental taboo against incest.

Whatever the reasons for the apparent increase in physical and sexual abuse of children, it demands our intervention. We should start with strong, unambivalent criminal prosecution of perpetrators. And a child's safety must take precedence over the preservation of a family that has allowed abuse to occur.

In his book *The Welfare of Children*, Duncan Lindsey, a professor at the School of Public Policy and Social Research at UCLA, argues persuasively that the child welfare system has been overwhelmed by the responsibilities assigned to it in the past two decades. With limited resources, it has proved unable to provide the full range of protective services for which it is responsible: intervening in emergencies, evaluating children's safety and removing them from the family when necessary, placing them in foster care and monitoring that care, counseling parents, deciding whether to prosecute parents, reuniting families, and coordinating services with schools, police, relatives, and other agencies. The burden of child protection not only has made it impossible for welfare workers to perform their historic mission of helping disadvantaged children but, according to Lindsey, "too often allows criminal physical and sexual assault of children to go unprosecuted and thus fails to protect children from continued harm."

Cases of physical or sexual abuse should be referred immediately to the police. If the police decide to proceed with charges against any adult in a child's home, even as an accessory to a crime, child protective workers should assist in deciding whether the child should stay in the home or be moved to safer ground. And social workers and courts should make decisions about terminating parental rights of abusive parents more quickly, rather than removing and returning abused children time and again. As the U.S. Advisory Board on Child Abuse and Neglect recommends: "The child's safety and well-being must be a priority in all child and family programs."

Physical and sexual abuse destroys the trust children need to feel secure. So does verbal abuse. If you wonder why I include it in the same breath, stop and listen to what's being said around you. Negative, belittling words directed at children pervade our culture.

You must have witnessed, as I have, parents who should know the hurtful effects of unkind words nevertheless humiliating their children over perceived shortcomings in athletics, academics, or appearance. You must have cringed, as I have, while a father or mother humiliates a child in public for no apparent reason. Not only parents, but many teachers, coaches, and other adults who have the upper hand are routinely disrespectful to kids. Perhaps they feel they must respond in kind to the aggressive and ugly attitudes some kids express toward authority. But like any kind of violence, verbal violence escalates if both sides continue to retaliate. And it wounds just as deeply. As Erik Erikson observed, the most deadly of all sins is the mutilation of a child's spirit. Adults should practice counting to ten and taking a deep breath before contributing to the climate of incivility and insecurity that surrounds us.

MY HUSBAND went alone to the theater to see his favorite movie, *High Noon*, again and again when he was six. What made it his favorite is the role Gary Cooper plays, which is the very thing that makes it different from other westerns. Cooper plays a sheriff who is afraid of what he has to do to protect his town from the forces of evil—and does it anyway.

When it comes to the dangers that pervade our homes and communities these days, we could take a cue from that sheriff. However fearful or uncertain we are, we have obligations to our children. Home can—and should—be a bedrock for any child. Communities can—and should—provide the eyes and enforcement to watch over them, formally and informally. And our government can—and should—create and uphold the laws that set standards of safety for us all.

It would be nice if there were a yellow brick road that would transport us magically to a place of absolute invulnerability. There's no place like that, and there never was. But there are many examples we can follow—in our homes and beyond them—that will lead us and our children toward the security we all deserve.

The Best Tool You Can
Give a Child Is a Shovel

You have brains in your head.
You have feet in your shoes.
You can steer yourself
Any direction you choose.

DR. SEUSS

O f the many extraordinary world figures I have met, Nelson
Mandela is a standout, not only for his political leadership
but for the moral authority he has provided, in word and deed,
since his release from prison in 1990, after twenty-seven years.
Having long admired him, I was deeply honored to attend his
inauguration as President of South Africa with the American dele-
gation headed by Vice President Gore.

The inauguration was an exuberant celebration of South
Africa's passage from apartheid to democracy, but for me, the high
point came after the official ceremony, at a luncheon President
Mandela hosted at his new residence. Addressing a crowd that
included representatives from almost every nation, some of whom
were at war with one another or were major violators of the
human rights of their own citizens, he spoke of his people's need

for love, loyalty, and reconciliation. He also mentioned that he had invited three of his former jailers to attend the luncheon and the day's celebrations.

I was dumbfounded. How many of us, I wondered, would have had the character, self-confidence, and faith to extend forgiveness to those who subjected us and our loved ones to brutal persecution?

In October 1994, Bill and I had a chance to return the South African President's hospitality. At a state dinner in Mandela's honor, my husband toasted him, quoting from a letter Mandela had written to one of his daughters during his long imprisonment: "There are few misfortunes in this world you cannot turn into personal triumphs if you have the iron will and necessary skills."

ONE OF THE family's—and the village's—most important tasks is to help children develop those habits of self-discipline and empathy that constitute what we call character. They enable us to be resilient in the face of the problems we encounter in life and to grow bigger, not bitter, in spirit.

Each of my parents had a different approach to character building. Both approaches were meant to give us the confidence to negotiate life's sharp edges without compromising our integrity. When difficult or challenging situations would arise, my mother always posed the same question to me: "Do you want to be the lead actor in your life, or a minor player who simply reacts to what others think you should say or do?" Asking myself that question has helped me through many difficult times.

My father's approach was vintage Hugh Rodham. When I was facing a problem, he would look me straight in the eyes and ask, "Hillary, how are you going to dig yourself out of this one?" His query always brought to mind a shovel. That image stayed with me, and over the course of my life I have reached for mental, emotional, and spiritual shovels of various sizes and shapes—even a backhoe or two.

Children can learn early on to grasp those imaginary shovels—or any tool that works for them—gaining from their parents and the other adults around them the essential skills of problem solving and coping with adversity that build character in daily life. Life itself is the curriculum, as are history, literature, current events, and, especially, religious teachings.

Nelson Mandela derived inspiration and guidance when he studied the actions and words of leaders like Mahatma Gandhi and Dr. Martin Luther King. The lessons men and women have learned over thousands of years are available to anyone, in the form of fables, stories, poems, plays, proverbs, and scriptures that have stood the test of time. A wonderful new anthology of such writings is found in *A Call to Character,* edited by Colin Greer and Herbert Kohl.

You never know where you might find such guidance when you need it. One of Chelsea's and my favorite nursery rhymes summed up the absolute unpredictability and frequent unfairness of life: "As I was standing in the street / As quiet as could be / A great big ugly man came up / And tied his horse to me." I thought often of that rhyme during our first year in the White House: My father died, our dear friend Vince Foster killed himself, my mother-in-law lost her battle against breast cancer, and my husband and I were attacked daily from all directions by people trying to score political points. To deal with my feelings I could turn to my religious beliefs, my husband and family, and my friends.

I also sought out and found new ways of thinking about my life and the challenges I faced. I read avidly about how my First Lady predecessors had played the hands dealt them during their turns in the spotlight. I reread favorite scriptures, quotations, and writings that had touched me in the past. I discovered new sources of support, inspiration, and clarity in books and people.

One of the people I encountered, through his writings and tapes, was the Reverend Henri Nouwen, a Jesuit priest and the author of meditations on his and our world's spiritual journey. His book *The Return of the Prodigal Son* analyzes that New Testament parable from the perspectives of the father and both his sons—the one who returns home after squandering his fortune and the dutiful older son who never left. One sentence hit me over the head like—well, like a shovel: "The discipline of gratitude is the explicit effort to acknowledge that all I am and have is given to me as a gift of love, a gift to be celebrated with joy."

I had never thought of gratitude as a habit or discipline before, and I discovered that it was immensely helpful to do so. When I found myself in a difficult situation, I began to make a mental list of all that I was grateful for—being alive and healthy for another day, loving and being loved by family and friends, experiencing the awesome privilege of working on behalf of my country and its citizens. By consciously reminding myself of my blessings, I could move myself from pessimism to optimism, from grief to hopefulness.

From the beginning, Bill and I have tried to equip Chelsea with her own batch of shovels. We have tried to help her to develop her own spiritual life. We have also tried to anticipate the challenges she will face and to assist her in meeting them. One of our chief worries, naturally, has been how to protect her from the inevitable fallout of her father's public career.

In 1986, my husband ran for reelection as governor of Arkansas. During his previous campaigns, Chelsea had been young enough that we could monitor what she heard or saw about her father's political activities. But now she was six, and much more a part of the village in her own right. She went to school, she could read, and she was generally more aware of what was happening in the world outside our home.

When two combative former governors decided to run against Bill, we knew we had to brace ourselves for a messy campaign. We discussed the situation and decided to prepare Chelsea so she would not be surprised or overwhelmed if she heard someone say something nasty about her father. It is not a pleasant duty, teaching harsh truths to a child, but we wanted her to develop the skills she would need to cope with whatever life sent her way. And we wanted to teach them in a way that would promote her confidence in dealing with the world, rather than making her cynical about it.

One night at the dinner table, I told her, "You know, Daddy is going to run for governor again. If he wins, we would keep living in this house, and he would keep trying to help people. But first we have to have an election. And that means other people will try to convince voters to vote for them instead of for Daddy. One of the ways they may do this is by saying terrible things about him."

Chelsea's eyes went wide, and she asked, "What do you mean?"

We explained that in election campaigns, people might even tell lies about her father in order to win, and we wanted her to be ready for that. Like most parents, we had taught her that it was wrong to lie, and she struggled with the idea, saying over and over, "Why would people do that?"

I didn't have a good answer for that one. (I still don't.) Instead, we asked her to pretend she was her dad and was making a speech about why people should vote for her.

She said something like, "I'm Bill Clinton. I've done a good job and I've helped a lot of people. Please vote for me."

We praised her and explained that now her daddy was going to pretend to be one of the men running against him. So Bill said terrible things about himself, like how he was really mean to people and didn't try to help them.

Chelsea got tears in her eyes and said, "Why would anybody say things like that?"

Our role-playing helped Chelsea to experience, in the privacy of our home, the feelings of any person who sees someone she loves being personally attacked. As we continued the exercise during a few dinners, she gradually gained mastery over her emotions and some insight into the situations that might arise. She took turns playing her father and one of his opponents, former governor Orval Faubus. She worked on her speeches and asked questions. For example, when she learned that as governor, Faubus had been responsible for closing Central High School in Little Rock in 1958, she mentioned in one of her pretend speeches that he closed schools to keep black children out, while she (Bill Clinton) would never do that.

Bill and I have continued our dialogue about politics with Chelsea over the years, helping her to discern motives and develop perspective so that she can form her own judgments regarding what she sees and hears. Looking back, I am glad that we started to prepare her at a tender age, because by the time her father ran for President, we were even less in control of the messages to which she was exposed. Each time she went out into the world I ached, afraid of what or whom she might encounter. But I reminded myself that we had done the best we knew how to do under the circumstances. We had tried to give her the tools to deal with the hurt from which we could not shield her, and we had to hope that as a resilient young woman, she would know how to use them.

Before and after we moved into the White House, I had the good fortune and honor to spend time with Jacqueline Kennedy

Onassis. I admired the way she had raised her own children under extraordinary circumstances, and I was eager to hear her thoughts on the challenges that come with parenting when it feels like the whole world is watching.

She stressed the importance of giving children as normal a life as possible, of granting them the chance to fight their private battles while protecting them from public exposure. She told me how, when John was a little boy, he had once been harassed by a bully while riding his bike in a park. The Secret Service had stepped in to prevent an altercation. Jackie told them that the next time something like that happened, they should let John fend for himself. He needed to learn how to take care of himself, because there wouldn't always be a Secret Service agent or a concerned mother two steps behind him.

These may sound like the problems of privileged parents and children, and they are. But they are not so different in nature from the balancing act every parent must attempt: when to protect and when to stand back, when to hold on and when to let go. Much as we want to keep our children from harm, we won't always be there for them, and sometimes the most sympathetic thing we can do is to let them tough it out for themselves.

When my family moved to Park Ridge, I was four years old and eager to make new friends. Every time I walked out the door, with a bow in my hair and a hopeful look on my face, the neighborhood kids would torment me, pushing me, knocking me down, and teasing me until I burst into tears and ran back in the house, where I would stay for the rest of the day. Such was the fate of the new kid on the block. After this had gone on for several weeks, my mother met me one day as I ran in the door. She took me by the shoulders, told me there was no room for cowards in our house, and sent me back outside. I was shocked, and so were the neighborhood kids, who had not expected to see me so soon. When they challenged me again, I stood up for myself and finally won some friends. It was not until much later that my mother told me she had watched from behind the dining room drapes, shaking with worry, to see what would happen.

Now that I'm a mother myself, I know how hard it is to make decisions like that. My daughter would describe me as overprotective, although she generally indulges me and puts up with my worrying good-naturedly. Of course, there are places where Bill and I draw the line to protect her. We have actively shielded Chelsea from the press, for example, believing that children deserve their childhood and cannot have it in the public limelight. It isn't fair to let them be defined by the media before they have the chance to define themselves. We have taken some flak for this, but more than a few reporters have privately told us that we are doing the right thing.

When it comes to everyday life, however, parents have to concentrate on instilling self-discipline, self-control, and self-respect early on, and then must allow their children to practice those skills the way they would let them exercise their muscles or their brains. As my mother taught me, even very young children can be given a sense of strength in the face of indifference or cruelty. Part of that strength comes from experiencing appropriate discipline.

THE NEED for discipline usually arises when children hit their "terrible twos." This is the time when kids begin to test the limits of their powers, issuing endless edicts and vetoes in an effort to control the world around them.

Many parents find themselves unsettled by their new role, which seems to change overnight from all-powerful caregiver to cop. Young parents, in particular, may be frustrated by a toddler's newfound assertiveness and stubbornness. Frustration can quickly give way to anger, and worse. We have all seen a parent slap a child for a seemingly trivial infraction.

People berate children, or strike them, when they don't know what else to do. Sometimes they are reacting the way their own parents did. What they may not know, or may forget in the heat of the moment, is that they are passing on a message of disappointment and low expectations. Whether they say it out loud or not, they are conveying, "You're a bad person, and you shouldn't expect good things to happen to you."

It may help to think of discipline not as a fixed, unbending recipe but as a continuum. As Dr. Brazelton explains in *Touchpoints:* "Discipline means 'teaching,' not punishment." Instead of just telling children what they can and can't do, we should be teaching them to weigh their options and to make responsible choices—first by making choices for them and explaining our decisions, then, little by little, by letting them choose for themselves. The goal is self-disciplined autonomy.

Experts may differ on the nature and timing of discipline, but they agree that it must begin with clear expectations and should be tailored to the child's stage of development and particular temperament. They also agree with Dr. Brazelton that "love comes first, and discipline second." He elaborates:

> Punishment may need to be part of discipline on certain occasions, but it should follow promptly on the misbehavior, be short, and respect the feelings of the child. After any punishment is over (such as a time-out or withdrawal of a treat), you should sit down with your punished child and assure her: "I love you, but I can't let you do this. Someday you'll learn to stop yourself, and then I won't need to stop you."

My parents divided between them the task of disciplining my brothers and me. My mother's method relied on pointing out the pluses and minuses of our behavior. When we behaved thoughtlessly, she would force us to consider why we had acted as we did.

My father, not one to spare the rod, articulated and emphasized his expectations for us. He told us repeatedly that he would always love us but would not always like what we did. We used to test him by asking if he would still love us if we murdered someone. He would reply that he would never stop loving us but would be deeply disappointed and hurt by what we had done. Occasionally he got carried away when disciplining us, yelling louder or using more physical punishment, especially with my brothers, than I thought was fair or necessary. But even when he was angry, I never doubted that he loved me. The message I heard loud and clear was, "You have a lot going for you—you'd better not screw it up." For the most part, the balance my parents used with me was an effective one.

When I began studying child development, I learned about three approaches to discipline, characterized by psychologists as "authoritative," "authoritarian," and "permissive." This distinction is difficult to apply as a formula to every dealing parents have with children, even within the same family, since most of our actions do not fall into neat categories. But my husband and I have found it useful as a general guide in our own parenting.

Authoritative parents try to do what Brazelton and others recommend: to strike a balance between control and autonomy by sending clear and consistent messages about what is right and wrong and what behavior is expected, backed up by discipline that suits the child and the occasion. Saying this is a lot easier than doing it. The tension between freedom-giving and limit-setting is constant and may be exacerbated by disagreements between parents, as was sometimes the case in my family. But being aware of that tension and need for balance helps adults to weigh the alternatives when confronted by the daily challenges children—and especially teenagers—pose.

Authoritative parenting stands between the extremes of author-
itarianism and excessive permissiveness. It acknowledges that,
looking ahead to the time of independence, a gradual increase in
children's freedom and the permission to make their own choices
is necessary. Such discipline might be called "explanatory," in the
sense that it is aimed at encouraging children to articulate why
something is bad or dangerous, to help negotiate rules and penal-
ties, and to develop their own sense of what is appropriate.

Authoritarian parents don't see alternatives. To them there is
only one way—their way. They try to control their children's
thoughts and actions with persistent verbal and physical discipline
that does not distinguish between important and minor infrac-
tions. The novelist Pat Conroy's father, as depicted in Conroy's
novel *The Great Santini*, is a classic example of an authoritarian.
Overbearing, harsh, even sadistic, he justifies his behavior by
believing he is creating tough kids who will be able to go toe-to-
toe with a cruel, harsh world. Conroy vividly captures how children either mimic the behavior of authoritarian parents or grow up
anxious and insecure.

Overly permissive parents lean to the opposite extreme.
Because of their uncertainty about parenting, or perhaps because
of difficulties in their own past or present lives, such as abuse or
divorce, they can't seem to muster the consistency needed to set
and enforce limits. Mothers—single mothers in particular—can be
especially vulnerable to this dilemma, which Bill's mother eloquently conveyed in her autobiography. Discussing how she came
to realize, after Roger was arrested for selling cocaine, that she had
overlooked his problems for years, she observed:

> We mothers—maybe especially when there's no
> father at home—want *so* for our children. We want to
> give them the good things and protect them from the bad

things. There's nothing wrong with that—until it's carried to such an extreme that it keeps the children from growing up. That's what I did with Roger, and that's what I was trying to change when I decided to "stop mothering" him. By then, though, the damage was done. All this became clear to me one day in the spring of 1985. I was working in the yard and I heard a chirping noise. I looked around and saw a baby bird on the ground. . . . There in the nest was the mother bird, just making an awful racket. . . . She had kicked her baby out of the nest and was now lecturing him about getting busy and learning to fly. And I thought, who's the bird brain here? That mother bird is smarter than I am.

Many intact couples also abdicate their responsibilities when it comes to discipline. They may be confused about their own values or the values they think are appropriate to teach to children, or they may be unwilling to make the effort. They may be afraid that if they impose rules and limits, their children won't like them. A parent who fears that discipline will alienate children is heading for trouble. What begins as "permissiveness" too often ends in negligence and confusion.

I am continually amazed by parents who know about their teenagers' drinking or cigarette or marijuana smoking and rationalize it, even going so far as to announce that they are glad their kids do it at home, where it's "safe." Is it "safe" to permit children to break the law and to engage in potentially self-destructive behavior anywhere? Each of us adults did things as a child or teenager that we are glad our parents didn't know about. We were testing their limits, which helped us to define our own. Today's children do the same—it's part of growing up. But when they push against a boundary that keeps collapsing because no one pushes back, they fall into uncharted, and often dangerous, territory.

Some children receive few explicit messages at all from their parents. Whether they are middle-class "latchkey" kids, ghetto kids, or kids whose parents are too wrapped up in their own lives to pay attention to them, they are raising themselves, like the band of stranded schoolboys in *Lord of the Flies*. And in the absence of parental guidance, children turn to other authority or pseudo-authority figures—to gang leaders, to older children who are also adrift, and to the dubious role models popular culture provides.

The teenage years, we all know, pose a special challenge for parents. The developmental changes of adolescence are second in pace and intensity only to those of infancy, and teens' need for parental supervision is second only to toddlers'. (A lot of parents would add that dealing with the fiery fifteens is a lot more stressful than coping with the terrible twos.) But telling a three-year-old not to play with matches is an unassailable decision. Figuring out whether to ignore your thirteen-year-old's emotional outburst or trying to arrive at a reasonable weekend curfew with your sixteen-year-old is another matter. And the difficulty of setting limits for adolescents is compounded by the growing pains we may unconsciously relive as we watch kids go through theirs.

Adolescence—as Bill and I are observing—is a time of approach and retreat, when young men and women insist on making their own choices regarding behavior, appearance, and values. It often demands not so much discipline from adults as self-discipline; we need the wisdom to anticipate errors that could be devastating, the restraint to pick our battles carefully, and the trust that, with what we have taught our children, they can handle the rest. Teenagers have the right to make decisions and make mistakes.

A couple I know who live in the public eye went away one weekend and returned to find their daughter in the kitchen—with a new Technicolor hairdo. They blew up. Suddenly the girl looked at her parents in that whimsical fifteen-year-old way that can stop you in your tracks. "Mom, Dad," she said, holding out a strand of her hair, "*this* is ruining your life?"

But teenagers often turn back to their parents when the temptations they confront today—drugs, alcohol, and sex, to name a few items at the top of most parents' worry lists—and the pressures to give in to them are overwhelming. The choices and consequences they confront are more complicated than those faced by earlier generations. Yet the biology of adolescence has not changed as much as our attitudes about what is and is not appropriate behavior. Adolescents want adults to reassert authoritative control over their lives—and much of their behavior is a plea for predictable rules to help them restructure their lives in the midst of great change.

I recently read a newspaper story in which teenagers, many from affluent neighborhoods in Washington, D.C., explained why they sneak out of the house at night to go to parties or to meet with friends. It was clear that in many cases the children did not take seriously the rules their parents set, or did not think their parents were going to check up on them anyway. As one psychologist explained in the article: "These kids are telling their parents, basically, 'To hell with the rules. I'll do what I want.' The parents are feeling too inept or too busy to say no, and want somebody else to fix the problem."

When parents are willing to take a "nonnegotiating posture" on the word "no," to be strict on curfews and appropriate discipline, children are less likely to be confused about the choices they confront.

At a recent gathering of journalists who cover family and children's issues, a reporter asked me how I felt, as the mother of a teenager, about sex education in the schools.

I said it would be great if we could get kids to postpone any decision about sex until they are over twenty-one, which provoked a round of nervous laughter from my listeners. In a culture that shouts sex from every billboard, movie screen, radio station, television set, and magazine (and now even computer monitors), they— and I—know that kids are confronted with sex every time they turn around, and they have to decide about it, early and often.

After many years of working with and listening to American adolescents, I don't believe they are ready for sex or its potential consequences—parenthood, abortion, sexually transmitted diseases—and I think we need to do everything in our power to discourage sexual activity and encourage abstinence. Young people can learn to value the intimacy of friendships with the opposite sex as well as their own, can enjoy being in groups as well as couples. Those kinds of relationships need adult support, including the time it takes to organize gatherings for kids, instead of turning them loose in malls, video arcades, or the streets. Homes, schools, churches, and communities should provide havens for kids who want an alternative.

These same entities have to pitch in when it comes to educating kids about sex. The Institute of Medicine, the health policy advisory arm of the National Academy of Sciences, recently published a scientific review of what is currently known about unintended pregnancy in our country. It concluded that families, schools, and religious and community institutions are all responsible for educating young people about sex, and it recommended that schools continue to develop comprehensive, age-appropriate programs of sex education, which emphasize teaching abstinence. The available evidence does not support fears that direct discussion of sexual behavior increases sexual activity; rather, it suggests many adolescents become sexually active without having had any formal sex education at all.

No matter how great an effort adults make, however, there will be some adolescents who are determined to embark on sexual experience. They, too, need straight talk about contraception and sexually transmitted diseases to help them deal responsibly with the consequences of their decisions.

As anyone who has studied the incidence of teen pregnancy and sexually transmitted diseases can tell you, many adolescents are woefully ignorant about the physical and emotional aspects of sexuality. I have interviewed pregnant teenagers who, impossible as it seems, could not explain exactly what they and their partner had done to cause the pregnancy, despite all the half-clad bodies and heavy breathing they have seen on television.

The result is tragic, especially for teenagers who are in difficult circumstances to begin with. Girls who become pregnant are usually a grade or two behind in their academic work. Frequently they come from disorganized families they would like to escape. Such girls often see little future for themselves, and a baby can look like a way out, or at least something they can call their own. Where sex is a quid pro quo for social status and security in the surrounding culture, these girls get little help from the village in persuading them that they have other options.

Many teenage boys are in a comparable bind. Lagging in school and frustrated by what they perceive as a lack of opportunity, they see in sex and fatherhood a route to tangible power and accomplishment. It is a primitive proof of manhood, but it is achievable.

When I talk with girls in their teens who have a baby or who are about to have one, they often say that they expect the child's father, who is usually older, to marry them. If I ask why he has not yet done so, they come up with a variety of excuses: he has to join the army or get a job or end a relationship with another girl first. There is always a reason, and however dubious it sounds, it does not prevent these girls from fantasizing about being loved and cared for. Girls pregnant with a second baby tend to be more cynical about marriage, but the sense of being unconditionally needed by an infant remains a powerful lure.

Girls with more advantages in life may decide to take chances with sex because "everybody else" is, or because they want to be popular with a certain boy or clique. They may forgo contraception and protection against sexually transmitted diseases because such planning requires that they acknowledge the choice they are making, and it doesn't mesh with the fantasy of being "swept away."

I wish we would all take a deep breath and remember that sex has been around for a long, long time and we are all here because of it. It is an important part of who we are and how we live, and there should be no shame in our children's curiosity about it. If we could accept that, we could begin talking to children, as soon as they could understand what we were saying, about the importance of honoring their bodies and entering into relationships responsibly. As children grow older, we could explain that there are stages in each human being's life, and that sex is an appropriate part of an adult's life, something that comes with maturity and readiness for commitment.

WHY DO some kids try risky behaviors when others don't? How can we create conditions in both our homes and our society that increase the odds that they won't? How are we to equip kids with the character and the skills they will need to make it safely to adulthood?

When it comes to substance abuse, the Center on Addiction and Substance Abuse (CASA) at Columbia University is providing some answers. Under the direction of its chairman and president, Joseph A. Califano, Jr., it has begun an annual survey of the attitudes of American adults and adolescents toward cigarettes, alcohol, marijuana, cocaine, heroin, and other illegal drugs, with the aim of alerting adults to what can be done to protect children. Califano spells out what is at stake: "Make no mistake about it. If our children get through the adolescent years, ages ten to twenty, without using drugs, without smoking, without abusing alcohol, they are virtually certain never to do so."

Some of the factors that increase the risk of substance abuse in those years deserve emphasis. Casual attitudes toward marijuana and minors' access to cigarettes raise the likelihood that teenagers will make a sad progression from cigarettes to marijuana to more serious drug use and earlier sexual activity. Dropping out of school puts the child at greater risk, as does having a parent who is an abuser of alcohol or drugs.

If this knowledge had been available years ago, Bill and his mother might have been aware that Roger, who for years witnessed his father's alcoholism and experienced its destructive consequences, was a prime candidate for alcohol and drug abuse. One reason my husband is adamant about curbing smoking among teens—and adults, for that matter—is the fact that he learned first-hand, in his own family, about the slippery slope that begins with the use of one addictive substance and leads to other destructive behaviors and attitudes.

Teens who participate in at least one after-school activity other than sports use drugs less often than those who don't. Ironically, adolescents with part-time jobs are more likely to use drugs—owing, perhaps, to their disposable income and early independence. Those who regularly attend religious services, however, use drugs less frequently than teens who attend rarely or never.

The CASA survey recommends steps we can take—if we have the will—to protect children: vigorously enforcing laws that prohibit the sale of cigarettes and alcohol to minors; establishing "drug-free" schools; paying for research about and treatment of addiction; halting the glamorization of alcohol, tobacco, and drugs in advertising and the entertainment media.

The characteristics that keep kids from using drugs are harder to quantify but not to understand. Children who truly grasp that they have a choice to make in the matter are more likely to make a responsible one. So are children with high self-esteem. Most influential of all is the optimism and awareness that comes from knowing their parents are interested in and involved in their lives. As the report noted: "What matters is not so much parents' work situation, or even their marital status. What really counts is their *involvement* in their children's lives. What really counts, finally, is firm guidance . . . or, as one parent put it, 'watching my kid like a hawk.'"

SOMETIMES, THOUGH, the tools families have at hand—discipline, watchful guidance, and love—just aren't up to the task. A teenage girl I know of killed herself at the age of fourteen, leaving a note that said, "I don't think I'm strong enough to be a teenager in today's world." More than anything it says about "today's world," that statement is testimony to the presence of severe depression and despair, which requires the intervention of sensitive, well-trained experts. As I and others have learned painfully through the suicides of friends and loved ones, too often individuals and families are reluctant or ashamed to reach out to the village for assistance. And too often, when they do, the village doesn't reach back. We need to see to it that such help is not only available but readily offered, without stigma, to those in need.

One way of offering help is to provide teenagers with variations of what societies in the past have always given them—powerful, creative, challenging, and life-affirming ways of moving from childhood to adulthood. Among Native American peoples, these have often taken the form of a spiritual journey mentored by a wise elder, from which the young people return strengthened and filled with a vision of their higher purpose. Young Jewish boys and girls study sacred texts and traditions to prepare for a bar or bat mitzvah, in celebration of their new maturity.

It is no coincidence that these movements into maturity are marked by a public affirmation. Our own culture is in need of such powerful rites. Teenagers need more than a driver's license to herald the passage from childhood to adulthood.

Great Transitions, a new report by the Carnegie Corporation on preparing adolescents for the upcoming century, recognizes that we have left kids adrift at this critical stage of transition. It recommends that our nation offer more youth-supporting events and activities. It should be no surprise that teenage gangs have flourished in their absence. Teenagers need a sense of belonging and want to be engaged in constructive activity. Community service for young people offers the combination of challenge and involvement that so many desperately need to stay on course in life.

However we go about it, we must recognize that the years of adolescence have traditionally been the times of greatest opportunity and greatest danger. Added to this is the indisputable fact that these are the most complex times in human history. Whether children are swept away in the undertow of confusion or reach maturity safely depends on how strongly and creatively we affirm our faith in their promise.

In the end, though, our children will reach a point of independence when we can't watch over them or counsel them or see that others do. That is when character takes over—and when they need their shovels. Few of us will ever be tested like Nelson Mandela, but challenges, crises, failures, and disappointments, will come. Developing the "iron will and necessary skills" to shovel our way out from under whatever life piles on is a lifelong task for us all. And doing what we can to see that all our children are similarly equipped is our lifelong responsibility to them and to the village.

Children Are Born
Believers

*Every child comes with the message that God is not yet
discouraged with Mankind.*

RABINDRANATH TAGORE

Some of the best theologians I have ever met were five-year-olds.

As children, my friends and I had long, serious discussions about what heaven would be like. One day a boy named David, who had bright-red hair and freckles, announced that he wouldn't go to heaven if he couldn't have peanut butter. We all argued over whether angels (which we all hoped to become) ever ate anything, let alone peanut butter. As the debate raged on, each of us sought guidance from a higher authority—our parents. When we compared answers the next day, we found that grown-ups could not agree on this critical theological point, either.

I sympathized with our parents years later, when Chelsea and her friends came to Bill and me with even weightier inquiries. By first grade, they were asking: "Where is heaven, and who gets to go there?" "Does God ever make a mistake?" "What does God look like?" "Why does God let people do bad things?" "Do angels have real bodies?" "Does God care if I squash a bug?" "Is the Devil a person inside or outside of us?"

Bill and I were struck by these questions, even as we struggled to provide thoughtful answers within the scope of a child's understanding. They reflected a much deeper spirituality than we generally give children credit for. And they strengthened my belief that children are born with the capacity for faith, hope, and love, and with a deep intuition into God's creative, intelligent, and unifying force. As child psychiatrist Robert Coles observes in his book *The Spiritual Life of Children*, "How young we are when we start wondering about it all, the nature of the journey and of the final destination."

Like the potential to walk or to read, the potential for spirituality seems to be there from the beginning. A wonderful little book, *Children's Letters to God*, contains messages that are filled with hope and trust, humor and sensitivity, and an awesome sense of familiarity. "Dear God," writes one young child, "I bet it is very hard for

PEANUTS® reprinted by permission of United Feature Syndicate, Inc.

you to love all of everybody in the whole world. There are only four people in our family, and I can never do it." Another asks, "How did you know you were God?"

The inclination toward spirituality does not need to be planted in children, but it does need to be nurtured and encouraged to bloom. One way we do this is by teaching children to translate the spiritual impulse into the shared form of expression, in words and rituals, that religion provides.

Religion figures in my earliest memories of my family. My father came from a long line of Methodists, while my mother, who had not been raised in any church, taught Sunday school. During a recent visit, she joked that she had begun doing so in order to keep Hugh from sneaking out of his class. When a friend of mine asked her what the essence of her spiritual teaching was, she replied, simply and sincerely, "A sense of the good."

We attended a big church with an active congregation, the First United Methodist Church in Park Ridge. The church was a center for preaching and practicing the social gospel, so important to our Methodist traditions. Our spiritual life as a family was spirited and constant. We talked with God, walked with God, ate, studied, and argued with God. Each night, we knelt by our beds to pray before we went to sleep. We said grace at dinner, thanking God for all the blessings bestowed. My brother Hugh had his own characteristic renditions, along the lines of "Good food, good meat, good God, let's eat!" But despite our occasional irreverence, God was always present to us, a much-esteemed, much-addressed member of the family.

Bill is a Southern Baptist who feels as close to his denomination as I do to mine. Over the years, we have attended each other's churches often, and Chelsea spent time in both until she was ready to decide, at age ten, to be confirmed as a Methodist. The particular choice was not as important to her father and me as was her commitment to being part of the fellowship and framework for spiritual development that church offers.

The anthropologist Margaret Mead felt that exposure to religion in childhood was important, because prayer and wonder are not so easy to learn in adulthood. She was also concerned that adults who had lacked spiritual models in childhood might be vulnerable as adults to the appeals of intolerant or unduly rigid belief. My own experiences confirm Mead's conviction. I have known parents who were not themselves religious but who conscientiously ensured that their children were exposed to at least one religious faith for these reasons. I have also met people who had turned away from the teachings or structure of the faith in which they had been raised but were inspired to return by their own children.

At a formal dinner recently, I sat next to a distinguished businessman who told me he had started reading the Hebrew Bible from the beginning. Even though he had been bar mitzvahed decades before, he had not thought of himself as a religious or spiritual man. But one day, while holding his daughter, he had pointed at the sunset and said, "Look at the beautiful painting God gave us tonight." His little girl asked, "Who is God?" He decided that he owed it to her to introduce her to religious faith, just as his parents had introduced him. There is no substitute for this. If more parents introduced their children to faith and prayer at home, whether or not they participated in organized religious activity, I am sure there would be fewer calls for prayer in schools.

CHURCHES, SYNAGOGUES, mosques, and other religious institutions not only give children a grounding in spiritual matters but offer them experience in leadership and service roles where they can learn valuable social skills. A friend, reflecting on the role of formal religion in her childhood, remarked one day, "My church was my finishing school." She recalled the first time she spoke in public, a one-line recitation as part of an Easter morning program when she was four. Each successive Easter, her part in the program grew larger. Her church leader showed her how to speak clearly and loudly. With every public performance, she gained greater self-confidence.

I knew what she meant. In my own church, I took my turn at cleaning the altar on Saturdays and reading Scripture lessons on Sundays. I participated in the Christmas and Easter pageants (learning a lesson in recovering poise the time I fainted in my angel costume in the overheated sanctuary) and read my confirmation essay on "What Jesus Means to Me" before the whole congregation.

Chelsea's Sunday school teachers in Little Rock and Washington have helped her and her peers to explore and express ideas, worries, and fears, from getting along with parents who "just don't understand" to dealing with teenage temptations. Churches are among the few places in the village where today's teenagers can let down their guard and let off steam among adults who care about them. Churches that make kids feel welcome and supported are doing more than involving them in worship. As I have mentioned, a survey of teenagers' attitudes and behaviors found that those who attend religious services regularly are less likely to experiment with risky behaviors like drug use. I wish more places of worship were open after school and on weekends to provide constructive activities for kids under adult supervision.

Some churches are becoming villages in themselves, offering members access to state-of-the-art technology, family centers, and adult discussion groups on topics like marriage and parenting.

Many churches, like mine in Little Rock, offer preschool and day care programs, and some now include athletic facilities and even restaurants. These churches provide a social center for people of all ages.

But no matter how broadly churches and other places of worship are redefining and expanding their religious and social roles, the right to religious and spiritual expression extends beyond their boundaries. How do we protect that expression under the First Amendment's guarantee of freedom of religion and its prohibition against any government "establishment" of religion? For children, this question often concerns the extent to which they may learn about religion and express their own religious convictions in our public schools. I share my husband's belief that "nothing in the First Amendment converts our public schools into religion-free zones, or requires all religious expression to be left behind at the schoolhouse door," and that indeed "religion is too important in our history and our heritage for us to keep it out of our schools."

On the other hand, we run into problems when people want to use governmental authority to promote school prayer or particular religious observances or to advocate sectarian religious beliefs. When public power is put behind specific religious views or expressions, it might infringe upon the companion freedom the First Amendment guarantees us to choose our own religious beliefs, including the right to choose to be non-religious.

To bring reason and clarity to this often contentious issue, my husband asked Secretary of Education Richard Riley and Attorney General Janet Reno to develop a statement of principles concerning permissible religious activities in the public schools. The complete guidelines, which are available at your local school district office or the Department of Education, include the following:

- Students may participate in individual or group prayer during the school day, as long as they do so in a non-disruptive manner and when they are not engaged in school activities or instruction.

- Schools that generally open their facilities to extracurricular student groups should also make them available to student religious organizations on the same terms.

- Students should be free to express their beliefs about religion in school assignments, and their work should be judged by ordinary academic standards of substance and relevance.

- Schools may not provide religious instruction, but they may teach *about* the Bible or other scripture (in the teaching of history or literature, for example). They may also teach civic values and virtue, and the moral code that binds us together as a community, so long as they remain neutral with respect to the promotion of any particular religion.

This last point is particularly important, because it defines an area in which the role of religious institutions overlaps with the role of parents, schools, and the rest of the village: the responsibility of helping children to develop moral values, a social conscience, and the skills to deal with the issues they will confront in the larger world. Just as it is appropriate, often necessary, for schools and other institutions to help build character by teaching the values at the heart of religious creeds, it is also necessary for churches to connect the development of personal character to life in the world beyond home and church.

My church took seriously its responsibility to build a connection between religious faith and the greater good of a society full of all kinds of people. I received my earliest lessons about how we were expected to treat other people by singing songs like "Jesus loves the little children / All the little children of the world / Red and yellow, black and white / They are precious in His sight." Those words stayed with me longer than many earnest lectures about race relations. (To this day I wonder how anyone who ever sang them could dislike someone solely for the color of his skin.)

My church's youth minister, the Reverend Donald Jones, arranged for my youth group to share worship and service projects with black and Hispanic teenagers in Chicago. We discussed civil rights and other controversial issues of the day, sometimes to the discomfort of certain adults in the congregation. Reverend Jones took a group of us to hear Dr. Martin Luther King, Jr., speak at Orchestra Hall (despite some church members' suspicion that King was a Communist). We argued over the meaning of war to a Christian after seeing for the first time works of art like Picasso's *Guernica*, and the words of poets like T. S. Eliot and e. e. cummings inspired us to debate other moral issues.

I wish more churches—and parents—took seriously the teachings of every major religion that we treat one another as each of us would want to be treated. If that happened, we could make significant inroads on the social problems we confront.

Many parents do make the teaching of these values an essential component of religious instruction, and many others see them as a focus in themselves. Like me, however, they have undoubtedly learned to recognize the look of young eyes glazing over at the first hint of a long-winded explanation of some principle. Better a story that demonstrates the spiritual and human qualities we wish to transmit to young people. In our bedtime reading and prayer ritual when Chelsea was younger, Bill and I read children's versions of Bible stories to her. Cain and Abel exemplified envy and its consequences. David's conflict with Goliath illustrated the power of faith in the face of overwhelming odds. Queen Esther's courage in saving the Jews underscored the need for courage and careful planning before taking risky action. The Good Samaritan parable is an example of compassion toward people who are of different backgrounds. Religion is not just about one's relationship with God, but about what values flow out of that relationship, how we follow them in our daily lives and especially in our treatment of our neighbors next door and all over the world.

Stories about contemporary or historical figures can also make the point about the power of faith to give courage. One of my heroes when I was growing up was Margaret Chase Smith, the first woman elected to both the U.S. House of Representatives and the Senate. I admired her courage in standing up to her fellow Republican Senator Joe McCarthy and his political smear tactics. In her essay "This I Believe," she explained the core of her courage. "I believe that in our constant search for security we can never gain any peace of mind until we secure our own soul. And this I do believe above all, especially in my times of greater discouragement, *that I must believe*—that I must believe in my fellow men—that I must believe in myself—that I must believe in God—if life is to have any meaning." I would add to Senator Smith's eloquent statement of her belief that she translated it into action, and so must we if our convictions are to have meaning beyond ourselves.

Preaching is a distant second to practicing when it comes to instilling values like compassion, courage, faith, fellowship, forgiveness, love, peace, hope, wisdom, prayer, and humility. By putting spiritual values in action, adults show children that they are not just for church or home but are to be brought into the world, used to make the village a better place. It is not always easy to live what we believe, however. For example, while I believe there is no greater gift that God has given any of us than to be loved and to love, I find it difficult to love people who clearly don't love me. I wrestle nearly every day with the biblical admonition to forgive and love my enemies.

THE STRUGGLE to live up to the spiritual values we profess is not only an individual one. Groups of people, even nations, can suffer from an absence or misuse of spirituality. The great physician and philosopher Albert Schweitzer likened the condition of the soul in modern life to sleeping sickness. He warned against the indifference and apathy that can overtake our lives in the absence of love for one another and for God.

For the United States, that same warning was sounded by Lee Atwater, one of the political strategists credited with the victories of Ronald Reagan and George Bush. When Atwater was dying, he told a *Life* magazine reporter: "Long before I was struck with cancer, I felt something stirring in American society. It was a sense among the people of the country, Republicans and Democrats alike, that something was missing from their lives, something crucial. . . . I don't know who will lead us through the '90s, but they must be made to speak to this spiritual vacuum at the heart of American society, this tumor of the soul."

I cut out that passage and put it in a little book of sayings and Scriptures that I keep. And I think the answer to his question— "Who will lead us out of this spiritual vacuum?"—must be all of us. Not just our government, not just our institutions, not just our leaders and preachers and rabbis, but all of us must renew our own sense of spirituality and work to live up to its expectations and values.

As we engage in that renewal, though, we have to beware of the misuse of religion to further political, personal, even commercial agendas. If we employ it as an excuse for intolerance, divisiveness, or violence, we betray its purpose, as did the extremists who employed religious rhetoric to justify assassinating Prime Minister Rabin of Israel. The "true believer" who proclaims that God or the Gospel or the Torah or the Koran favors a particular political action and that anyone who opposes him is on the side of the Devil is asserting an absolutist position that permits no compromise, no deference to the will of the majority, no acceptance of decisions by those in authority—all necessities for the functioning of any democracy.

Religion is about God's truth, but none of us can grasp that truth absolutely, because of our own imperfections and limitations. We are only children of God, not God. Therefore, we must not attempt to fit God into little boxes, claiming that He supports this or that political position. This is not only bad theology; it marginalizes God. As Abraham Lincoln said, "The Almighty has His own purposes." Even in dealing with political issues that have serious moral implications, we must be careful to avoid demonizing those who disagree with us, or acting as if we have a monopoly on truth.

People of faith belong to the larger village along with other citizens, the majority of whom share many—but not all—of their values. Our laws are designed to permit us to live in harmony, even when we have serious differences over religious and political matters. But to achieve that harmony, more than law is required; mutual tolerance and respect are also necessary.

I have been privileged to meet some of our world's great religious leaders, among them Roman Catholic, Protestant, and Orthodox Christians, Jews, Muslims, and Buddhists. Despite their profound differences, each speaks from a deep wellspring of love that affirms life and yearns for men and women to open their hearts like children to God and one another. Indeed, given the spiritual inclination of children, it is fitting that in many religious traditions they lead the way to spiritual awareness and enlightenment. As the Bible says, "And a little child shall lead them." When we find ourselves growing impatient, ungrateful, or intolerant, children can remind us to appreciate our daily blessings, to practice kindness, even to love our enemies. As children's spirituality blossoms, it will—if we let it —open in the hearts of adults a greater capacity to care for all children, to take responsibility for them and to pray for their futures. And when we pray for others, we often find in ourselves the energy to put ourselves to work on their behalf.

At the same time, prayer allows us to let go of our children and to let them find their own ways, with faith to guide and sustain them against the cruelties and indifference of the world. In her book of prayer, *Guide My Feet*, Marian Wright Edelman looks back upon a childhood that was a marvelous mixture of spiritual joy and exuberant, though disciplined, family and communal life. She writes: "We black children were wrapped up and rocked in a cradle of faith, song, prayer, ritual, and worship which immunized our spirits against some of the meanness and unfairness . . . in our segregated South and acquiescent nation." I have seen that immunity at work in my own life and the lives of others. But someone must inoculate each new generation, and then administer "booster shots" through example and ritual.

In the first part of her autobiography, *I Know Why the Caged Bird Sings*, Maya Angelou recounts the rape she experienced as a

child, which left her mute for several years. Her life today represents a triumph of spirit that she attributes in part to the deep spirituality she developed as a traumatized child. "Of all the needs . . .
a lonely child has, the one that must be satisfied, if there is going
to be a hope of wholeness, is the unshaking need for an unshakable God." Amen.

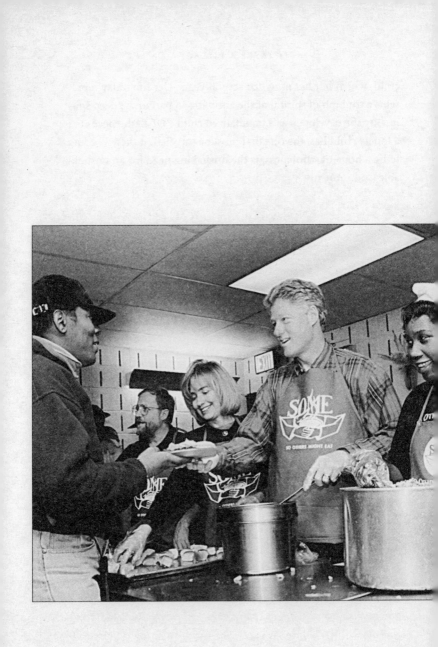

Childhood Can Be
a Service Academy

A candle loses nothing of its light by lighting another candle.

JAMES KELLER

For a few weeks every autumn, when the fields around Chicago were ripe for harvesting, children of Mexican migrant workers joined our classes at the Eugene Field School in Park Ridge. They never stayed long, because their families were always moving on to the next harvest. One year, a boy who was older than I and big for his age took to pushing me and my friends around on the playground. Whatever motivated him, his bullying quickly aroused my fear and dislike. My reactions to this one boy might well have spilled over to my feelings about the rest of the migrant kids if my mother had not encouraged me to volunteer, along with other girls in my church youth group, to baby-sit for the migrants' younger children on Saturdays so that their older brothers and sisters—my classmates—could join their parents working in the fields.

Just seeing the camp where the families lived made me think for the first time about how my classmates spent their time when they were not in school. I had never before known people who lived in trailers. When we went inside, the mothers seemed nervous about leaving their babies and toddlers in the care of twelve-year-olds who spoke no Spanish. I began to realize that the lack of familiarity cut both ways.

The day passed uneventfully, and when the mothers returned, they expressed their pleasure at seeing their children well cared for. It was the return of the fathers, though, that made the greatest impression on me. When the buses dropped them off at the base of the long road to the trailer camp, the children ran as fast as they could to greet them. They were filled with excitement, the same excitement I felt when my own father came home from work at the end of the day. Suddenly those migrant children didn't seem so different from me. This brief encounter helped me begin to appreciate the importance of making judgments about individuals instead of stereotyping whole groups. It also gave me a lot of satisfaction at an early age to be serving families who worked so hard for so little.

There is probably no more important task parents—and the rest of the village—face than raising children not only to tolerate but to respect the differences among people and to recognize the rewards that come from serving others. I call this affirmative living—the positive energy we derive from taking pride in who we are and from having the confidence and moral grounding to reach out to those who are different. As Elie Wiesel, winner of the Nobel Peace Prize, has said, "Everything becomes possible by the mere presence of someone who knows how to listen, to live, and to give of himself."

Learning to live affirmatively begins with the way we feel about ourselves. Children who grow up thinking of their own lives in positive terms are more likely to value the lives of others as well. Religious teachings remind us that we are to love others as we love ourselves. Loving oneself is not a matter of narcissism or egocentrism; it means respecting yourself and feeling affirmed in your identity.

I have described in this book some of the many ways in which parents and the village can help children to develop a positive sense of themselves. When we give children the nurturing, time, and care they need, they are more likely to develop emotional intelligence, confidence in their intellectual abilities, and the capacity to cope with life's adversities. These qualities are important not only in themselves but because they help children to become good citizens who contribute to the quality of life in their communities and to our ongoing civilization.

As educator William Damon writes in *Greater Expectations:* "Even if our children were being raised to become the best informed, most artistic, and healthiest children that the world has ever seen, it would all come to nothing unless they found some things beyond themselves. . . . They would still need to develop a sense of social responsibility. . . . Otherwise they could not live together in a decent society, nor pass along what is left of the culture to their own children."

A first step in teaching children to live affirmatively is to give them a strong sense of identity, rooted in their heritage. But that is only half the task. We know what happens when children are raised to think that their particular heritage makes them better than everyone else. A false sense of superiority or self-righteousness can lead to the exclusion, ridicule, and harassment of other people and, in extreme cases, to violence, as we have seen with ethnic cleansing in Bosnia, tribal warfare in Rwanda, religious conflict in the Middle East.

Therefore, as we help children create a positive identity, one with meaning and purpose in the world, a sense of responsibility toward and respect for others needs to be nurtured along with it. The remarkable lives of A. Elizabeth (Bessie) and Sarah (Sadie) Delany, whom I had the privilege to visit when they were 103 and 105 years old respectively, are testimony to this point. Anyone who has read their books or seen the Broadway play based on *Having*

Our Say has learned the importance of never forgetting who you are. The Delany sisters' father had been a slave, a fact he did not hide; instead, he used it to pass on to his children a profound belief in their worth and potential. The Delany children learned to honor their parents and the sacrifices they had made. Their parents not only suffused them with love but instilled in them a sense of right and wrong, an ethic of hard work, and a clear understanding of their responsibilities as human beings.

The results speak for themselves: Bessie became a dentist and Sadie a high school teacher, each of them among the first African-American women to achieve those positions. When they encountered prejudice and discrimination, they had the internal fortitude to move beyond it; as Sadie says, "Life's not easy for anyone, despite how it may look. Sometimes you just have to put up with a lot to get the little bit you need." (The long-living Delany sisters— Bessie died six months after my visit—are also prime examples of what researchers are discovering about the positive role an affirmative outlook on life can play in physical health. Certainly it lowers our levels of anger and hostility, freeing up energy for more constructive purposes.)

The family is not only children's heritage; it is also the first "civilization" they know, the first context in which they can learn about their rights and obligations. Research summarized in a study by psychologists at the National Institute of Mental Health shows that children are ready to begin their instruction at a very early age. Precursors to empathy begin to manifest themselves in infancy, when a baby will cry in response to another baby's cry. Between the ages of one year and two and a half, children begin to help, share, and comfort. Toddlers pat one another reassuringly or hug an upset parent. Around this time, they begin to display feelings of guilt or shame when they cause distress or disobey a clear standard of conduct. These are signs that children's moral sense is beginning to emerge.

Whether or not it continues to develop depends largely on the actions of the adults around them. Everyday experiences and conversations—showing a toddler how to touch a pet or a baby sister gently, or asking a six-year-old to imagine how it would feel to be a homeless person—provide ongoing opportunities to teach core values and beliefs.

At the same time, adults must help children to distinguish between appropriate and inappropriate behavior. Teaching tolerance, for example, should not be confused with giving children the sense that anything goes. They should learn that some behaviors, such as violence, abuse, or harassment, are unacceptable. And they should not be afraid to make judgments that reflect an understanding of the real world. It is realistic, not racist, to be cautious when walking through a high-crime neighborhood, or to want to avoid a corner where a drive-by shooting has taken place. Such judgments become biased only when they are motivated by negative stereotypes rather than common sense.

Awareness of racial, ethnic, and other differences occurs by the age of three or four, when they readily notice variations in skin color, for example, and are not shy about pointing them out. They do not automatically assume that people who do not look and speak as they do are persons they should fear, mistrust, or dislike, however.

Yet rather than taking their observations as ready-made opportunities to teach children respect for others, many parents ignore or stifle such comments. They may be afraid that they will say the wrong thing, or that simply talking about difference makes them bigots. But when parents ignore what children notice, they abdicate their role as teachers to the media and to their children's peers, who will be quick to supply negative stereotypes. By keeping silent, these parents are teaching bias as surely as if they blatantly voiced it.

"Every one of us has been made aware of a simple truth," my husband said in a speech in Austin, Texas, in October 1995. "White

Americans and black Americans often see the same world in drastically different ways. . . . The reasons for this divide are many. Some are rooted in the awful history and stubborn persistence of racism. Some are rooted in the different ways we experience the threats of modern life to personal security, family values, and strong communities. Some are rooted in the fact that we still haven't learned to talk frankly, to listen carefully, and to work together across racial lines." He was speaking of racial conflict, but his prescription applies more broadly to all forms of bias in our multiracial, multiethnic society.

As always, the solution begins at home. Parents must learn to talk with children about the diversity of human experiences and traits, answering their questions simply and directly and giving them an appropriate vocabulary to describe what they see. Religion can play a key role. I remember once as a child having diversity explained to me this way: If God had made a garden with only one kind of flower, it would not be nearly as beautiful as a garden with many different flowers. We can also point out to children that scientists who study genetics are learning that despite our superficial differences, human beings are more alike than unlike; we share common ancestors and are all members of the human family.

At the same time, adults should be alert to the language they themselves use, even when they are not addressing children directly. Especially in the early years, when children are voraciously acquiring vocabulary, what adults say makes a lasting impression, even if it is not intended seriously. Children are not born bigots, but they are quick learners. As the lyrics to the song "Carefully Taught" from *South Pacific* remind us, you have to be taught, "Before you are six or seven or eight / To hate all the people your relatives hate."

Within and beyond their homes, adults must speak out against racial, ethnic, religious, or gender slurs. We can say simply, "We don't talk like that in this house," or, as a friend's father always told her, "That kind of comment has no place in this world." We can also say to others, "Please don't speak like that in front of my family." Standing up for tolerance and respect in front of children gives them models for how to confront bigotry on their own, whether it is directed at them or others.

When children are the target of bias, open and honest talk is critical, to acknowledge the pain and to underscore that what causes it is bigotry, not identity. Adults can often comfort children by reminding them that those who resort to name-calling and finger-pointing do not know the first thing about them.

The village should also help prevent negative stereotypes from taking root in the first place, whether through more sensitive portrayals of people in the media or through adorning the walls of classrooms and day care centers with images that acknowledge and celebrate diversity. Toys, games, and books that promote positive images of women and minorities have an impact too. There is no substitute, however, for giving children experience with people who are not like them and cultures that are not like their own, as I learned in my own childhood. Boy Scouts and Girl Scouts, school clubs, church groups, and other community programs offer children of different backgrounds the opportunity to share activities and to discover their common interests. Sports teams in particular can be havens of cooperation and teamwork.

Clearly, schools and day care centers, where many children are first introduced to people from a variety of backgrounds, have an important role to play in shaping their attitudes and expectations. At the Washington Beech Community Preschool in Roslindale, Massachusetts, director Ellen Wolpert has children play games like Go Fish and Concentration with a deck of cards adorned with images—men holding babies, women pounding nails, elderly men on ladders, gray-haired women on skateboards—that counter the predictable images. Some schools are reinventing the old tradition of "pen pals," arranging for students to exchange letters, artwork, or even videotapes with children from other countries and cultures. Others have developed history and social studies lessons about the unfair treatment—and accomplishments—of women and minorities, which are often overlooked. Special opportunities like Black History Month can be used to expose students to the contributions of particular groups of Americans. In some school districts, teachers and staff undergo training to make them more comfortable with the topic of diversity and to expose them to innovative ways of dealing with it in the classroom. Schools in districts where there are children of different races or ethnicities have formed parent-staff committees to promote potluck dinners, family-to-family visits, and workshops for parents and staff.

Yet no matter how hard schools work to teach tolerance and empathy, conflicts will arise, especially when children bring with them different cultural assumptions and expectations. My parents drilled into my brothers and me that familiar refrain "Sticks and stones may break my bones, but words will never hurt me" and the advice to "take a deep breath and count to ten" to give us ways to avoid hostile confrontations.

Schools can help to equip children with the tools to prevent harsh words and playground taunts from escalating into aggressive behavior. In April 1995, I visited a peer mediation project at Seward Park High School on Manhattan's Lower East Side. Every day, nearly three thousand youngsters arrive there from homes in which they have grown up speaking different languages, celebrating different holidays, belonging to different religions, and experiencing different family cultures. I watched college students from New York University who are AmeriCorps members teaching the high school students techniques for mediating their peers' disputes, working in groups to negotiate nonviolent resolutions rather than relying on teachers and administrators to "police" them.

Some of the most effective approaches to promoting affirmative living are those that involve the entire village. A World of Difference, a national educational project sponsored by the Anti-Defamation League, helps teachers, administrators, students, and parents to promote tolerance and diversity in their schools and communities. Workshops throughout the year teach students to recognize and resist prejudiced behavior and to share their reflections about racial and cultural issues. An annual event in Boston called Team Harmony brings middle and high school students and teachers together with local sports figures and business leaders to take a stand against prejudice and bigotry. Local television and radio stations, newspapers, churches, and synagogues get involved.

After the Team Harmony event in 1994, many students wrote about the positive messages they received. "Since the event, I want to do all that I can to stop racism," one of them wrote. "I want everyone to live in peace and harmony, where there is no hatred and no violence. I don't care that some of my friends are black, white, Chinese, Vietnamese, or Portuguese."

When racial tensions surfaced in the town of Lima, Ohio, following the verdict in the Rodney King beating trial, Mayor David Berger initiated a series of dialogues about race relations. In firehouses and living rooms, classrooms and church halls, residents came together to discuss their perceptions of one another and of their community, an all too rare opportunity. As one resident put it, "It's not like you can walk up to someone on the street and say, 'Hey, what do you think about race relations?'"

Members of the community were trained as discussion leaders, with the task of seeing that the conversation stayed focused and that everyone's viewpoint was included. The ground rules were much the same as those the peer mediators at Seward Park were taught: listening carefully, speaking freely and honestly but respectfully, asking for clarification rather than letting a misperception fester, maintaining an open mind.

The ongoing dialogues have proved successful in allowing citizens to confront stereotypes and to move beyond them. As the Reverend James McLemore of St. Paul AME Church in Lima says, "Once people get past the issue of race, they start looking at the problems they have in common."

In Billings, Montana, organized bigots began to perpetrate a series of hate crimes against blacks, Hispanics, Jews, and Native Americans in 1993. After this had gone on for several months, someone threw a chunk of cinder block through the bedroom window of a five-year-old Jewish boy in which a menorah was displayed to mark the festival of Hanukkah. The boy was not hurt, but the town had finally had enough.

Margaret MacDonald, a local woman who calls herself "the church lady," recalled hearing how, in Denmark during World War II, ordinary citizens had decided to wear Stars of David when the Nazis ordered Jews to wear them. MacDonald convinced members of her church to display menorahs too. The local newspaper ran a picture of a menorah so that people could cut it out and tape it to their windows, and the editors urged all citizens to participate. "Let all the world know," they wrote, "that the irrational hatred of a few cannot destroy what all of us in Billings, and in America, have worked together so long to build." Within a very short time, thousands of homes had menorahs prominently displayed. The hate crimes have ceased, but concerned citizens stress the need to maintain vigilance. Respect is an ongoing lesson in today's village, where so many cultures and races live and work together.

NEVER HAS our nation been as diverse in its population as it is today. Nor has any previous generation of children been confronted so urgently with the task of learning to respect and empathize with one another and to recognize a common humanity. At a time when democracy depends so much on our finding common ground, and when so many adults are unsure about how to bridge societal divides, there seems to be one idea on which most people agree: we need to find ways to offer our children a vision of affirmative living that can be applied in their daily actions and interactions.

One way in which young people have historically come together and expressed their sense of humanity and compassion is by giving their service to a greater cause. This is an American tradition that extends from the YMCAs and YWCAs and the Boy Scouts and Girl Scouts, begun around the turn of the century, to the Civilian Conservation Corps and National Youth Administration of the Great Depression, and the Peace Corps, which was launched in the early 1960s. As civil rights leader Martin Luther King, Jr., reminded us, "Everybody can be great because everybody can serve."

Throughout our history, American thinkers and philosophers have recognized that public service is crucial to safeguarding democracy and to maintaining national unity in peacetime as well as in war. Harvard professor Robert Putnam observes that people who join the PTA or their local garden clubs or bowling leagues learn lessons that are central to democracy: mutual trust, cooperation, the habit of expressing their opinions openly and listening to those of others. In the words of former senator Harris Wofford, who helped to found the Peace Corps and who now heads the Corporation for National Service, "The service ethic should be to democracy what the work ethic is to capitalism."

But the service ethic does not magically appear upon adulthood. Educator Ernest L. Boyer notes: "If we want good citizenship among older people, it surely must become a part of children's lives." Compassion and empathy are more likely to take root if they are grounded in daily life. Service can begin at home, with children performing chores—setting the table, vacuuming the rug, watering the plants—on behalf of their families. My mother taught my brothers and me that helping others was not only an obligation but a privilege. She encouraged us to get involved in drives to collect money and goods for needy people through our church and school, and she came up with ways of making service fun. One year, she helped us organize a neighborhood athletic competition modeled on the Olympics to raise money for our town's United Way.

Children need to hear from authoritative voices that kindness and caring matter. Even more important, they need to see adults helping others if we expect them to follow suit. In the words of Rabbi Lyle Fishman, service is "caught rather than taught." Psychologist Julius Segal recalled: "When my friends and I were young children, we used to see our elders regularly empty their carefully saved pennies from a 'charity box' and offer them to anyone who came to the door seeking help. My own father's ability to pay the next month's rent was chronically in doubt but never his readiness to reach out to people he viewed as 'even worse off than I am.' Such acts set tangible standards for children. They fix in the soul a posture of caring."

My husband's mother also set an example of service for her children. One Thanksgiving when Bill was ten, Virginia sent him to the corner store for some last-minute shopping. One of his classmates was there, eating a doughnut and drinking a soda. When Bill asked him where he was having Thanksgiving dinner, the boy held up his doughnut and said, "Right here." Bill did not hesitate to invite him home, knowing his mother would have done the same.

From the time Chelsea was a toddler, we have tried to give her opportunities to serve, at home and through church and school. Thanksgivings, we took her with us to volunteer at shelters. At Christmas, we bundled up and played Santa to needy families. But we have also tried to teach her, as we were taught, that service is a part of daily life—as the saying goes, the rent we pay for living. There is no shortage of needs waiting to be met: an elderly neighbor who needs someone to carry groceries, a park or block or strip of highway strewn with litter, a single mother who could use some extra baby-sitting help, a playmate home with a broken arm. We should remember that just as a positive outlook on life can promote good health, so can everyday acts of kindness. The great psychiatrist Karl Menninger reportedly advised a man who said he was on the verge of a nervous breakdown: "Lock your house, go across the railroad tracks, find someone in need, and do something for him."

Children who are raised with an ethic of service learn to give beyond what is asked of them. Sarah Pollack graduated from high school in Virginia in 1994. Her parents promised to buy her a car for high school graduation if she got good grades and a college scholarship. Sarah got straight A's and won a scholarship of more than five thousand dollars a year. When it came time for her to spend the fifteen thousand dollars her parents had set aside for her car, Sarah asked if she could take the money and start a college fund for needy students at her high school. Asked by a reporter what prompted her to use the money to benefit others, she replied: "They were friends. They were people I respected, with talent. It really just killed me that they could go nowhere. . . . I'm just passing something on that I've been fortunate to have. That doesn't make me any more special than anybody else."

My husband met another extraordinarily giving teenager, thirteen-year-old Brianne Schwantes of South Milwaukee, Wisconsin, when he visited Des Moines, Iowa, during the 1993 flood. Brianne suffers from brittle bone disease, which means that her bones have broken so easily and so often that her growth has been stunted. Yet when she heard about the flooding, she persuaded her parents to bring her to Iowa to help fill sandbags. There she was, barely four feet tall, fulfilling her obligations to her fellow citizens.

It is often said that children are our last and best hope for the future, and that if we want society to evolve, we must teach the next generation the importance of active citizenship. Teaching children how to become good citizens and giving them an appreciation of governance is another way to elicit their natural empathy, compassion, idealism, and thirst for service.

It is never too early to start on the path of political participation and leadership. My husband and thousands of other American boys and girls have participated over the years in Boys and Girls State and Boys and Girls Nation. I know many young people who have also learned about current events, diplomacy, and statecraft through their participation in the Model United Nations program.

Another impressive forum for teaching governance was the international conference sponsored by the Elie Wiesel Foundation for Humanity, which brought together teenagers from five regions of the world. Called "Tomorrow's Leaders," the conference offered these students the chance to hear from world leaders and to try to develop peaceable solutions to conflicts around the world.

If youth service is, as our collective history demonstrates and as my husband and I believe, "a spark to rekindle the spirit of democracy in an age of uncertainty," it must not be left solely to individual acts of altruism. We need to create frameworks and contexts that will allow it to flourish and to become habitual.

I wish every school adopted the model of the Washington Elementary School in Mount Vernon, Washington, where service is integrated into the curriculum. The school's motto is "Service is a life-long commitment." Students in every grade perform individual acts of service, from tutoring younger children to serving on safety patrols. Each classroom also plans a class service project. One year, the second graders made a quilt for a homeless shelter and the third graders planted flowers as part of a school beautification project.

Some individual school districts require community service. Recently, Maryland, whose lieutenant governor, Kathleen Kennedy Townsend, is a longtime champion of the idea, became the first state to do so, making service a learning experience for students as well as a benefit for their communities. At one Maryland middle school, home economics students make outfits for homeless children and deliver them to a local shelter. At another school, students read Charles Dickens's *A Christmas Carol*, focusing on the theme of poverty, and work with local organizations to provide assistance to needy single mothers and their children. At yet another school, students studying ecology help to clean up and maintain the stream that serves as their "outdoor classroom."

Creating a framework for service is the driving idea behind the National Service Corporation, the public-private enterprise that includes AmeriCorps, which gives young people sixteen and older an opportunity to serve their country in return for financial assistance for college or job training and a modest living allowance during their service. Recruits commit to at least one year (with the opportunity to serve two if they choose), during which time they are trained to help communities solve educational, environmental, health, and public safety problems.

In its second year, AmeriCorps has already recruited more than twenty-five thousand young people. They are working with local churches and synagogues and nonprofit and public organizations in more than twelve hundred communities. AmeriCorps members also help existing charitable and service organizations like City Year, Habitat for Humanity, and the Red Cross to make the best use of part-time volunteers.

In many cases, AmeriCorps members are filling needs that no other organization or government agency can meet. In Simpson County, Kentucky, for example, they have helped to raise the reading scores of more than a third of the county's second graders by an average of two or more grade levels in a single year, recruiting more than two hundred parents to join in the effort. In Texas, Iowa, and Idaho, AmeriCorps members have helped to immunize hundreds of thousands of children who might otherwise have remained beyond the reach of state health authorities. In Kansas City, a team of AmeriCorps members has worked with the police department to close down more than two dozen crack houses and set up a score of neighborhood watch groups.

PROGRAMS LIKE AmeriCorps offer a socially meaningful transition from childhood to adulthood. They also offer a model for bridging private charity and government programs that we can all learn from. It was these rewards—material as well as spiritual, collective as well as individual—that a group of seventeen religious leaders emphasized recently when they asked Congress to support Ameri-Corps because it builds and strengthens the bonds that make community possible.

No matter how well our children learn the ethic of service, there will always be far more needs than individuals or charities can meet. That's why so many charities—some of which depend on a measure of federal support—have objected to suggestions that they can fill the holes in the social safety net left by cuts in social programs, particularly those affecting children. Neither government nor charitable organizations alone can keep the net intact, but working together, they can manage it.

Partnerships between government and the volunteer community are most clearly visible when disaster strikes, as my husband and I have observed firsthand following hurricanes and tornadoes in the South, floods in the Midwest, fires in the Northwest, and earthquakes in the West. Volunteers come alone or with friends, as part of church groups or service clubs, all offering their most precious gift, themselves. Government sends experts to help coordinate relief efforts. In tragic situations such as these, people commit acts of extraordinary compassion and readily overcome what might in ordinary times seem to be great differences.

After the bombing in Oklahoma City, we saw a country united in shock and love. When the first survivors emerged injured and bloody from the federal building, we did not see blacks or whites, Christians or Jews, but fellow human beings and children who might have been our own. Fire and police officers, medical crews, and emergency workers who put their own lives in jeopardy in their search for survivors did not pick and choose whom they would rescue; every life was valued and worth fighting to save.

Why does it take a crisis to open our eyes and hearts to our common humanity? As my husband said in his 1995 State of the Union address: "If you go back to the beginning of this country, the great strength of America, as de Tocqueville pointed out when he came here a long time ago, has always been our ability to associate with people who were different from ourselves and to work together to find common ground. And in this day, everybody has a responsibility to do more of that. We simply cannot wait for a tornado, a fire, or a flood to behave like Americans ought to behave in dealing with one another."

Men and women acting selflessly in the midst of tragedy remind us what really counts. They also remind Americans of our fundamental goodness, and of the essential strength of our nation. No democracy has survived as long or tried as hard to live up to its ideals. Nowhere on earth do so diverse a people live and work side by side every day, and for the most part get along so well.

Children can be our conscience, and the agents of the changes that are needed, if we don't burden them with stereotypes. If we teach them affirmative thinking and feeling, they will learn to live affirmatively—to measure their own lives by the good they do, not just for themselves but for all their fellow villagers.

Kids Are an Equal Employment Opportunity

*Caring can be learned by all human beings, can be worked
into the design of every life, meeting an individual
need as well as a pervasive need in society.*

MARY CATHERINE BATESON, *COMPOSING A LIFE*

Both of my parents loved sports. My father would stand in front of our house and throw a football to my brothers and me as we ran pass patterns around the elm trees. My mother hit thousands of tennis balls over the net, trying in vain to make worthy opponents of us. Each of them spent summer weekends hitting fly balls for us to field, teaching us to dive, and trying to interest us in golf. (At least they succeeded with my brothers on that one.) My father was focused on our excelling and winning, while my mother wanted us to have fun and get exercise.

Both my parents also cooked. My mother prepared by far the bulk of our daily meals, but most Saturday nights my father made up his special hamburgers. He also had a knack for soups and grilling. My brothers and I did not think it odd that our mother could hit a fastball or that our father could cook. Even within their apparently traditional marriage, we saw each doing things that didn't fit the stereotypes.

More than twenty years ago, when I was working for the Carnegie Council on Children, I heard the trailblazing social philosophers Erik Erikson and Erich Fromm discuss the different roles mothers and fathers traditionally played in bringing up children. From listening to them, I concluded that the conventional parental roles could be summed up by saying that men typically acted as breadwinners and rulemakers, while women were homemakers and caregivers.

What struck me even then was that there are many variations on the traditional parental division of labor that have worked over time and are working today. But it remains true that raising children, like most important work in our society, requires a constellation of skills and perspectives. Children deserve the benefit of what society has traditionally considered to be male and female traits and skills to meet their physical, emotional, and intellectual needs, and to offer them models for a range of human behaviors.

Even in the best of circumstances, it is difficult for any one of us to raise children alone. And when single parents try, they have to perform roles outside their usual repertoire, or get others to take on those roles. Even families with two parents rely on the village for functions that are beyond their scope.

Yet as obvious as it is that children's needs exceed what any individual or pair of individuals can provide, society continues to characterize child rearing as "women's work." Even when women with children share the breadwinner and rulemaker roles with their husbands, they almost always bear the primary—and disproportionate—responsibility for caregiving and homemaking. One of the greatest gifts we can give our children is the awareness that these roles can and should be shared more fairly and flexibly. In the meantime, stereotypes about women's roles persist.

A recent study done by a University of Michigan psychologist purports to show that young women are exhibiting more "masculine" behavior because they are becoming more assertive, ambitious, and self-confident, while young men are not exhibiting more "feminine" behavior like expressing empathy and caring. Why not consider all these to be human behaviors that both men and women display, depending on their particular temperaments and circumstances?

Is a mother who is assertive or ambitious on behalf of her children or husband acting "feminine," while a mother who is ambitious and assertive on behalf of her own career or a public issue she cares about acting "masculine"? Is a father who rocks a crying baby or soothes a teenager's hurt feelings "feminine," while a father who refuses to comfort either child "masculine"? Sometimes we fall into the trap of sexual stereotyping as we grapple with new ways of articulating our changing experiences and responsibilities.

We like to think we've come a long way from the limited range of roles that were considered "proper" for each gender in the past. Most of the women my mother knew stayed home because society expected them to, and they aligned their own expectations with society's, even if they wished they had different choices.

Some of us can recall an aunt who longed to go to college, a grandmother who kept voluminous journals she showed to no one, a female cousin with a head for figures. Much of the fiction written by and about women over the centuries contains an undercurrent of disappointment, dissatisfaction, or simple wistfulness about roads not taken. Part of the reason girls of every generation who read *Little Women* identify with Jo March is that they see her as unafraid to take action on her own behalf, to turn away from a predictable path and chart her own course.

In fact, many women defied convention in the past, by choice or necessity. All through our nation's history, women have worked outside the home as well as in it. Even during the 1950s, plenty of women with and without children were working in factories, offices, schools, and other people's homes. But because these women's lives did not match the conventional image, their work remained largely invisible. Often the official portrait of American life has omitted the diversity of women's experience as well as their needs and desires.

WHEN I look back on my childhood, I see how my mother and my girlfriends' mothers worked to push open doors of opportunity for us. They supported our academic and athletic pursuits and ferried us to and from lessons and practices. They held us to high standards, even if they spoke of their aspirations for us mostly in terms of their wanting us to do well enough in school so that we could go to college or get training for a job that could provide a good living if we had to support ourselves.

Perhaps because my mother's background dimmed her own prospects for higher education, she was more outspoken in her support of me. From the very beginning she believed that her greatest responsibility to me was getting me prepared to make the choices that were right for my life, even if they weren't the ones she would have—or could have—made. She shared my dismay when, at fourteen, I wrote to NASA asking how I might become an astronaut, only to be told that women were not being considered for the job (a policy I was delighted to see changed eventually).

It wasn't that the mothers I knew growing up did not want to be full-time homemakers and caregivers. Their dedication and discipline reflected how important they considered those roles to be. But they had the wisdom to know that the years devoted to child-rearing come to an end, and that divorce or the death of a spouse can leave women on their own, with decades of productive life ahead. And they saw—as their daughters came to see more clearly—that the larger society gave more lip service than real respect or reward to their efforts to nurture families and communities. Because of them, the women's movement, and increasing economic pressures, more and more women began to take up paid work that the marketplace valued: "men's work."

As with any major societal shift, there have been trade-offs and unanticipated consequences for both women and men. The struggle to give work and family the time and attention they need can be emotionally as well as physically exhausting. By and large, however, as columnist Ellen Goodman observes, "Women still see their lives as better than their mothers'. This is the generation that has traded depression for stress—not a wholly bad bargain. They have more options and more power as well as more obligations."

Goodman's observation is supported by the findings of a 1994 survey of more than 250,000 working women of every income level, job category, and family status, conducted by the Women's Bureau of the U.S. Department of Labor. Their responses, which Vice President Gore and I presented and discussed in a public forum, are detailed in a report, "Working Women Count!" For working women with children at home, the number one issue was the struggle to integrate work and family and to find and pay for decent child care. A working mother from Milwaukee spoke for thousands of women when she wrote: "Between balancing home and work and job, you always feel like you are doing four things at one time. You're doing your job but you're thinking about what you are going to cook for supper and who is going to pick up the kids." The women's descriptions of their lives are peppered with words like "hectic," "tough," "hard," and "rough." Many women said they were tired all the time.

Mothers working outside the home believe their employers could be more understanding about children's illnesses and doctor's appointments. They say they need expanded leave policies to care for children or ailing relatives, but many note that they cannot afford to sacrifice pay for long or at all. In general, women in lower-paid jobs found their workplaces less family-friendly and flexible than women in executive and management positions.

Before I had Chelsea, I noticed that in all the offices where I worked, most of the female workers began whispering into their phones every afternoon at around three o'clock. Finally, it dawned on me that they were making sure their children arrived home from school safely and were doing their homework or whatever else they were supposed to be doing. They whispered because they felt they might be penalized for carrying out their family obligations.

Underlying all the survey responses was a familiar refrain: women believe that their work contributions and responsibilities are undervalued, including their responsibilities to children. They know how hard they work for their families, and they believe that other sectors of society, including their employers, should do more to help. Their concern for the well-being of children fuels their opinions on broader issues and their desire to be heard. As the report notes, "They care deeply about their jobs, their co-workers, their workplaces, and the state of the national economy."

Although the personal demands on women are heavy, they take pride in their contribution to the family's income, and eight out of ten respondents say they "love" or "like" their jobs. But they are not stereotypes—neither "upbeat super-moms that unequivocally love their jobs and never have a problem or a hair out of place" nor the equally stereotypical "angst-ridden women so torn apart by competing demands that they return to the home" or "driven career women who give up their personal lives to 'make it' in the world of men." They are responsible adults with real lives and real needs, including the need to contribute according to their talents and abilities and to be granted the assistance that will enable them to do a good job at work and at home.

The survey responses are a reminder that we still haven't broken the mold—or, more accurately, broken the mold that makes the molds, the mechanism that insists on forcing complicated needs and desires into neat little boxes. Are we "career women" or "stay-at-home moms," "traditionalists" or "new traditionalists"?

The attempt to attach labels to our lives takes us backward. Whenever we pose women's options as an "either/ or" choice— most commonly between work and family—we do a disservice all around. In earlier generations, we lost artists, doctors, and engineers. My generation lost good mothers and dedicated community volunteers among women who did not see a way to combine their work life with making a home or nurturing a family. We are fond of saying that women "juggle" work, marriage, children, and myriad other obligations. I used the phrase too, until author and scholar Mary Catherine Bateson pointed out that when you juggle, eventually something gets dropped.

Now I prefer the metaphor of composing that Bateson illuminates in *Composing a Life*—making something beautiful, like a patchwork quilt, of the elements we choose. Perhaps it would be easier if the stuff of our lives were cut from a uniform social and familial pattern, even if the cloth is not the pattern we would have designed for ourselves. Easier maybe, but not so beautiful or well suited to our particular needs, desires, and circumstances.

THE FOOLISHNESS of stereotyping was brought home to me when I was a young lawyer but not yet a mother. I was asked by a client, an insurance company, to attend on its behalf a juvenile court hearing at which two brothers, ages ten and twelve, were to appear because they were accused of vandalizing a neighbor's house.

I will never forget the mother of the boys as she testified on their behalf. Fierce as a lioness defending her cubs, she denied—in the face of overwhelming evidence—that her sons were the vandals. They couldn't be, she explained, because she had quit work and stayed home to raise them. (That was the first time I really understood the meaning of the saying "Denial ain't just a river in Egypt"!)

Pitting stay-at-home moms against work-outside-of-the-home moms makes everyone a loser. There is no magic formula for raising children. You will find successes and failures among parents who do the work of staying home with their kids and among those who leave home to go to work. What makes the difference is whether parents have the competence and commitment to give children what they need for healthy development.

It is time for us to make our peace with the past. We can begin by taking care not to denigrate the roles of women as mothers and homemakers and by not jumping to conclusions about the mothering skills of women who work outside the home. I suggest that, in private and in public, we stop paying lip service to motherhood and start giving parents—men as well as women—the physical, financial, and emotional support they need to raise children well.

As I said in my speech at the United Nations Fourth World Conference on Women in Beijing, "We need to understand that there is no formula for how women should lead their lives. That is why we must respect the choices that each woman makes for herself and her family. Every woman deserves the chance to realize her God-given potential."

I HAVE had my own experiences with the power of stereotypes, most notably when the response I gave to a reporter's question during the 1992 Presidential campaign led to the infamous cookies-and-tea tempest. I had understood the question to refer to the ceremonial role of a public official's spouse, and I replied that I had chosen to pursue my law practice while my husband was governor rather than stay home as an official hostess, serving cookies and tea to guests.

Now, the fact is, I've made my share of cookies and served hundreds of cups of tea. But I never thought that my cookie-baking or tea-serving abilities made me a good, bad, or indifferent mother, or a good or bad person. So it never occurred to me that my comment would be taken as insulting mothers (I guess including my own!) who choose to stay home with their children full time. Nor did it occur to me that the next day's headlines would reduce *me* to an anti-cookie—and therefore obviously anti-family—"career woman." Many people jumped to conclusions about me, both positive and negative, based as much on how they interpreted what I said as on the words themselves. Few heard my full comments or knew much about me before labeling me in one way or another.

I learned important lessons from the whole episode, one of which is that when I am asked a question that relates to me personally, I have to be aware that my answer may be measured by how people feel about the choices they've made in their own lives. But the incident also highlighted for me the amount of energy that is wasted on public and private sniping over women's and men's choices and on stereotyping their values, abilities, and predilections. Whatever our differences of opinion on these matters, they pale beside the needs of children, which demand all our varied resources.

Raising children isn't like other jobs, for men or women. There is no exam to pass, no license to hang on the wall. There aren't any vacations, sabbaticals, or leaves of absence, either. You may be a "full-time" lawyer or secretary or teacher or construction worker, but you're a parent around the clock. In addition to being breadwinners, many women are frequently primary caregivers not only for children but for aging parents, shouldering a punishing triple load.

It may be that women will achieve economic and social parity with men only when mothers and fathers fully share responsibility for rearing their children and other household tasks. That day, however, is not likely to dawn anytime soon. In the meantime, we can do two things that will make a difference over time: give both mothers and fathers the time and encouragement to become actively involved in the process of parenting; and help our sons and daughters to avoid the limitations imposed by stereotyping.

WHEN I became pregnant in 1979, my law firm did not have a maternity leave policy. When I tried to raise the subject, I encountered embarrassed silence. As the months went on, I noticed that my male colleagues averted their eyes from my swelling body. When I went to court, judges asked with more concern than usual if anyone needed a recess.

I wound up with a four-month maternity leave that enabled me to spend much-needed time with Chelsea, getting accustomed to my new role as a mother. But most new parents don't meet with anything like this kind of accommodation.

As I have mentioned, the Family and Medical Leave Act guarantees unpaid leave to employees in firms with more than fifty workers. That is a good beginning. Many parents, however, cannot afford to forgo pay for even a few weeks, and very few employers in America offer paid maternity and paternity leave. (Some notable exceptions are outdoor-wear manufacturer Patagonia, ice cream maker Ben & Jerry's, Beth Israel Hospital in Boston, the Sara Lee Corporation, and NationsBank.) Only about half of all female workers of childbearing age are eligible for short-term disability benefits that would cover pregnancy and childbirth, because the Pregnancy Discrimination Act of 1978, while it prohibits discrimination against these conditions, does not mandate coverage where none already exists.

Other countries have figured out that honoring the family by giving it adequate time for caregiving is not only right for the family and smart for society but good for employers, who reap the benefits of workers' increased loyalty and peace of mind. The Germans, for example, guarantee working mothers fourteen weeks' maternity leave (six weeks before and eight weeks after delivery) at full salary. Mothers are also guaranteed job-protected leave for up to three years after childbirth, for the first two years of which they receive a maternity grant equal to about one fifth of the average German woman's salary. While this financial benefit is not adequate to support most families, it is a helpful supplement to family income.

Other European countries provide similarly generous leave, some of them to fathers as well as mothers. In Sweden, for example, couples receive fifteen months of job-guaranteed, paid leave to share between them. The pay is approximately 90 percent of salary for the first twelve months and is reduced further in the last three months.

Yet few Swedish fathers take advantage of the policy. According to a University of Wisconsin study, attitudes and beliefs play a significant role in the decision, along with practical considerations. Many Swedish men, like their American counterparts, believe that men should be the primary breadwinners, lack exposure to male role models who care for infants, and, not least, perceive that there is little social acceptance and encouragement for taking paternal leave.

In our country, even when paid paternity leave is offered, few men take it. One exception to this pattern is Lotus Development Corporation, which offers four weeks of paid leave to new fathers and adoptive parents. Of the 305 Lotus employees who took family leave in 1994, more than a third were men, "an unusually high percentage in American business," according to *Working Mother* magazine, which adds that Lotus's "cutting edge culture . . . makes men feel safe taking time away from work to care for their children."

Many employers are not supportive even when leave laws apply. Kevin Knussman, a Maryland state trooper for nearly two decades, applied for extended parental leave to care for his new baby while his wife recuperated from a difficult pregnancy. The state police personnel office informed him that unless his wife was "in a coma or dead," he didn't qualify as a "primary care provider." He was ordered back to work after ten days leave. Earlier this year, Knussman filed a lawsuit against the state of Maryland, claiming that the police department's refusal was a violation of the Family and Medical Leave Act.

Despite institutional resistance, more fathers are beginning to put time with their families high on the list when they make job decisions. A recent survey of more than six thousand employees in professional and manufacturing jobs found almost as many men as women reporting that they made adjustments in their work lives such as refusing promotion offers, transfers, extensive travel, or overtime. Business may be starting to hear and to respond. Another study showed that working men and women who ranked family over work earned more in the long run than those who did not.

As the saying goes, no one on his deathbed ever says he wishes he'd spent more time at the office. Many divorced men who form second families vow they won't neglect their children the second time around. But children from a first marriage aren't training wheels, and they don't get a second chance at childhood.

More men are beginning to acknowledge the tough choices parenthood sometimes entails. My husband's former deputy domestic policy adviser, Bill Galston, decided that he couldn't combine his work at the White House with the time he wanted to spend with his son. Galston spearheaded the administration's efforts to strengthen families and support children, and he takes seriously his obligations to his own child. He says, "Fatherhood for me has been the most deeply transformative experience in my life. Nothing else is a close second. It is a prism through which I see the world." He tried hard to integrate time with his son into the demands of his work, bringing him to the White House after school to do homework or to dine with him. But when his son wrote him a letter in which he said, "Baseball's not fun when there's no one there to applaud you," Galston decided to leave a job he loved to return to teaching. He told my husband, "You can replace me, but my son can't."

Most men, however, are unlikely to participate wholeheartedly in the care of their children until they are not only accepted as but expected to become active caregivers by the culture at large. Gender roles change slowly, and more than legislative change or progressive business policies is required. It is an age-old problem, and not a uniquely American one by any means.

In a poor section of Santiago, Chile, I visited La Pintana Community Center, which offers a variety of programs to strengthen and preserve families. Two working-class couples spoke to me of their experiences in a program designed to strengthen fathers' involvement with their wives and children. The men told me how they used to spend their nonworking hours having a good time with their friends, leaving their wives home to care for the children. The counseling program, however, had helped them to discover how rewarding time spent with their families could be.

If a Latin American culture that has strong notions about gender roles is attempting to find ways to promote the idea that fatherhood is as challenging and rewarding as anything in the so-called real world, so can we. Perhaps the most effective way we can involve men in parenting is simply to do so.

I remember how tentative my father was about even holding

my baby brothers at first. In contrast, my brother Tony is an active caretaker for his son, and my husband was an eager participant in caring for Chelsea. He held her and sang and talked to her for hours. He had never tended a baby before, though, and I had to back off to create enough space for him to figure out how to get comfortable with her. I forced myself to stop hovering over them and to let him learn for himself how to tell a "wet" cry from a "hungry" one, or how to change a diaper without fear.

I also had to accept that he wouldn't always tend to Chelsea the same way I did. When Chelsea was learning how to turn over, Bill had her on our bed one day, watching with amazement as she turned first one way, then the other. He called excitedly to me to come see and, when I arrived, told me in all seriousness that he was sure she understood gravity. A few minutes later, she rolled off the bed and fell onto the carpet. So much for her grasp of physics!

A father who cares for his own child needs to be appreciated as a responsible parent rather than relegated to the role of "baby-sitter" or ill-trained assistant. Inexperience may result in occasional mishaps—an unsecured diaper that falls down or some other minor inconvenience. My friends and I often shake our heads over what our husbands will let kids do when we're not around. Bedtimes get pushed back, and meals become junk food extravaganzas. But the time children spend with their fathers builds a special bond that is more enduring than the occasional cranky, sleepy, stomachachy aftermath.

No one can dictate exactly how a given household should divide labor. It depends on the unique needs and abilities of each member and what seems right for the family as a whole. Two of my dearest friends illustrate two of the different ways it can be done.

One, a friend since grade school, quit teaching school when the first of her three children was born. For many years, she led a life much like my mother's, devoting herself full time to her children and her home. Now that her youngest child is in junior high, she has again taken a paying job. Her husband has been the family's consistent breadwinner, but he has also participated daily in the care of their children. In addition to sharing household chores, he has done, in his words, "dad things" like coaching their sports teams.

My other friend married after she was forty and had a child when she was forty-five. Her husband, who has a job that enables him to work from home, has assumed the bulk of the cooking and the daily care of their son, while she has continued a hectic professional career that includes frequent travel. The two of them are at ease with this division of labor, and their son is thriving. They remind me of what Shirley Abrahamson, a distinguished judge, said when she accepted an award from the American Bar Association. In thanking her husband for his support, she noted that he had managed to combine marriage and career—but that no one ever asked him how he does it!

CHILDREN LEARN what they see. When they see their fathers cooking dinner or changing the baby's diaper, they'll grow up knowing that caregiving is a human trait, rather than a female one. When they see their mothers changing tires or changing fuses, they'll accept troubleshooting as a human quality, rather than a male one. We should be mindful of the messages we send them as well as the behavior we demonstrate.

Differences in adults' treatment of girls and boys begin well before they reach their first birthdays, as has been demonstrated by studies in which infants in diapers or snowsuits are left in the care of adults who think they know the child's sex because of the names they are told. The same baby is treated differently depending on whether the adult thinks it is a boy or a girl. For example, an adult might identify and respond to the same infant's cry as anger in a "boy" and fear in a "girl."

These early signals continue in school. When a girl does poorly on an exam, adults are inclined to say things like, "Never mind, you did the best you can." Boys are more likely to be told, "Try harder. You can do better." The message that children hear—and internalize—is that effort pays off for boys more than for girls. They also learn that being a boy means taking risks, being active, and trying to do things on your own, while being a girl means needing adult assistance to do whatever you have trouble doing.

Stereotypes start to have an impact during the preschool years, when children tend to notice behavioral and other differences between boys and girls for the first time, and to be concerned with trying to define sex roles. Adults have the authority with children this age to do much to counter the messages they receive from the media and their peers. We can encourage girls to be active and dress them in comfortable, durable clothes that let them move freely. We can choose gifts that transcend gender stereotypes —building blocks for both girls and boys, for example. We can be equal opportunity chore-givers, enlisting girls in yard work and boys in housework.

We can also take care to talk to children in a way that counterbalances the stereotypes coming thick and fast from the media. We can make a point of asking girls about their activities rather than commenting just on their appearance, and we can encourage boys to describe their feelings. We can also acquaint them with the diverse opportunities that exist for women and men out in the world as well as at home. From the time Chelsea was small, Bill regularly took her with him to the governor's office, where he kept a tiny desk stocked with paper and crayons so that she could do her "work" while he did his. We need to make the effort to give boys and girls alike a clear idea of what their parents and other adults do when they leave the house.

It's important that we equip our children with solid, sensitive models of what men and women can be, both as caregivers and as achievers, because when they go out into the world, they'll discover what men and women who try to put children first already know: the village has a long way to go to accommodate their diverse and changing roles both in the working world and at home.

Change starts with each of us. And despite the pressures and frustrations, the more time and energy mothers and fathers put into their parenting, the more joy they'll get out of it. And the richer the models they'll be providing for their children, now and as they begin to compose their own adult lives.

Child Care Is Not a Spectator Sport

At work, you think of the children you've left at home.
At home, you think of the work you've left unfinished.
Such a struggle is unleashed within yourself; your heart is rent.

GOLDA MEIR

I magine a country in which nearly all children between the ages of three and five attend preschool in sparkling classrooms, with teachers recruited and trained as child care professionals. Imagine a country that conceives of child care as a program to "welcome" children into the larger community and "awaken" their potential for learning and growing.

It may sound too good to be true, but it's not. When I went to France in 1989 as part of a group studying the French child care system, I saw what happens when a country makes caring for children a top priority. More than 90 percent of French children between ages three and five attend free or inexpensive preschools called _écoles maternelles_. Even before they reach the age of three, many of them are in full-day programs.

In France, there is a national consensus that the child care system should not just warehouse kids but prepare them for school and for life. Preschool teachers and directors have the equivalent of a master's degree in early-childhood and elementary education. Infant-toddler educators have a degree that is roughly equivalent to two years of college in the United States, as well as a two-year professional course in early-childhood education and development. And the buildings where these child care centers are located are modern and inviting, designed by well-respected architects with children in mind. Walls are specially constructed to absorb sound and shock. Interiors are bright and colorful. Spaces are designated for play, sleeping, eating, and even for good-byes and big hello hugs with parents. It is no wonder that so many French parents— even mothers who do not work outside the home—choose to send their children to these government-subsidized centers.

For the small percentage of French children who are cared for in family day care, the system also works well. Three out of four home providers are licensed, and the law limits the number of children they care for to three per home. The incentives to get licensed are substantial: employee benefits, regular mailings of up-to-date information from the government, and periodic visits from a specially trained pediatric nurse.

Do I believe the French love their children more than we do? Of course not. Nor do I believe that their system can or should be duplicated wholesale here. France is a country far smaller and more homogeneous than ours. And the price for such generous social programs is felt across the board in higher taxes. What I do believe, however, is that the French have found a way of expressing their love and concern through policies that focus on children's needs during the earliest stages of life. While I was in France, I had conversations with a number of political leaders, from Socialists to Conservatives. "How," I asked, "can you transcend your political differences and come to an agreement on the issue of government-subsidized child care?" One after another of them looked at me in astonishment. "How can you not invest in children and expect to have a healthy country?" was the reply I heard over and over again.

IF YOU WANT to open the floodgates of guilt and dissension any-where in America, start talking about child care. It is an issue that brings out all of our conflicted feelings about what parenthood should be and about who should care for children when parents are working or otherwise unable to.

Even though I enjoyed better options than most mothers, I still worried constantly about child care when Chelsea was small. At the time she was born, we lived in the governor's mansion, sur-rounded by a ready-made village of adults who were willing to pinch-hit when I needed extra help. But for two years when Bill was not governor (and Chelsea was still very young), our only help was a woman who came during work hours on weekdays. And like all child care systems, ours broke down from time to time.

My version of every mother's worst nightmare happened one morning when I was due in court at nine-thirty for a trial. It was already seven-thirty, and two-year-old Chelsea was running a fever and throwing up after a sleepless night for both of us. My husband was out of town. The woman who normally took care of Chelsea called in sick with the same symptoms. No relatives lived nearby. My neighbors were not at home. Frantic, I called a trusted friend, who came to my rescue.

Still, I felt terrible that I had to leave my sick child at all. I called at every break and rushed home as soon as court adjourned. When I opened the door and saw my friend reading to Chelsea, who was clearly feeling better, my head and stomach stopped aching for the first time that day.

I often think about what I would have done about child care if I had not had the time and money to make careful decisions. Could I have left my daughter in a stranger's home, in front of the TV all day, or in a big room with dozens of cribs lined up against a wall? Would I have felt comfortable choosing a nursery school for Chelsea when she was two if I had not been able to take off from work several times at the beginning, to accompany her there and observe how she and the other children were treated? Many mothers, for financial and logistical reasons, do not have any choice in these matters.

We all have war stories about the heartache and heartburn of trying to find—and keep—decent child care. But the low priority we place on child care as a nation has led to a system that, unlike the one I saw in France, looks more like a patchwork quilt than a security blanket. Ten million children under age five rely on surrogate care, and many of the approximately 22 million children between ages five and fourteen whose mothers work require care during nonschool hours. While only one in five infants under age one were in day care thirty years ago, more than half are today. And many of those receive care for thirty hours a week or more.

The variety of arrangements these children are left in is dizzying. Neighbors trade child care duty with each other, or relatives are called in to help. When those options do not exist, parents must turn to a marketplace that is complex, confusing, costly, and extremely uneven in quality. Their choices include family day care homes in which one adult takes care of several children from the neighborhood; day care centers that run the gamut from very good to very bad; preschools attached to religious institutions and universities; nannies, au pairs, relatives, and full- and part-time baby-sitters.

In choosing care, cost is a primary factor for many families. Those who cannot afford to pay high prices may end up leaving their children in unlicensed, poorly staffed, and often unsafe environments. According to the National Child Care Survey in 1990, families earning less than $18,000 a year, for example, spent an average of $54 a week for child care. Though often not enough to assure quality care, that $54 represented a huge portion of their household income—about 25 percent on average. By contrast, families earning $54,000 or more spent only about 6 percent of their household income for child care.

Does this mean that children from poorer families never receive loving, patient, and attentive care? No, it doesn't. But from what experts tell us, there is a link between the cost and the quality of care. Many lower-income parents are in a double bind because of their work schedules, which often conflict with available child care. The survey showed that one third of mothers with incomes below the poverty line and more than a quarter of those earning less than $25,000 worked weekends. Yet only 10 percent of day care centers and an even smaller percentage of family day care homes provide care on weekends. Almost half of working-poor parents are in jobs with rotating schedules, making child care arrangements even more complicated.

For parents, particularly those working long hours for low wages, finding child care can present a serious dilemma. Like immigrant mothers at the turn of the century who left their children alone in tenements while they worked in sweatshops, many parents today feel there are no good options when it comes to child care.

In 1990, a woman in New Jersey left her five-year-old daughter locked in her car while she worked a part-time job on Saturdays. When the little girl was discovered, she was temporarily removed from her mother's care. It turned out that the woman was a single parent struggling to support her daughter and had nowhere else to leave her while she worked. The car seemed to her the safest of a bad set of options.

This may be an extreme example, but I bet a lot of parents can relate to that mother's desperation. Ask parents sitting around their kitchen tables to talk about child care, and many will say the situation is dire. The more than 250,000 women who responded to the federal Working Women Count! survey were uniform in their observations about child care. A woman in Oregon who has two grown children, two foster teenagers at home, and a grandchild conveyed the sentiments of most respondents when she wrote: "Child care is a disgrace in this country. On the one hand it's too expensive for many women considering their salaries, on the other hand, it does not provide the child care provider a decent wage. Locating good child care is a nightmare."

A single mother in Illinois who works in a clerical job said: "Working moms already have limited time on their hands, but . . . they feel like they're searching for a needle in a haystack when it comes to child care." She described herself as falling into the child care netherworld because she makes too much to qualify for state programs but finds that the price of private day care "is well out of reach."

Paradoxically, while many parents say that finding affordable child care is a major worry, the vast majority claim to be happy with their arrangements. Often they feel satisfied because the location is convenient, the price is affordable, or the caregiver seems nice. In some cases, parents—who have spent days searching high and low for care—are simply relieved to find any solution that meets their needs.

Yet two recent studies point to an alarming fact: Faced with options that range from wonderful to terrible, many parents do not know what to look for when choosing child care. They often overlook important measures of quality, such as basic safety requirements, the experience and training of child care workers, and whether the setting is appropriate for their child's stage of development.

Child care facilities for infants and toddlers were recently rated in a national study and found to be generally low in quality. Only one in seven was rated as being developmentally appropriate for the children being served. Two hundred twenty-five infant and toddler rooms were evaluated and found to be particularly inadequate. Many had safety problems, poor sanitation, unresponsive caregivers, and a lack of toys and other materials for children. A study of an equal number of home-based child care providers in three communities, conducted by the Families and Work Institute, turned up similar serious concerns about quality. Not unexpectedly, these problems were more prevalent in settings serving low-income children.

As Geraldine Youcha reminds us in her history of child care in America, the most important thing for a child is the quality of care he receives, not necessarily the setting he receives it in. "Children have been helped and hurt by any system, whether orphanages, foster care, upper-class nanny care or mother care. The best was good; the worst was bad."

Why isn't child care in America as good as it should be?

The sad fact is that, unlike the French, we Americans have never sufficiently valued the work of caring for children. It is only recently that we have even begun to acknowledge the contributions of mothers who stay at home—and to appreciate that "mothering" is really a form of early-childhood education. Historically, we also have undervalued the outsiders whom we rely on to care for our children. As far back as Colonial times, raising children was frequently the responsibility of apprenticed girls or indentured servants. Children were cared for by slave women who served as wet nurses, maids, and nannies. Too often a child care worker can be just about anybody who asks for the job. And what does it say about our view of child care when we pay more to the garage attendant who parks our car than the person who is responsible for our children all day?

This devaluation of child care workers is due in part to our nation's long history of ambivalence about whether surrogate child care is an acceptable part of American life. The extraordinary settlement houses that Jane Addams and other social reformers founded in the late nineteenth century to assist the children of immigrant working mothers went out of fashion years ago. The pioneering efforts of early-childhood experts like Dr. Bettye Caldwell to turn schools into family centers that also provided child care never fully caught on, in part because they represented a new idea about using schools for broader community purposes. And Americans continue to be divided over what role, if any, the federal government should play in helping working parents pay for child care.

The fact is that the federal government has subsidized child care at various points in our history. During the Civil War, there were federally sponsored nurseries for mothers working in hospitals. There was a substantial system of federally funded day care during World War II, when mothers went to work in factories to support the war effort. By 1945, approximately 1.6 million children were in day care centers, most of them for six days a week, twelve hours a day. With factories operating around the clock, child care was a patriotic necessity that had to be funded.

But as much as the nation depended on the labor of millions of "Rosie the Riveters," mothers were still criticized for entering the workplace and putting their children in day care centers. There was extensive public debate and many warnings about the expected damage to children from institutionalized care. Even when follow-up studies of parents and children failed to produce any evidence of the predicted ill effects, the critics would not be silenced. As soon as the war ended, federal support for child care was cut off and most women returned home.

For twenty years after the end of World War II, a booming economy made it possible for most families to support their children on one income, typically the father's. When mothers worked, out of necessity or desire, the care of children was usually entrusted to siblings, relatives, or older women like Mrs. Walters, whom Bill's mother employed to care for him and Roger.

Over time, however, child care became a political issue, as women, responding to a changing economy and exercising their hard-won rights to enter the paid workforce, again began joining men on the job. In 1971, President Nixon vetoed federal child care legislation, explaining that it "would commit the vast moral authority of the National Government to the side of communal approaches to child rearing over against the family-centered approach." In retrospect, what is more interesting is what he said he could support: increased funding of day care for welfare recipients and the working poor; tax deductions to subsidize day care for families with two working parents; increased funding for the construction of day care facilities; expanded nutrition and health care services for poor children; better targeting of maternal and child health services to low-income mothers; and expanded funding for Head Start. Now even these measures are controversial in some quarters.

Meanwhile, the need for child care has continued to grow. Global economic changes since the early 1970s have resulted in stagnant wages and benefits for many people. On one income, many families cannot enjoy what is considered to be an American standard of living. Most single parents face a stark choice: either they work or they end up on welfare. But they cannot work without a safe place to leave their children.

In the late 1980s, the federal government forged a bipartisan consensus that significantly increased funding of child care for low-income children. States also increased their contributions. Yet even at its peak, the amount of assistance provided has not come close to meeting the needs of families.

IN PART because we have done so little to encourage better training and compensation for child care workers, a culture has evolved in which child care is more often viewed as "baby-sitting" than as a vehicle for nurturing the emotional and intellectual development of children. Like the French, we should make sure that child care offers our kids the opportunity to learn and grow in warm, stimulating environments that help prepare them for school.

Finding quality child care should matter to parents. Although studies show that children are not affected adversely by having parents who work outside the home, there is evidence that poor care has damaging consequences. Children enrolled in family child care—care in a private home—are more likely to be in settings without licensing or standards than are children in child care centers. Family care is generally less expensive and more convenient than center-based care, which makes it especially popular with single parents. But unlike in the French system, family caregivers in America are often not regulated. In 1993, almost half of the states did not limit the number of children who could be cared for in these home settings. And roughly half of all states did not require a full range of basic health and safety protections. Child care centers, too, suffer from a hodgepodge of regulations, which vary from state to state.

Parents often assume that cost is the biggest barrier to good care, but another problem may be their inability to recognize good quality and demand it for their children. Parents need to be alert, engaged, and informed consumers, just as they need to be self-aware in their own parenting. I have visited child care facilities all over the country, and I can testify to the superb conditions in some settings and the abject inadequacy of others. While many centers offer bright, pleasant surroundings and an assortment of toys, others are dreary and spartan, with no open spaces for play. In some centers, the caregivers seem bored, distracted, and uninterested in the children. But in the best settings, the workers are creative, energetic, and focused on the children. And you can tell immediately that they also take seriously the responsibility of their jobs.

Zero to Three, an organization devoted to informing the public about young children's needs, tells us that caregivers should be "well trained in pediatric first aid, rescue breathing, sanitation, and prevention and detection of early signs of contagious disease" and that the setting should meet or exceed local and state health standards and provide health information to parents.

Having enforceable state licensing requirements for child care providers also helps raise standards of care. A study of Florida's child care centers measured the quality of care children received before and after state regulations went into effect. These laws put more adults in charge of fewer children and required that at every licensed center at least one staff person have a Child Development Associate credential or its equivalent for every twenty children served. Researchers observed that the day care workers were more responsive and positive in dealing with the children after the regulations went into effect. The children themselves exhibited greater language and social development, and the number of behavior problems went down.

Even when caregivers meet legal standards, there is no guarantee that the quality of their care is what children deserve. Parents can learn a lot about child care by making unannounced visits to a site before *and after* enrolling their children. Every parent ought to find out the ratio of adults to children in a particular child care setting. Experts agree that one adult should watch no more than three or four infants, for example.

Parents should ask questions about the training of child care workers, which can range from a few hours a week as a neighborhood baby-sitter to a master's degree in early-childhood development. And parents should feel they have the right to ask about salaries: a caregiver making only the minimum wage might have one eye focused on finding a new and better-paying job. Continuity is important. Turnover is high among low-wage workers, and that can be problematic, as children form attachments with people who suddenly vanish from their lives.

In scouting out child care, what we observe tells us a lot. The room where kids play does not have to be opulent, but it must be clean. It does not have to be filled with every toy advertised on television, but it should have a variety of toys, books, stuffed animals, and art supplies suited to your child's stage of development. The Child Care Action Campaign, a nonprofit coalition of individuals, organizations, and businesses dedicated to helping parents recognize and find quality child care, advises that "jigsaw puzzles and crayons may be fine for preschoolers but are inappropriate for infants." It may seem obvious, but when parents are feeling pressed to find a place for their child, these factors are sometimes ignored.

Zero to Three illustrates easy ways to understand the impact "quality of care" can have on small children and how parents can be partners in promoting it. Let's say Tim is two and a half years old and his mother drops him off for the first time at a child care center. She may have visited the center before but has not made a point of finding out who her son's primary caregiver will be. It turns out no one is assigned that role and Tim is left to fend for himself. He is bullied, and when no one attends to him when he starts to cry, he takes it upon himself to fight back. Within a few weeks, he, too, has become a class bully, who is regularly yelled at and assigned to "time-outs." He has learned his lessons well: his feelings are not valued, and in this day care center it is every toddler for himself.

In an alternate scenario, Tim and his mother spend time with his primary caregiver, a woman named Mindy. She asks Tim and his mother questions, and learns from Tim's mother about his temperament and particular needs. When another child intentionally bumps Tim, Mindy pulls him aside to talk and then introduces the two boys. Whenever Tim's mother leaves him, Mindy gives him extra attention and reassurance. Within a few weeks, Tim is playing happily with the other children and is no longer anxious about his mother's return. With Mindy's help, he has come to feel safe and valued.

These are steps we can take as individuals to ensure that our own children receive the care they need. But what can we do as a society to make sure that all children are cared for the way we want our own children to be?

We can begin by insisting that the federal government not turn its back on children by depriving low-income and working families of the assistance they need to be assured quality child care. As battles rage over the federal budget, it is important to remember that much of the best child care for low-income children is subsidized in one way or another by the federal government. Child care for working and low-income parents has been subsidized through the Child Care and Development block grant and other federal programs, along with additional state funding. Other forms of assistance help subsidize care for children whose families are on welfare.

Earlier this year, I visited the Linn County Day Care Center in Cedar Rapids, Iowa, which, supported by federal, state, and local funds, enrolls nearly seventy children from low-income families. I was impressed by the center's range of activities. In one room, children were gleefully feeding guinea pigs; in another, they were busy making valentines with paper and glue. Every classroom and every activity I saw reflected the center's emphasis on developing the language and social skills of each child.

It was also clear that the center understood that quality child care and strong families go hand in hand. There was not one parent I met who was not either working, actively involved in job training, going to college, or trying to get a high school equivalency diploma. Having access to child care they could trust enabled them to pursue goals that would benefit both their families and society.

Many states have worked to address the patchwork problem by creating integrated systems of support and supervision of child care. Beginning in August 1993, North Carolina merged its state and community funds to establish the Smart Start initiative to improve the health and well-being of its young children, in part by improving the training of child care providers and creating high-quality programs to prepare children to enter school. In Ohio, even in an era when the state's overall spending has grown at its slowest rate in forty years, legislators have increased funding for select programs for children and families by one third since 1991 through the Ohio Family and Children First Initiative. Its goals are to assure healthier infants and children, to increase access to quality preschool and child care, and to improve the state's outreach efforts to promote family stability. These programs are successful in part because they expand on a base of federal support delivered through the states.

One of the most hopeful signs I have seen is the growing interest of the business community in assisting employees with child care. More and more, businesses are recognizing that when employees miss work to stay home with sick children or when parents are distracted by child care problems, the bottom line suffers too.

The Du Pont Company was one of the first large companies to institute work-family programs such as job sharing and subsidized emergency child care. A study of Du Pont employees confirmed the view that family-friendly policies are a good business practice, because they make the workforce more committed and more engaged. "If you do something to meet the employees' needs, they return the favor," said Charles Rodgers, whose firm conducted the study.

Eastman Kodak provides a backup child care service in which a nurse or similarly trained professional will come to an employee's home when regular child care arrangements fall through. IBM allows some of its employees the flexibility to work at home and sponsors day care centers that offer children a wide range of activities. The *Fort Worth Star-Telegram* in Texas allows employees to work from home via computer and has set up a private room at its headquarters where new mothers can nurse their infants. Local governments and nonprofit organizations, too, are discovering the benefits of policies that help families. In Kansas City, Missouri, for example, city employees are granted four hours of paid leave annually to participate in children's school activities. And the YWCA of New York City offers employees reduced tuition for children's summer camp.

On October 31, 1995, I hosted an event at the White House honoring twenty-one companies in the American Business Collaboration for Quality Dependent Care that have pledged to contribute $100 million for child and dependent care in fifty-six cities nationwide. Allstate, AT&T, Chevron, Citibank, Hewlett-Packard, Johnson & Johnson, Mobil, Texaco, and Xerox were among the companies honored. James Schiro, the chairman of Price Waterhouse and one of our guest speakers, said: "All of the companies participating believe in our theme: 'Doing together what none of us can afford to do alone.'"

Hundreds of other companies around the country have also been listed on the Department of Labor's "honor roll"—a list of employers who pledge to initiate workplace policies that help parents and families, such as flexible work schedules, paid leave to attend children's school activities, and tax-deductible set-asides from employees' paychecks that can be used to pay for child care.

Susan O'Neil, an employee of Deloitte & Touche, who spoke at the White House, described the hectic pace of her life as a mother working full time outside the home. She credited her employer with helping her find child care through a company referral service and giving her flexible hours to meet her family's needs.

"This is real, America," she said. "We ask you the government, and you the employer, to help us, the working people, to make it work. We can't do it alone."

She is right. As a nation, we must make child care a priority and begin to value the important work of raising strong, healthy, and happy children.

Education = Expectations

Children are likely to live up to what you believe of them.

LADY BIRD JOHNSON

I have never met a stupid child, though I've met plenty of children whom adults insist on calling "stupid" when the children don't perform in a way that conforms to adult expectations.

I remember a six-year-old girl I tutored in reading at an elementary school in Little Rock. I'll call her Mary. She lived in a tiny house with six siblings, her parents, and an assortment of other relatives, who came and went unpredictably. There was so much commotion in the evenings that she was rarely able to sleep for longer than a few hours, and she always looked tired. She seemed uncomfortable talking, but she didn't want to read, either. Sometimes her eyelids would droop and she would lay her head on the desk.

One day, desperate for a way to hold her attention, I asked Mary if she liked to draw. Her brown eyes lit up and she nodded eagerly. Her colored-pencil drawings of people and animals were technically advanced and rich in detail. Awkward as she was with words, Mary communicated vividly through her art. Her pictures of a small house crowded with many people and lacking space for her to draw or to play provided us with a way to begin talking about her life. When I complimented her on them, though, she repeated what other adults must have said to her: The drawings were just silly "baby" stuff and not very good.

When her teacher observed what we were doing, she cautioned me that my purpose was to help Mary learn to read, not to play. I suggested that encouraging Mary to express herself in her drawings and then helping her to write stories about what they conveyed could lead her to reading. But the teacher could only see that Mary and I had failed at our assigned task, which was to read stories in the class workbooks.

Mary was obviously intelligent, but her intelligence was expressed in the pictures she drew and not by trying to read from a printed page. Yet her artistic interest and talent were not being praised at home or in school. It wasn't surprising that she often seemed withdrawn or unhappy. How could she not notice that her talents were ignored, even penalized? It does not take long for children like Mary, whose intelligence is expressed in a way that is not customarily recognized or appreciated, to lose a sense of how valuable their particular gifts are, and, along with it, their confidence and sense of self.

When this happens, teachers, parents, and other adults often write them off as "slow" or "unmotivated" and come to expect less of them in the way of academic performance. Tragically, the children are thus deprived of the opportunity to master the basic skills they will need to realize their particular gifts. This is a loss not only to them but to the entire village, which could benefit from all our talents.

In his 1983 book, *Frames of Mind*, Howard Gardner outlined the theories about multiple intelligence that he had formulated while working with gifted children and children who had suffered brain damage. He discovered that the loss of certain mental capacities, such as language ability, was accompanied by an enhancement of others, such as visual or musical abilities. These findings prompted Gardner to explore how parts of the brain seem to promote different abilities. He uncovered what he describes as the capacity people have to express themselves through various forms of intelligence.

Even within the same family, it's easy to see that different children are good at different things. From very early on, some seem to be drawn to words and learning from books, although the abstract, logical reasoning mathematics requires may come less easily to them. Other children excel at math, because their minds travel most easily in the worlds of numbers and symbols, but they may have difficulty expressing themselves in words.

Verbal and mathematical abilities stand children in good stead in most classrooms. Other kinds of intelligence may go unrecognized. Children who think in visual images may not thrive when limited to words and symbols. An early knack for music, like my husband's, might be ignored if it is not accompanied by more conventional skills. So might the strong intuitive skills that allow people to read the moods and temperament of others. We have all known children who seemed to think with their bodies—who can rapidly learn a new sport, for example—and yet seem restless and uncomfortable when they are forced to sit still at a desk. The brilliant choreographer Martha Graham once said, "If I could say it, I wouldn't have to dance it." Yet rather than celebrate our children's multiple forms of intelligence, too often we elevate one form over another or caricature kids accordingly, labeling them "jocks" or "nerds."

Howard Gardner's list of intelligences takes into account verbal, mathematical, visual, physical, and musical intelligences as well as psychological skills like the ability to understand and interact well with others. These forms of intelligence are not mutually exclusive. Every one of us has all of them to some degree. Their particular constellation may determine not only what we are good at but how we learn—if we are given the encouragement and opportunity to develop them.

Whatever the range of intelligences includes, it is increasingly clear that standard IQ tests capture only a fraction of it. The tests were originally designed to measure only the aptitudes that fall within Gardner's first two types of intelligence, verbal and mathematical. Yet much classroom work engages only that part of a child's potential. Schools often categorize children's intelligence according to their performance on IQ and other narrowly conceived tests and adjust their encouragement and expectations accordingly. Even "slow" children are quick to catch on to the categories schools have put them into, and learn a simple equation: If adults don't think I can achieve, I can't and I won't.

The philosopher Nelson Goodman suggests that we would do well to learn to ask *how* rather than *whether* someone is smart. That question would shift the emphasis to helping individuals realize their potential, rather than whether they have potential in the first place. The main point I want to make here is that virtually all children can learn and develop more than their parents, teachers, or the rest of the village often believe. This has great implications for how we approach our children's educations.

One of the striking differences international studies have repeatedly turned up between American parents and students and their counterparts in other countries, particularly in Asia, is the greater weight our culture currently gives to innate ability, as opposed to effort, in academic success. I don't know all the reasons for this preoccupation, which seems to be linked to an obsession with IQ tests and other means of labeling people, but some possible explanations are not particularly flattering to us.

Believing in innate ability is a handy excuse for us. Too tired to read to a child or enforce rules on TV-watching or phone use? Too preoccupied to seek out extra help for a child who needs more practice with math or a foreign language? Why bother, if none of that really makes much of a difference anyway? More concerned with how a daughter looks than whether she's reading at grade level? More interested in a son's jump shot than in how he conjugates verbs? If that's what gets our attention, you can bet it's what kids will think is important too. But how can we parents see the connection between effort and appearance, or between effort and athletic prowess, but not between effort and academic success?

The bell curve lets the rest of us off the hook too. What's the sense of reforming schools, especially if it costs any money? What is the point of figuring out how to tailor teaching to the unique ways children learn? Why puzzle over what they should learn, and why bother to articulate it to them? Cream will rise to the top no matter what we do, so let nature take its course and forget about nurture.

If we are permitted to write off whole groups of kids because of their racial or ethnic or economic backgrounds, then the occasional academic shooting star will be seen as a fluke. And when whole groups of kids succeed despite the odds, like the poor Hispanic high school students Jaime Escalante coached to succeed on the Advanced Placement calculus examination, their success can be ascribed to a unique brand of charismatic teaching and motivation that can't be replicated anywhere else.

I began to work on behalf of education reform in Arkansas in 1983, when my husband asked me to chair a committee that would make recommendations for improving Arkansas's education system. That was also the year that "A Nation at Risk," the landmark report about our schools, was issued. I couldn't begin to describe in a single chapter all the effort since then that has gone into promoting preschool and kindergarten programs, raising academic standards, establishing accountability, professionalizing teaching conditions, improving vocational and technical education, and many other changes. But after a dozen years of involvement in education reform, I'm convinced that the biggest obstacles many students face in learning are the low expectations we have of them and their schools.

I've mentioned the impact President Eisenhower's post-Sputnik call for higher math and science performance had on my generation. Performance standards were upgraded; new classroom equipment was purchased. Our parents and teachers demanded more from us. Nearly forty years later, though, education is more important to success in the global village than ever. Now we have no clear and immediate enemy to frighten us into improving education for our own children; we have to do it for ourselves. But the starting point is the same: High expectations begin at home.

MY PARENTS made learning part of our daily activities, from storytelling and reading aloud to discussing current events at the dinner table to calculating earned run averages for Little League pitchers. They taught me and my brothers in all sorts of informal ways before we started school, and they continued teaching us in partnership with our teachers at school.

When I was in fourth grade, I was having trouble with arithmetic. My father said he would help me if I got up as early as he did each morning. The house was cold, because the furnace was turned off when we went to bed. I would sit shivering at the kitchen table as the house slowly warmed up and my father drilled me on multiplication tables and long division.

Some parents do not easily assume the role of teacher. They

may lack the confidence, be unwilling to devote the time, or simply not know, for example, that reading aloud to babies and toddlers is the single most important activity we can do with children to ensure that they will read well in school. But the village has found ways to help parents start teaching children when it counts most, in the preschool years.

In Arkansas, I introduced a program that had been developed in Israel. Called HIPPY—the Home Instruction Program for Preschool Youngsters—it works like this: A staff member recruited from the community comes into the home once a week and role-plays with the parent (usually the mother), demonstrating for her how she can work with her child to stimulate cognitive development. Along with special activity packets, the program employs common household objects to illustrate concepts. For example, a spoon and a fork might be used to demonstrate differences in shape or sharpness, or the volume control on the TV might be turned up and down to teach the concepts of loud and soft. The material in the activity packets, designed for parents who may not read well themselves, is outlined in straightforward fifteen-minute daily lesson plans arranged in a developmental sequence. The usual starting age is four, and most children participate for two years. Some programs add a third year, so children can begin the program at the age of three.

When we brought HIPPY into rural areas and housing projects in Arkansas, a number of educators and others did not believe that parents who had not finished high school were up to the task of teaching their children. Many of the parents doubted their own abilities. One mother whose home I visited told me she had always known she was supposed to put food on the table and a roof over her children's heads, but no one had ever told her before that she was supposed to be her son's first teacher.

Not only did the program help kids get jump-started in the

right direction; it also gave the parents a boost in self-confidence. Many of them became interested in learning for themselves as well as for their children, going back to school to get a high school equivalency degree or even starting college. This is a particularly important development, because researchers cite a mother's level of education as one of the key factors in determining whether her children do well in school. It stands to reason that when a mother furthers her own learning, she becomes more engaged in her child's.

There are similar—and similarly successful—efforts going on elsewhere, such as the Parents as Teachers (PAT) program started in Missouri, which also uses home visits to coach parents on preparing children for school.

The importance of early learning is also one of the driving ideas behind Head Start, the thirty-year-old federally funded preschool education program that has consistently helped to prepare disadvantaged children for school. But Head Start doesn't reach children until they are four, when we now know from research that many of them are already behind their peers. So when Congress reauthorized Head Start in 1994, at the President's recommendation it established Early Head Start to target low-income families with infants and toddlers.

So far, however, Head Start reaches only about 750,000 of the estimated two million children who need it, and Early Head Start is just getting under way. Despite the proven success of investments like Head Start, it and many other preventive programs are caught in the battle over federal budget priorities. Our nation can afford to invest in early childhood education and balance the budget. There are few more important investments at the federal, state, or local level than programs focused on helping parents to develop the confidence and skills to teach young children.

We work at home to prepare children for learning, in anticipation that much will be demanded of them when they reach school. Too often, however, expectations are undermined by a piecemeal approach to educational change. Nearly every problem in education, including the plague of low expectations, has been tackled successfully somewhere. Leading education reformers like James Comer, Theodore Sizer, Ernest L. Boyer, and Deborah Meier have diagnosed our ills, prescribed strategies for recovery, and put them to work. They usually boil down to a few crucial ingredients: clear expectations that all children can and should learn; manageable school and class size; an orderly classroom environment; the close personal involvement of at least one teacher with each child; a commitment to tailoring instruction to how different children learn; active parental participation. Reciting this wish list is easy. Figuring out how to put it into practice in the face of bureaucratic opposition, parental qualms, some teacher resistance, and the host of other obstacles reform faces is another story.

I once spoke to a group of school superintendents about model programs that had been effective in transforming poorly performing students into motivated achievers. I asked if anyone in my audience had visited any of the programs I mentioned. A long silence fell over the room. Finally, one superintendent confessed that he couldn't see himself explaining to his school board that a nearby school was solving a problem that had stumped him. There wasn't anything new in education anyway, he added, so he couldn't see the sense in getting worked up about some "experiments."

That superintendent would doubtless brush off as "experimental" Reading Recovery, a program started in New Zealand, which is considered among the most literate countries in the world. Reading Recovery has demonstrated consistent success in getting nearly nine out of ten first graders who read poorly to grade level in a few months. In 1984, a group of educators at Ohio State University's

College of Education launched a Reading Recovery pilot in selected Columbus, Ohio, public schools. The program was astonishingly successful, and gradually it won widespread support. Reading Recovery teachers are now being trained in school districts in forty-seven states. Yet many schools continue to pursue remedial reading methods that are not nearly as effective. Why?

The first problem is money, especially in urban school districts, which generally have less money to begin with and more students in need of help. Even though children move through the Reading Recovery program quickly and, after leaving it, usually do not need additional help, saving money in the long term, a front-end investment is needed to train teachers in the strategies that make the program a success: one-on-one tutoring, with an emphasis on phonics and language skills. The failure to make a sufficient initial investment creates a self-fulfilling prophecy: When large numbers of first graders still can't read at the end of the year, the program will be judged a failure.

Concerns about career advancement sometimes work against innovative programs, too. The success of a program like Reading Recovery may not be enough to outweigh the preconceptions of teachers and administrators who have long affiliated themselves with other approaches or are intent on preserving their budgets, staff, and political clout.

Such misplaced adult priorities divert our efforts and energies from where they are most productively spent—on paying attention to how children learn and doing our best to personalize the learning process so that each of them can meet high standards.

It is precisely this concern that motivated social psychologist Jeff Howard to create the Efficacy Institute in Lexington, Massachusetts. The Institute has trained twenty thousand teachers in school districts throughout this country to rethink their assumptions about children's intelligence. In Tacoma, Washington, where two thirds of the teachers in the district have gone through Efficacy training during the past three years, results of this new approach are already visible. On standardized tests, the scores of fourth and eighth graders rose significantly in just two years. Part of the reason for this increase in achievement is that teachers go back into the classroom and share their new knowledge about learning with the students, explaining to them how important it is for them to work hard so they can "get smart." Students absorb the message that smart is not something you simply are, but something you can become.

Another innovator who has pioneered a more effective approach to learning is Bob Moses, who is revered for his efforts to mobilize black voters in the South during the civil rights movement. Thirty years later, he has brought the same passionate commitment to a different kind of work.

Helping his own daughter to struggle with her algebra homework in the early 1980s, Moses, who had been a teacher before he became a civil rights leader, began volunteering at her school, trying to get students to be comfortable with numbers and more engaged in the process of problem solving. He knew that without strong math skills poor children would be at a disadvantage in the highly competitive world of higher learning. His determination gave birth to the Algebra Project, which addressed the crisis in math education among minority students through a middle school curriculum that was designed to bridge the conceptual gap between arithmetic and algebra.

Moses developed a five-step model that mimicked the natural learning process he had observed in children and brought abstract concepts down to earth. When working with students in Boston, for example, he treated a route on the subway as a number line, assigning negative and positive values to various stops. After the kids rode the subway, they returned to the classroom to test out their concepts. In the early 1990s, Moses returned to Mississippi, this time to crusade for the right to learn algebra, early and effectively.

Moses's method of teaching students mathematical concepts through real-life examples seems as if it should be an obvious one. But in many classrooms, teachers still treat the subject in purely abstract terms, assuming that some students are "naturally" able to grasp the concepts, while others—girls and minority students, for example— cannot. The methods Moses pioneered demonstrate that most students can grapple with advanced math. They have been so successful that programs like the Algebra Project are being instituted in schools around the country.

Such programs are particularly important because studies show that the strongest single indicator of whether students will go on to college is whether they have taken both algebra and geometry. Armed with this knowledge, the College Board's Equity 2000 Project is working to ensure that students receive at least two years of college preparatory mathematics before graduating from high school. So far, the program has been adopted in six urban areas around the country. Preliminary results show a rise in teachers' expectations for students' performance and a dramatic increase in student enrollment in algebra, with only a small increase in course failure rates.

Forward-thinking teachers and school administrators across the country are creating a whole range of alternatives to cookie-cutter teaching and evaluation methods, such as the use of student portfolios and exhibitions in addition to conventional exams to assess students' progress. Such educators also put a premium on getting parents involved in kids' learning.

Schools are frightening places for many parents. When Bill and I went to our first parent-teacher conference when Chelsea was in kindergarten, we were apprehensive. For the first time, another adult was going to pass judgment on our child, and our many years of schooling did nothing to ease the anxiety.

If a child's parents have not finished school or were poor students themselves, they may be even less at ease in a school setting. Many parents stay away except when a child gets into trouble. Knowing how important parental involvement is to their success, however, more schools are making efforts to involve parents actively as their partners in educating children.

Dr. James Comer, a child psychiatrist at the Yale Child Study Center, created the School Development Program as a means of reducing barriers between home and school. More than six hundred schools in twenty-one states have adopted Comer's approach, which teaches parents how to help their children learn, encourages parents to help plan academic programs, and brings parents, teachers, and other school staff together in relaxed settings.

In Camden, New Jersey, the idea of "family schools" emerged in the early 1990s. As in other communities where family stability is threatened by drugs, violence, and abuse, school must be a safe haven for the family as a whole if children are to prosper. As Annie Rubin, principal of Coopers Poynt, one of Camden's family schools, says, "For every child at risk, there's also a family at risk."

At Coopers Poynt, parents and guardians find an array of social services. Nurses provide prenatal screening and conduct classes in parenting and child development. The presence of a full-day parents' center encourages parents to volunteer as classroom aides. Coopers Poynt opens its doors early each morning—before classes begin but not before many students' parents start their workday—and doesn't shut them until late afternoon. "We don't have any magic formula," Rubin says. "We just care. I just feel that if [families] are touched by us, they're all going to do a little better."

A number of independent programs exist to strengthen parents' involvement in their children's schooling. The Family Math program, based in Berkeley, California, was developed to give parents the confidence and skills to help their children learn math. Parents and children come together for weekly classes, held in four- to eight-week cycles at schools, community centers, and libraries. Teachers and parents who have been trained as Family Math instructors demonstrate math activities that parents and children can do together at home, none of which require more than pencil and paper and ordinary household items like beans, buttons, and toothpicks. The program has been so successful that it has been replicated in a number of communities around the country. As with HIPPY, it has inspired some parents to return to their own education.

Kent Salveson, an Orange County–based developer in Southern California, has offered an innovative example of how businesses can help to promote an entire community's involvement. In conjunction with the University of Southern California, he created a low-income housing project called EEXCEL Apartments. (EEXCEL stands for Educational Excellence for Children with Environmental Limitations.) Salveson's idea was to strengthen the ties between home and school, and to make education, child and health care, and family counseling more accessible to the poor. Explaining the thinking behind his brainchild, Salveson said, "If we want to change a neighborhood, a community, our country, we have to change the home. I don't care if it's in Beverly Hills or in South-Central. Children are being neglected. A nation is the sum of all its homes."

The original forty-six-unit complex has spawned other EEXCEL buildings in California, and more are in the works in several other states. All of them are in low-income areas that don't generally have access to the family support services they need. Each has space set aside for classrooms, which are equipped with computers, books, and school supplies. In exchange for course credit, local university students are available four hours a day, four days a week, to provide one-on-one tutoring to children who live in the complex. At the end of each semester, EEXCEL holds a banquet for the parents, children, and tutors to celebrate the children's school achievements and awards gift certificates from local bookstores to children who get good grades. The complexes also sponsor other activities and services designed to bring neighbors together—résumé and job training programs, Campfire Girls and Boys, bookmobile visits, a food share program, literacy and art classes, and community holiday parties. Salveson says that one of his goals is to "break down the massiveness of the city to a smaller community of people who live in the building."

NOWHERE IS the partnership of parents and the rest of the village more crucial to the schools than in the expectation that discipline and order are necessary for learning to happen. One spring morning, my brother Tony came downstairs for breakfast and found my father in his customary place at the kitchen table, reading the sports page. Instead of talking sports, though, as they usually did, my father began to quiz Tony about what he had done in school the day before. Tony answered with vague descriptions of a day like any other at his junior high. Only then did my father show him the photo in the sports section. Prominently featured in the bleachers were my brother and several friends who had skipped school to join the crowd celebrating the Chicago Cubs' opening game at Wrigley Field. That day, the boys got in trouble both at home and at school.

Skipping school is one thing. Today drugs and violence lead the list of offenses foremost on parents' and teachers' minds. How do we reassert adult authority?

First, we parents have to back up school authority and quit making excuses for our kids when they misbehave. Does that mean teachers and principals are always right? Of course not, but they deserve to be given back the presumption that they are.

Schools have to do their part by stating the rules clearly and punishing violators. Habitually disruptive students should be removed from regular classes until they are able to attend without interfering with other students. Standards of conduct should be explained and enforced, and parents should say "Hallelujah" instead of "I'll sue!"

Schools could take a big step toward improving discipline by sending kids the clear message that school is their work and they are expected to behave and dress accordingly. I agree with those who advocate dress codes and even uniforms in some school districts because they appear to diminish the frictions caused by brand-name consumerism and gang identification. I'd much rather have students worrying about their homework for the next day than whether they have the right clothes to wear or who might attack them if they wear the wrong color sneakers.

In 1994, the Long Beach School District in California became the first district in the nation to mandate uniforms for its elementary and middle school students. That year, school violence decreased to half the rates of the previous year. Other districts are taking note and beginning to follow suit.

Long Beach leaves the precise details of the uniform to each school's principal so long as the elements fit the overall dress code. The school system has sought financial assistance to enable low-income families to purchase the uniforms, but a group of parents and students has filed suit anyway, claiming they cannot afford the costs and that the school district has not helped. Without going into the merits of the case, I find it hard to understand why energy is being spent litigating that could be used to raise money for uniforms or to tackle some other school problem. Other schools with voluntary uniform codes, like those in Fulton County, Georgia, have used school funds to subsidize uniform purchases and have started an exchange program for outgrown uniforms.

Robert E. Lee High School in Houston, Texas, provides a good example of the effect community-wide involvement can have on curbing violence in schools. Several years ago, the school set out to enlist the support of families and community members in dealing with a serious gang problem. The city of Houston initiated a school-day curfew, imposing a two-hundred-dollar fine on parents if their children were found on the street when they were supposed to be in school. At the same time, the high school implemented a "zero tolerance for gangs in the school" policy. Bilingual administrators combed the neighborhoods the school serves, speaking with families and "cutting contracts" with them to enlist their help in enforcing the policy. A core group of teachers, administrators, police officers, and school district security guards worked to identify gang members and to take steps to evict them from the school if they became violent. Since then, the climate in the school has changed dramatically, and students' scores on state exams have steadily improved. An honors English class has been established for the first time. As the principal said, "We can now concentrate on our academic problems, not our sociological ones."

ULTIMATELY, THOUGH, what schools need most from the village are high standards to live up to. Some people disagree, claiming that even voluntary standards interfere with local control, permitting outsiders to determine what children are taught. I have never accepted that argument, which confuses what standards are for: They establish what children should know, not how they are taught or measured. Algebra is algebra, from Little Rock to Atlanta, from Seattle, Washington, to Washington, D.C. And even before I started working on standards in Arkansas, I knew of many schools, particularly in poor areas, that needed help designing appropriate curricula.

Education is fundamental to our country's future and to the future of our children, who will have to be prepared to compete in a national and global economy. High standards will help ensure that all of them—no matter where they live—will have access to quality education.

I think often of a young man I met at an annual reception for high school honors graduates and their parents that Bill and I started hosting at the governor's mansion in 1979. He told me he had long dreamed of becoming a doctor. But when he went for an interview at the local college, he was told that, although he was his graduating class's salutatorian, his school had not adequately prepared him for the rigors of a premed course of study. What he had been taught as "algebra" was arithmetic with a few x's thrown in. He was advised to take a fifth year of high school somewhere with more challenging classes or go to college prepared to take remedial courses. What a rotten choice to be confronted with after he had kept his side of the bargain by studying and performing well!

When I worked on education reform in Arkansas, the proposals we made for a standardized curriculum and course content recommendations to accompany it encountered opposition from administrators who claimed in all sincerity that their students didn't want or need higher standards. One superintendent told me that very few of "his kids" went to college, so he couldn't see what difference it would make. Another superintendent ushered me into his office and pointed at a sign on his desk that said, "This too shall pass." He told me that was what he thought of my husband's efforts to reform education. Standing in front of the new gymnasium they had built, he and the school board solemnly assured me that they knew the kids in their district, and none of them were interested in taking foreign languages, art, or advanced sciences.

Thankfully, their attitude was not representative of the majority of citizens or legislators, and Arkansas passed a sweeping education reform in 1983 that has changed the expectations—and lives—of thousands of students. But all too often, in too many places, the concept of "local control" is still used to justify having low expectations of students, particularly poor ones, and to resist holding all students and schools accountable for their progress in meeting explicit goals.

IN 1989, President George Bush convened the nation's governors in Williamsburg, Virginia, to kick off an effort to establish national goals for education, a movement that received support from all but one of the assembled governors and that quickly took on national momentum. My husband represented the Democratic governors at that gathering, only the third such working meeting in our nation's history. As President, he and Secretary of Education Richard Riley, who had championed effective education reform as Governor of South Carolina, brought the goals-setting process to fruition in 1993 when they presented to Congress the Goals 2000: Educate America Act, which passed with strong bipartisan support and the backing of almost every major national parent, education, and business organization.

The genius of Goals 2000 is that it marries the ideas of high standards for *what* children should learn, local control over *how* children learn, and accountability for *whether* children learn. The act reaffirms the traditional principle of local control of education, acknowledging that each community is the best judge of what will work in its schools. But it also recognizes, as I learned in Arkansas, that many parents and schools need guidance in setting goals that will prepare children for future challenges, as the Information Age changes the ways we live and work.

Under the legislation, states are expected to establish their own academic content standards and assessments of student perform-ance. Goals 2000 gives schools help in determining where, amid the daily flurry of demands, they need to focus their attention and what skills students need to acquire. The National Assessment of Educational Progress, administered by the federal government, acts as a report card, a tool for charting the results of state and local reform efforts.

As soon as Goals 2000 passed, it was attacked by extremists, who stirred up anxious parents with visions of totalitarian control over their children's minds and of "secular humanists" stealing their children's souls. One teacher told me that a local church had protested when she moved the chairs in her classroom into a circle for discussion purposes, citing the insidious influence of Goals 2000 because "everyone knows that's how witches' covens meet." The inci-dent would be laughable except that her principal ordered her to put the chairs back in their neat rows.

What are these goals that promote such passionate reactions?

By the year 2000:

1. All children in America will start school ready to learn.

2. The high school graduation rate will increase to at least 90 percent.

3. All students will leave grades four, eight, and twelve having demonstrated competency in challenging subject matter, including English, mathematics, science, foreign languages, civics and gov-ernment, economics, the arts, history, and geography; and every school in America will ensure that all students learn to use their minds well, so that they may be prepared for responsible citizen-ship, further learning, and productive employment in our nation's modern economy.

4. United States students will be first in the world in science and mathematics achievement.

5. Every adult American will be literate and will possess the knowledge and skills necessary to compete in a global economy and exercise the rights and responsibilities of citizenship.

6. Every school in the United States will be free of drugs, violence, and the unauthorized presence of firearms and alcohol and will offer a disciplined environment conducive to learning.

7. The nation's teaching force will have access to programs for the continued improvement of their professional skills and the opportunity to acquire the knowledge and skills needed to instruct and prepare all American students for the next century.

8. Every school will promote partnerships that will increase parental involvement and participation in promoting the social, emotional, and academic growth of children.

These goals are hardly the stuff of revolution—and are not likely to be fully achieved easily, or by the year 2000. We cannot expect to reverse decades of declining standards in a few years. A recent report showed that the country has made progress in some areas, such as math and science achievement. There has been little or no progress in areas such as reading achievement. And there have been greater problems with respect to juvenile drug use, especially marijuana, and classroom disruption.

But the whole point of goals is to encourage a process in states, school districts, and individual schools that will set standards and offer real guidance as to what should be taught and how student performance should be measured so that progress toward the goals can be assessed. Why should we accept goals, standards, and performance measures in business or sports but not in our schools? Can you imagine a successful CEO telling stockholders that their company has nothing new to learn from anyone and that it can't be expected to improve in any case, because, after all, look who its employees and customers are?

I was privileged to know the late Sam Walton, the legendary founder of Wal-Mart. He regularly visited Wal-Mart stores, literally dropping in unexpectedly in the small plane he piloted with his bird dogs in the back, landing in a nearby field if necessary. He would walk up and down the aisles, asking employees what they thought could be improved. Until he became too recognizable, he also walked the aisles of competitors' stores, asking employees there the same questions. He was never too proud to take an idea from anywhere if he thought it would improve customer service and value.

Children and their parents are customers of public education, but they are rarely asked what could be improved. Teachers are the lifeblood of any school, but they too are often ignored or marginalized when decisions are made. All citizens have a direct stake in how well our schools perform. The process of setting—and meeting—goals is one way to make sure all stakeholders in public education are involved.

SOME CRITICS of public schools urge greater competition among schools and districts, as a way of returning control from bureaucrats and politicians to parents and teachers. I find their argument persuasive, and that's why I strongly favor promoting choice among public schools, much as the President's Charter Schools Initiative encourages. I also support letting public schools determine how they can best be managed, including allowing them to contract out services to private firms.

Charter schools are public schools created and operated under a charter or contract. They may be organized by parents, teachers, or others from the community. The idea is that they should be freed from regulations that stifle effective innovation, so they can focus on meeting goals and getting results. By 1995, a total of nineteen states had enacted charter school laws, and about two hundred schools had been granted charters. The amount of autonomy and flexibility the schools have been granted varies from state to state. Some are authorized to operate independently from the outset, while others have to appeal to their local districts to waive individual rules.

The O'Farrell Community School is a charter school in San Diego, California. It has a racially diverse student body of fourteen hundred sixth, seventh, and eighth graders. Students are clustered in "families," with a head teacher who stays with them all three years. Cutting the red tape and regulations has freed teachers to work together. They have implemented a code of conduct known as "the O'Farrell way" (which includes community service as a graduation requirement), built course requirements around portfolios of students' work, and arranged for a health and counseling center to help students with nonacademic problems.

The Improving America's Schools Act, passed in October 1994 with the President's strong support, provided federal funds for a wide range of grassroots reforms, including launching charter schools. In addition, some states are using Goals 2000 funds to support charter schools like O'Farrell. Federal encouragement and funding are necessary in many places to break through bureaucratic attitudes that block change and frustrate students and parents, driving some of them to leave the public schools.

OUR REFUSAL to recognize diverse forms of intelligence and to uphold standards for all are most unfair to the majority of students who do not go on to obtain a four-year college degree. One in seven students does not even get a high school diploma or obtain a GED by the age of twenty-five.

From 1986 to 1988, I participated in a study sponsored by the William T. Grant Foundation called Youth and America's Future. The title of its report, "The Forgotten Half," referred to "the young people who build our homes, drive our buses, repair our automobiles, fix our televisions, maintain and serve our offices, schools, and hospitals, and keep the production lines of our mills and factories moving. To a great extent, they determine how well the American family, economy, and democracy function. They are also the thousands of young men and women who aspire to work productively but never quite 'make it' to that kind of employment."

Speaking plainly, we don't do much for these young people, and the consequences—for them and for us all—are severe. The 1990 Census showed that young people without college degrees earn significantly less on average than those with degrees. Those who go out into the job market with a high school degree or less are at a much greater disadvantage than they were fifteen years ago. Even if they performed well in school, few employers will even ask to see their transcripts.

In 1994, the President, again with bipartisan support, signed the School-to-Work Opportunities Act, aimed at improving the odds for those forgotten kids. The legislation offers incentives for improving vocational education in high schools and community colleges, and it enables more states, cities, schools, and employers to set up apprenticeship programs that lead to good jobs.

The key to helping students at risk of dropping out to stay in school is to make learning relevant in their lives by linking their schooling with "real world" experience. The Oakland Health and Bioscience Academy in Oakland, California, is one example of how that can be done. With the help and support of an interested community, the academy prepares students for a wide range of health and bioscience careers. Academy teachers work closely with staff from local community colleges and area hospitals to design relevant curricula, and one community college is developing a program that will grant credit to students at the academy and other area schools for the anatomy and physiology courses they take. Formal clinical apprenticeships at area hospitals are also in the works.

School-to-work programs like this one are providing students who are often disregarded in traditional classrooms the chance to learn specific skills. They are also improving academic performance. A recent report noted that the Oakland Academy students scored significantly higher in reading, language, and math than other students from similar backgrounds. School-to-Work programs are a chance for the whole community to get involved in educating our youth, by opening up internship opportunities and workplace visits.

AS A NATION, we are at a crossroads in deciding not only what we expect from education, but what education can expect from us, individually and collectively. The degree of our commitment will determine whether we graduate to a new era of progress and prosperity or fail our children and ourselves. Like education itself, our decision involves something beyond pragmatism. It is also a test of our values.

Do we believe children can learn if they are taught in a way that takes account of their particular talents and holds them to high and clear expectations? Do we believe all children deserve an orderly learning environment? Are we willing to set national goals for educational performance and provide incentives for teachers, schools, and students to meet them? Are parents ready to become partners with schools again, for the benefit of their own—and other—children? And how about the other members of the village, those who are childless or whose children have passed school age? Are they—are all of us—ready to join this partnership?

If we can answer yes to questions like these, we can be successful in educating children to move confidently into the future, carrying the village with them. The root of the verb "to educate," after all, means "to lead forth."

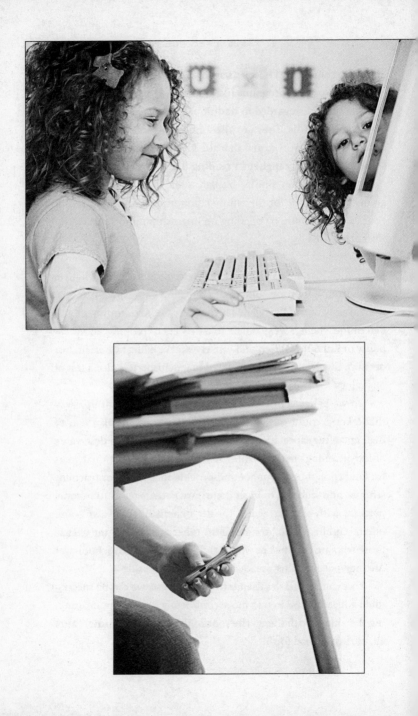

Seeing Is Believing

As television has ravenously consumed our attention, it has weakened the formative institutions of church, family and schools, thoroughly eroding the sense of individual obedience to the unenforceable on which manners and morals and ultimately the law depend. Obviously, we need to rebuild our families, our schools and our churches. But we cannot complete these reforms until something is done about television, for in both its advertising and its programming it has created demands that appeal, not to the best in our natures, but to the worst.

JOHN SILBER

A friend of mine told me about a visit she made to a family with five children. Down in the basement, she could hear the two teenage boys and their buddies singing along to the latest "gangsta"-rap CD. On the first floor, the six-year-old and the eight-year-old were slouched at either end of the couch, motionless in front of the screen, "surfing" the channels. Click. A futuristic battle scene. Click. Graphic images of a recent murder in the city. Click. Two men fighting. Click. What appeared to be a "docudrama" about rape. In an upstairs bedroom, their twelve-year-old sister was watching an "R"-rated video with a friend. It was a clear case of media assault.

When my friend gently raised the issue of the poison that was pouring into those children's minds, her harried hostess could only say, "Look, I'm doing my best." Clearly, this mother, like nearly every parent I talk with, could use some assistance from the village.

Some of that assistance has come from Tipper Gore, whose 1987 book, *Raising PG Kids in an X-Rated Society*, sums up the challenge parents face. Long before I met her, I admired Tipper for having the courage to stand up and say what millions of other fathers and mothers were thinking: that some of the media our kids are exposed to is doing them harm.

Tipper and her watchdog group, the Parents' Music Resource Center, were leading forces behind the effort to get record companies to put warning labels on music recordings with violent, degrading, and sexually explicit messages that are inappropriate for children. Yet Tipper was attacked and ridiculed for her outspokenness, and accused of supporting censorship for advocating voluntary warning labels.

Finally, other public figures have taken up her call for action. C. DeLores Tucker, head of the National Political Congress of Black Women, teamed up with William Bennett against "gangsta" rap. They confronted media giant Time Warner, which has since decided to sell its stake in Interscope Records, the company that produced some of the music with the most offensive lyrics. Although it has taken a long time, public opinion seems to be mobilizing to force the entertainment and news industries as well as the government to address concerns about the effects of the media on our children and our society.

The recent attention that has been brought to bear on the content of movies is also overdue, given their powerful influence on the culture. At least we have a movie ratings system, although there is much we can do to refine it and to improve the content of films in the first place. For example, we can look to countries such as Great Britain and Australia, which have stricter codes for violent content. But in this chapter the focus is primarily on what happens all day on our television screens, both because that is where most people see the movies Hollywood makes and because its presence and influence so pervade our society.

Former Federal Communications Commission chairman Newton N. Minow sounded the alarm long ago. In 1961, Minow decried television as a "vast wasteland" and urged that the networks be held to a high standard of public interest. Since then, Minow has devoted himself to this vitally important issue in a variety of communications and public service positions. Most recently, in *Abandoned in the Wasteland: Children, Television, and the First Amendment*, he and Craig L. LaMay catalogued the overwhelming evidence of television's negative effects that has accumulated over the past three decades and took broadcasters to task for evading the consequences of their decisions by hiding behind the First Amendment.

Minow's portrayal of how deeply televised violence has embedded itself in our national psyche is as shocking as the violence itself:

> So routinely do Americans accept television's version of their lives, that on January 18, 1993, when seventeen-year-old Gary Scott Pennington walked into his high-school English class in Grayson, Kentucky, and fired a .38 caliber bullet into his teacher's forehead, killing her, one of the students who witnessed the murder remembered thinking, "This isn't supposed to happen. This must be MTV." Must be. The average student in Gary's senior class had already seen 18,000 murders on television. The average student in the class had spent between 15,000 and 20,000 hours watching television, compared with 11,000 in school; every year the average American child watches more than a thousand stylized and explicit rapes, murders, armed robberies, and assaults on television.

Since the 1950s, a steady stream of articles, books, and studies have documented the harm television does to children. The American Psychological Association's Commission on Violence and Youth points to three major reports, each a decade apart—by a surgeon general's commission in 1972, by the National Institute of Mental Health in 1982, and by the American Psychological Association's Committee on Media in Society in 1992—which reviewed hundreds of studies to arrive at the same unshakable conclusion: that "viewing violence increases violence" and "prolonged viewing of media violence can lead to emotional desensitization toward violence."

Ninety-eight percent of American homes have at least one television set, which is watched each week for an average of twenty-eight hours by children between the ages of two and eleven, and twenty-three hours by teenagers. Children who grow up in lower-income families, with fewer organized activities or places to play, watch even more TV than their more affluent peers.

Children themselves report that certain television shows encourage them to engage in sexual activity before they are ready, to behave aggressively, and to be disrespectful to their parents. Eighty percent of Americans responding to a 1993 Times-Mirror poll said that they believe TV is harmful to society and especially to children. And we know that saturating young minds with increasingly graphic and sensational depictions of violence prevents them from developing the emotional and psychological tools they need to deal with the threat and the reality of violence. Shootings, beatings, even killings, begin to seem normal and, in an odd way, painless. Children become numbed—"desensitized"—to violence.

Whether, and under what circumstances, the violence people see on television and at the movies actually incites violent acts is a question researchers have debated for years, ever since the surgeon general's 1972 report. As with smoking and lung cancer, however, we know that there *is* a connection. Yet just as somebody—most often somebody well paid by the tobacco companies—is sure to stand up each time a new finding confirms the linkage between smoking and lung cancer and shout, "That's not definitive," every time a new report draws a connection between the violence on our television screens and the violence on our streets, some in the entertainment industry try to refute, or at least to dilute, the claim.

You don't have to conduct research worthy of a Nobel Prize to grasp that what most children are seeing on television can't be good for them. Just turn on your television, any time of the day, any day of the week, and see what is competing for their attention. I'll bet that if a stranger came into your home and began telling your kids stories about the same kinds of characters and events, using the same kinds of words and pictures, you'd throw him out. You wouldn't wait for a surgeon general's report to validate what your instincts as a parent told you was a hazard to your children's mental and emotional health.

Defenders of television argue that children are subjected to images of violence in all sorts of media—including fairy tales and other literary classics—and complain that it is not fair to hold television to a higher standard. But as Minow points out:

> The tradition of oral and written storytelling embodied in both fairy tales and modern children's literature developed in the service of children's moral education, and its lessons helped to define the boundaries between childhood and adulthood. In traditional settings, violence was but *one* possible outcome of conflict, not the only one or even the primary one. Moreover, stories that included violence surrounded it with meanings created by adults for instructing children, not by adults for entertaining adults.

Television executives are also quick to say that they are a major provider of information as well as entertainment. They stress that it is the duty of journalists to report what goes on in the world. It's true that children now get most of their information about events at home and around the world directly from the media instead of filtered through their parents, teachers, or other adults. And it's also true that we need to be made aware of crime and violence so that we can take actions to protect ourselves, such as supporting measures to impose sensible gun control. But why, when we turn on the evening news these days, do we find ourselves awash in depictions of sensationalized violence that are increasingly difficult to distinguish from the gore that permeates the latest "action" series?

In 1992, the Center for Media and Public Affairs counted the acts of violence on ten television channels in the course of a single eighteen-hour broadcast day. When the study was repeated just two years later, the center found that the incidence of television violence had increased by 41 percent, with the greatest rise occurring in news shows. Another recent study found that local news coverage of murders tripled last year, even though there was no corresponding rise in the recorded murder rate. The explanation is obvious. News executives are acting more single-mindedly from the same motive that drives their colleagues in the entertainment business: violence sells. Ellen Hume, a senior fellow at the Annenberg Washington Program in Communication Studies, points out in her recent report, "Tabloids, Talk Radio, and the Future of News," "News about crime and violence is cheap and easy to cover."

The exhaustive coverage of violence and bad news in general contributes to young people's increasing sense of alienation and to the dysfunctional, antisocial behavior that accompanies it. Many kids become depressed or have nightmares because of the barrage of bloodshed they see on TV. It numbs them to the pain and destructiveness of actual violence, encouraging a stance of ironic detachment. At worst, it contributes to what social scientist George Gerbner has identified as "the mean world syndrome," where children internalize the negative attributes of the world as they see it portrayed in the media.

Children also learn from television that we prize celebrity above all else, regardless of how it is achieved. At the same time, television may leave them with the impression that people hardly ever do anything good or right and that few, if any, adults are worthy of respect. We are saturated with stories about priests who molest children, gangs of young thugs who vandalize and victimize indiscriminately, and families that are nightmares of abuse and neglect. The lurid accounts tend to eclipse positive stories about priests and other clergy who help people come to terms with loss and find meaning in their lives, teenagers who feed the homeless, clean up our parks, and help the elderly, and families who pull together in times of stress.

Small wonder, then, that many children grow up skeptical that organized religion can offer guidance and sustenance, that they or their peers can be a force for good, that families can be a lasting source of strength and stability. The merciless, minute scrutiny of crimes and victims emphasizes and exaggerates the powerlessness of individuals, especially in the minds of children, whose own lack of power in the world is all too plain to them. More insidiously, it undermines their faith in institutions, their belief that individuals can band together for good as well as for evil.

Leonard Eron, a psychology professor at the University of Michigan and a leading expert on the effects of television, warns: "In the same way television teaches violence, it now teaches youngsters that . . . dysfunctional families are par for the course." Professor Froma Walsh of the University of Chicago echoes him. Consistently seeing the sensational way families are portrayed on most talk shows and many prime-time programs encourages people to "view their own families through a glass darkly and look for pathologies," even when families are "just trying to cope as well as they can." Such research suggests that whatever is provided as a steady diet on television becomes reality in the minds of frequent viewers. That's not good news for any family, given what's currently on the menu.

And the menu is expanding. Video games have transformed millions of television sets into scenes of blood and violence that children not only watch but participate in. Agile fingers race across the controls of best-sellers like Mortal Kombat and Killer Instinct, directing characters on the screen to execute the most desired outcome—a brutal murder. There are also moves like the Neck Breaker, the Skeleton Grab, the Skull Rip, and the Death Scream. In Mortal Kombat, a computer-generated voice urges "Finish him!" as blood continues to spray.

Recently, a fourteen-year-old boy from a Maryland suburb where actual violence rarely intrudes described his fascination with electronic violence to *Washington Post Magazine* staff writer David Finkel. "I like violence," he said. "I like seeing violence. I just really like watching violence." This boy's parents are involved in their son's life—they go to the movies with him and try to interest him in reading—but they also believe he is old enough to watch what he wants to see, listen to what he wants to hear, and play the games that amuse him. This boy assures Finkel that his life would be very different without this connection to violence. "I'd be scared to be with anyone else," he explains. "I wouldn't be able to relate to anybody else because *they've* all seen it."

It is too early to evaluate the effects of video games fully. But already some psychologists have pointed out that children's direct control of the violence in video games could be more harmful than what they only observe passively. Dr. Carole Lieberman, a UCLA psychiatrist and former chair of the National Coalition on Television Violence, refers to video games as a "new drug." "I think it's worse than television violence because children are pushing the buttons themselves," Dr. Lieberman says. "They are getting rewarded for destroying people in a game."

We already know that television doesn't just affect what we think; it also affects *how* we think. The medium, as Marshall McLuhan pointed out, is itself the message. The episodic, reactive, almost frantic pace of what is broadcast makes children feel and act frantic and shortens their attention spans and their patience for activities that take time and problems that don't yield immediate solutions.

Children—and teenagers—need stimulation, but there is a limit to how much they need, and what kind. Consider for a moment what it means to put the remote control in the hands of a pre-schooler. She does not have to work hard to be entertained, to use her imagination as she would if she were listening to a story or playing make-believe. She does not have the ability to screen out what she sees and hears, let alone to evaluate it. And least of all, faced with the dancing images and bright colors and exciting sound effects, is she equipped to walk away.

The pull of television is irresistible to children, riveting their attention the way traffic accidents draw rubberneckers. The homes in America where television sets blare night and day are like high-ways clogged with accidents. Only, in this case, the children gawk-ing mindlessly, overstimulated and underchallenged, are the victims.

MY PARENTS did not worry so much about the content of the televi-sion shows my brothers and I watched as they did about the amount of time we would spend at it, if they let us. They wanted us reading, doing chores, or playing outside, so they regulated our viewing hours strictly. Bill and I restricted both the amount and the kind of televi-sion Chelsea watched as a child, and even now we check up from time to time on her TV and movie watching. Parents are beginning to come up with other ways of defending themselves and their children from the excessive influence of television. They may eventually get some help from technology, such as the V-chip included in proposed telecommunications legislation. The V-chip is a computer chip with which parents could block television programs designated as containing material unsuitable for children. Making the technology available is only half the battle; putting it to good use will require a strong, clear rating system like the one we now have for movies.

In the meantime, parents are on their own in making sure children are not watching inappropriate shows or too much television, period. They can continue to trade their own "ratings" informally. They can encourage the newspapers and magazines that are beginning to gear reviews of movies and music toward parents to cover television in this way as well. They can also teach their children *how* to watch television, the same way they teach them to cross the street: carefully.

A publication entitled "Taking Charge of Your TV: A Guide to Critical Viewing for Parents and Children" is available from the Family and Community Critical Viewing Project, an initiative sponsored by the National PTA and the cable industry to teach television viewing skills to parents, teachers, and children. It suggests ways parents can talk to kids about what they are watching, which not only makes television a less passive pastime but transforms it into a learning tool. We can ask children why characters act as they do and help them to distinguish between responsible and irresponsible acts. We can get them to talk about how the families on television are different from theirs and from other families they know. We can relate television to real-life situations. When Roseanne and Dan fret over bills because Dan's business is going under, for example, we can explain to our children that sometimes parents need to figure out ways to make sure they can meet all their responsibilities.

Used wisely, television can help children to distinguish between fantasy and reality—precisely because the fantasy it projects feels so real to them. Identify aspects peculiar to "TV land" that may seem obvious to an adult but aren't necessarily clear to a child. For instance, when watching a thirty-minute drama or sitcom, point out that it's not realistic to solve a problem in the span of a half hour. Explain that this is how writers and directors adapt to scheduling needs and discuss how the situation might have played out in real life.

There is another option parents might consider: Just turn the televisions, video games, and VCRs off—for an evening, a week, a regular day each week. When I made this suggestion in an interview with *Woman's Day*, readers responded enthusiastically. Some parents, fed up with not only depictions of violence but the excessive influence of television in general, wrote to say they had already tried out the idea.

Imagine what might happen if we all turned off our televisions for an entire week. The quiet—and the other activities we could take up—might be habit-forming.

Here and there, parents are banding together and discovering their collective strength. The South Florida Preschool PTA monitors children's programming on the Miami television stations, with members volunteering to watch programming for one- or two-week blocks to determine whether the stations are complying with the law.

The Children's Television Act of 1990 limits the amount of time the networks can devote to commercials during children's programming. It also directs the FCC more broadly to review, as part of the licensing procedures, whether stations air shows that "serve the educational and informational needs of children." In three years, the Florida group found, the networks failed to meet the law's requirements. In their 1995 report, they noted that Miami commercial television stations were devoting only 1 percent of total programming time to educational programs for children.

The Miami group is among the many parent and consumer groups urging the FCC to enforce its regulations and to strengthen them, by requiring the networks to air more educational programming. In 1951, twenty-seven hours of quality children's programming aired each week. The President and FCC Chairman Reed Hundt would like to see the FCC require each network to broadcast at least three hours a week. As of this writing, the FCC has not yet taken action on this proposal. In response to public petitions, however, Westinghouse, which has recently purchased CBS, has voluntarily made such a commitment. The FCC's decision will not affect cable stations, since they are considered exempt from government regulations because they do not use the public airwaves.

The advent of cable television has dramatically expanded offerings available to children, for better and worse. Channels like Disney, Discovery, Nickelodeon, and A&E are staples of Clinton family viewing. But only 65 percent of American households now have access to cable, and the demographics of the remaining 35 percent includes a disproportionate share of the nation's children. As with many other social changes of the past fifty years, the children hardest hit by the negative impact of the media, television in particular, are those in low-income families.

That's why public television, which has consistently provided educational programming for children, deserves our tax dollars and charitable contributions. Shows like *Sesame Street* entertain while they teach math and reading. *Where in the World Is Carmen Sandiego?* makes learning geography fun and exciting. With the help of music videos and special effects, *Bill Nye, the Science Guy* transports science out of the classroom and into the world. Many "hit" educational shows are creations of the Children's Television Workshop, which was founded in 1968 to explore television's potential as an educational medium.

In May 1995, John Wright and Aletha Huston, professors of

human development at the University of Kansas, released the results of a four-year study on how television influences the academic skills, school readiness, and school adjustment of low-income children. They found that preschoolers who watched as little as twenty-five minutes per day of educational children's programs like *Sesame Street* did significantly better on standardized verbal and math tests when they started school and consistently spent more time on reading and other educational activities than did children who watched primarily noneducational cartoons and adult programming.

Educators, community leaders, church groups, and others can join in the effort to demand support for public television and better commercial programming. They can also organize boycotts of gratuitously violent, sexually explicit, or otherwise offensive programming. One household won't have much of an impact, but a village or two can make or break a Nielsen rating percentage point, and ratings are TV's most critical barometer for making programming decisions.

Teachers can play a part, both directly and indirectly. First and most important, they can do their best to make reading fun. They can also assist parents in helping to educate children about how television manipulates them and undermines values like compassion and kindness that they are learning at home, in their place of worship, and at school.

Journalists and news executives have responsibilities too. When violence is newsworthy they should report it, but they should balance it with stories that provide children and adults with positive images of themselves and those around them, taking care not to exacerbate negative stereotypes. To report the truth in a thoughtful manner, mindful of the potency of the written word and the televised image, is to be not only a good journalist but a responsible citizen.

Acknowledging that commercial television is driven by the

need to make a profit does not let executives and programmers off the hook. As Newton Minow said in a 1995 keynote address to a conference of Children Now, a leading nonpartisan, nonprofit organization for children: "In an ideal world, the people who work in television would have to take an oath like the Hippocratic oath: 'Do no harm.'" How could they uphold it? They could begin by asking themselves if they would allow their own children, grandchildren, nieces, nephews, and neighbors to watch the shows for which they are responsible. They could form their own advisory panels—preferably of parents—who could be counted on to put children's interests ahead of financial ones.

Journalists and broadcasters tell me they have been talking among themselves about these issues and looking for ways to fulfill both their professional and public responsibilities. At their annual Family Conference, held this year in Nashville, Al and Tipper Gore brought together broadcasters, children's advocates, advertisers, researchers, and parents to discuss the media's impact on children and families. Oprah Winfrey has decided to steer her show in a more positive direction. One television station decided not to carry the more lurid talk shows, and another is considering dropping them. A few local TV stations have decided to abandon the tabloid approach and get back into the news business.

There may be monetary as well as moral rewards for such choices. When he was a news director at WCCO-TV in Minneapolis, John Lansing realized that the more his station's local news coverage resembled an entertainment program, the weaker its connections to its community were becoming. He decided to convene town meetings to allow the station to reacquaint itself with the expectations of its viewers. As a result, the news operation dropped its tabloid-style coverage, and WCCO became a pioneer in "family-sensitive viewing," reducing or eliminating descriptions and images of violence during designated early evening hours.

Even so, WCCO has managed to maintain its first-place market share.

Numerous journalism associations and programs encourage balanced and open-minded reportage. One such organization is the Casey Journalism Center at the University of Maryland, which awards fellowships to reporters, editors, producers, and news directors. The recipients get the chance to participate in conferences and meet with experts on these issues. The intent is to encourage thoughtful, in-depth, well-documented reporting.

Television could take a cue from the several newspapers that have developed children's beats and long-term reporting projects focusing on family issues. The Cleveland *Plain Dealer*, for instance, has added a new "family section" that runs every Saturday. So far, it has run stories on children's television viewing habits (along with tips on how to make TV watching a more constructive activity), on ways grandparents and grandchildren can spend time together, and on building stronger families (accompanied by personal stories about people in the region). The section also includes a regular family finance column, with information on everything from the cost of buying a family pet to how to take a family vacation without breaking the bank.

Television, movies, video games, and music are here to stay and will continue to be influential in shaping opinions and behaviors in the years to come. As parents, we must be willing to reassert our authority over what enters our households. As creators and consumers of the media, and as citizens of the village, we must be willing to join with one another to press for improvements in what our children see and hear. A single act has little impact, but millions of decisions—to turn off television sets or to reject certain movies or CDs or video games—give us the voltage to send a message to advertisers and programmers that will reach them loud and clear.

Every Business Is
a Family Business

The Golden Rule does not mean that gold shall rule.

BARBARA REYNOLDS

My father distrusted both big business and big government. When I was growing up, he never tired of quoting President Eisenhower's warning against the military-industrial complex and the dangers of concentrated, unaccountable power in anyone's hands. I thought of him during a trip I made to South America in October 1995, when I happened to hear a reference to the words of an earlier President, Theodore Roosevelt. I was to give a speech to students and faculty at the University of Chile in Santiago. When the rector of the university introduced me, he referred to remarks that Roosevelt had made in the same hall eighty-two years before. The former President, he said, had warned against the excesses of unchecked corporate power.

Intrigued, I tracked down a copy of Roosevelt's speech and was struck by how relevant his message remains today:

> By allowing, with no control, this concentration of enor-
> mous enterprises in the hands of a few . . . many evils
> have arisen. . . . We must recognize that the great corpo-
> rations have established themselves, and that we must
> control and regulate them, so that big business does not
> obtain advantages at the expense of the smaller. More-
> over, we must insist on the principles of cooperation and
> the mutual sharing by employer and employee in the
> gains produced, so that the future prosperity of the great
> corporations is divided in the most equitable way
> among all those who participate in creating it.

Roosevelt's words reflected the popular view that would domi-
nate much of this century. As the private sector grew, people
assumed that the excesses of unbridled competition had to be
restrained by government. As a result, consumers have been protected by antitrust laws, pure food and drug laws, labeling, and
other consumer protection measures; investors have been protected
by securities legislation; workers have been protected by laws gov-
erning child labor, wages and hours, pensions, workers' compensation, and occupational safety and health; and the community at
large has been protected by clean air and water standards, chemical
right-to-know laws, and other environmental safeguards.

Doubtless, mistakes were made in drafting some of these laws
and in writing and applying the regulations that put them into
effect. But on balance, it is hard to quarrel with the results. Over
the course of the century, our environment has become cleaner, we
have become healthier, our workers safer, our financial markets
stronger. Now our economy, still the world's most powerful and
productive, is on a roll again, with small-business formation,
exports, and the stock market all at record levels, more than seven
and a half million new jobs created in less than three years, and

the combined rates of unemployment and inflation at a twenty-seven-year low.

In an era in which it has become fashionable to blame many of our nation's ills on government, however, our public debate seldom turns to the impact of economic forces on American families and children. Those who do raise the question are likely to be accused of insufficient devotion to the free market system. Yet if we care about family values, we have to be concerned about what happens to those values in the marketplace.

Like my father, I support capitalism and the free market system. But I also know that every human endeavor is vulnerable to error, incompetence, corruption, and the abuse of power. To paraphrase Winston Churchill's famous aphorism about democracy, capitalism is the worst possible form of an economy—except for all the alternatives.

There is built-in tension in a free market system like ours, because the same forces that make an economy strong—the drive to satisfy consumers' demands by maximizing productivity and profitability—can adversely affect the workers and families who are, after all, those very consumers. While we want to encourage competition and innovation—hallmarks of American capitalism— we need to be aware of the individual and social costs of business decisions. In every era, society must strike the right balance between the freedom businesses need to compete for a market share and to make profits and the preservation of family and community values. If either is undermined, the consequences will end up costing us all more in the long term, materially and otherwise, than we can possibly gain in the short term.

In this book I have talked about the responsibilities of individuals and institutions for the future of our children and the village they will inherit. No segment of society has a more significant influence on the nature of that legacy than business. We live in an era of what political scientist Edward Luttwak calls "turbo-charged" capitalism, which is characterized by intense competition; breathtaking technological changes; global financial, information, and entertainment markets; constant corporate restructuring; and relatively less public control and influence over the private economy.

This combination of changed circumstances poses new problems for families and communities, and for the children who grow up in them. Business affects us powerfully as consumers, as workers, as investors, and, more broadly, as citizens of the society it helps to create and as inhabitants of the environment it has a strong hand in shaping. Our circumstances therefore require new and thoughtful responses from every segment of society, particularly from business.

OUR ECONOMY grows as it gives consumers more and better products to choose from, at competitive prices. On the whole, this system has been a boon to us, not only allowing us to live comfortably but providing more Americans with jobs. But one of the conditions of the consumer culture is that it relies upon human insecurities to create aspirations that can be satisfied only by the purchase of some product or service. If all of us said today, "Okay, I have enough stuff. From now on I will buy only the bare necessities," that would be a disaster for our economy. But spurred on by cultural messages that encourage us to feel dissatisfied with what we have and that equate success with consumption—messages fueled by the advertisements that constantly bombard us— we face the far more likely danger of allowing greed to overshadow moderation, restraint, and the stability that comes from saving and investing for the future rather than satisfying short-term desires.

The threat is greatest to our children, who will inherit that future and the values that shape it. "As a society," writes David Walsh in *Selling Out America's Children*, "we Americans of the late twentieth century are sacrificing our children at the altar of financial gain," and, in Walsh's phrase, to the lure of "adver-teasing." Those of us who believe in the free market system should worry about what we are in danger of becoming: a throwaway society sustained on a diet of unrealizable fantasies, a society in which people—especially children—define self-worth in terms of what they have today and can buy tomorrow.

Walsh documents the careful calculation—and hundreds of millions of dollars—that go into advertising campaigns directed at children, whose desire for instant gratification and lack of sophistication make them easy targets. Children parked in front of the television for hours on end are particularly susceptible, and advertisers know it. After the Federal Communications Commission repealed regulations that limited the amount of time that could be devoted to commercials during children's television shows in 1984, the number of commercials again increased, and program-length commercials—shows that revolve around toy-based characters—exploded.

The Children's Television Act passed by Congress in 1990 again set limits on commercial time during children's programming, but compliance has not always been strictly enforced, although the FCC is trying. "Kids today," observes FCC chairman Reed Hundt, "can identify more cereals than Presidents." Nor is the drumbeat to buy, buy, buy confined to commercials; advertising permeates children's lives. Even their sports heroes have become walking (and slam-dunking) advertisements for everything from Nikes to Pepsis to Big Macs.

Mass consumerism and "adver-teasing" have parents competing with multinational corporations not only for their children's values and beliefs but for their health. According to one study, Joe Camel, the cartoon mascot of Camel cigarettes, is now as recognizable to six-year-olds as Mickey Mouse. Cigarette brand names have become affixed to virtually every professional sport, from soccer to skiing to sailing. If you doubt that tobacco companies target children as prospective consumers, ask yourself what gets three thousand American children to start smoking on any given day, or talk to Dave Goerlitz, an actor who appeared in commercials for Winston cigarettes for seven years, until he became so disgusted by the company's blatant attempts to lure children that he left the business and joined an antismoking crusade. Or take a look at the previously secret documents from Philip Morris, which produces two out of every three cigarettes American children smoke, that U.S. Representative Henry Waxman of California read into the *Congressional Record* in July 1995. Among the revelations was that the company, as Waxman put it, "studies third-graders to determine if hyperactive children are a potential market for cigarettes."

In cases where children are directly and seriously endangered by products, the government can and should step in, as the President has done in his proposal to have the Food and Drug Administration restrict children's access to cigarettes and smokeless tobacco, curtail cigarette advertising that appeals to them, and require tobacco companies to fund an educational campaign designed to counter the message that smoking is "cool." (Predictably, the tobacco companies are spending millions of dollars to fight the proposal through legal action in the courts and through an advertising campaign against "government bureaucrats.")

But government is a partner to, not a substitute for, adult leadership and good citizenship. Parents must become more willing to stand up to consumer pressures from advertisers and from their own children. They can resist the impulse to "prove" their love by showering children with things they do not need and give them precious time and attention instead. They can make a moral statement to their children and to manufacturers by refusing to buy products that promote gratuitous violence, sexual degradation, or plain bad taste. In the summer of 1995, clothing designer Calvin

Copyright 1995 by Herblock in *The Washington Post*.

Klein withdrew an advertising campaign targeted at teenagers that featured young models in sexually suggestive poses after consumers objected.

If parents do not take a stand, how can we expect children to resist the consumer culture's message that style is more important than substance? We can measure its potential for destruction in the young lives already lost to murder over a ski jacket or a set of fancy new hubcaps. Parents need help from the village to counteract and to curtail the force of this message. The broadcasters and publishers who provide time and space to advertisers must exercise greater restraint and better judgment. Business must work with government and families to find ways of balancing the interests of industry with the interests of children.

• • •

THE CONSUMER culture's assault on values adds to the pressures families are under in today's fast-changing economy. Most of us remember a time when business was an anchor in our communities. After World War II, when America had about 40 percent of the world's wealth and only 6 percent of its population, our nation enjoyed an economic boom in which businesses were expected to produce goods and services of high quality, not only for the purpose of bringing in profits for stockholders but also to create the jobs and higher incomes that would build the middle class. After all, if no one had jobs or incomes, who would buy the goods and services that businesses were producing?

In recent years, however, long-established expectations about doing business have given way under the pressures of the modern economy. Too many companies, especially large ones, are driven more and more narrowly by the need to ensure that investors get good quarterly returns and to justify executives' high salaries. Too often, this means that they view most employees as costs, not investments, and that they expend less and less concern on job training, employee profit sharing, family-friendly policies, shared decision making, or even fair pay raises that share with workers— not to mention their families and communities—gains from productivity and profits. Even workers' jobs may be sacrificed as executives seek short-term profits by "downsizing" or "outsourcing" (farming out to independent contractors work previously done in-house) or moving production to countries where wages are lower and environmental and other regulations less stringent. Instead of "We're all in this together," the message from the top is frequently "You're on your own."

Despite record profits for many companies, the gap in income between top executives and the average worker has widened dramatically. In 1974, the CEO of a large corporation typically made thirty-five times what an average factory worker earned. In 1993, CEOs made almost 150 times the average factory worker's wage—if he or she was lucky enough to have a job still. At the same time, as Stephen Roach, chief economist and director of global economic analysis for Morgan Stanley, notes in a recent report, "Between 1991 and 1995, nearly 2.5 million workers have fallen victim to corporate restructuring—a carnage without precedent for a U.S. economy in the midst of ongoing recovery." American workers, he observes, have "been left with a profound sense of insecurity regarding job and earnings prospects."

Changes in the economy, such as technological innovations and the globalization of commerce, have combined over the past two decades to produce what economists Robert H. Frank and Philip J. Cook call a "winner-take-all society." The middle class, the backbone of our nation, is splitting, with more and more falling into the "anxious class" of honest, hardworking Americans who go in debt every time a child falls ill or the family car breaks down. Midlevel managers and white-collar workers are increasingly vulnerable to becoming what Secretary of Labor Robert Reich calls "frayed-collar workers in gold-plated times." Hardly the stuff of which the American Dream is made.

This growing inequality of incomes has serious implications for our children. America's turbo-charged economy has produced cheaper and better goods and services and greater efficiency and competition, but it also has created serious social dislocations that undermine family and community values. As Alan Ehrenhalt, author of *The Lost City,* in which he examines the decline in community life since the 1950s, observes:

> The unfettered free market has been the most radically
> disruptive force in American life in the last generation,

> busting up neighborhoods and communities and erod-
> ing traditional standards of social life and personal con-
> duct. . . .
>
> It is the tyranny of the market that has destroyed the
> loyalty of corporations to their communities; customers
> to their neighborhood merchants; athletes to their local
> teams; teams to their cities. . . . Politicians have every
> right to endorse such changes. But to endorse them and
> then in the next breath tout the traditional values of
> neighborhood and family is to defy common sense.

The decision by a profitable company to lay off workers in the name of corporate efficiency affects not only those workers but their children, families, and communities. So does its decision to impose a part-time workweek to avoid paying employee benefits. And who suffers most when a company decides to make do with fewer employees, forcing parents to work extra shifts at night or on weekends—times when child care is virtually nonexistent?

To be fair, while corporate restructuring is eliminating many jobs, the economy is also creating millions of new jobs, with small businesses starting at a record pace. In short, it is a great economy for successful entrepreneurs and for well-educated employees in strong companies that are worker- and family-friendly. Still, until recently, downsizing reduced the number of jobs that our rate of growth normally would have created, and fewer of the new jobs carry health care and pension benefits.

For those who live in urban areas with few businesses of any kind, the impact of changes in the private sector is most direct and devastating, with high rates of unemployment and crime, drug abuse, welfare dependency, and school failure. By now we know, however, that problems elsewhere eventually affect us all. Government has a big responsibility to help remedy them. But its resources are limited, partly because, in an effort to support growth, it takes less of people's incomes in taxes than does almost any other advanced economy.

Other developed countries, including some of our fiercest industrial competitors, are more committed to social stability than we have been, and they tailor their economic policies to maintain it. Although Japan's economy, for example, has grown sluggishly in the last four years and is currently experiencing its longest postwar slump, government and corporations there continue to support a system in which many workers enjoy much greater job security. To them, the trade-off is worth it.

In Germany, too, there is a general consensus that government and business should play a role in evening out inequities in the free market system and in increasing the ability of all citizens to succeed. Compared to Americans, Germans pay for higher base wages, a health care system that covers everyone but costs less than ours, and perhaps the world's finest system of providing young workers who do not go on to college with the skills they need to compete in the job market. As a result of such investments, German workers command higher wages than their American counterparts, and the distribution of income is not so skewed as ours is.

We have chosen a different path, leaving more of our resources in the hands of the private sector. We get much greater job growth and more new business starts than our competitors, but we also endure more of the harsh consequences of a more open economy. As a society, we have a choice to make. We can permit the market-place largely to determine the values and well-being of the village, or we can continue, as we have in the past, to expect business to play a social as well as an economic role. That means we have to look realistically at what government must require business to do, principally in the areas of health, safety, competition, fair practices, and the environment; what government should attempt to per-suade business to do through partnerships and other incentives; what consumers and workers have to do for themselves; and what business leaders should do, on their own, for their customers, employees, investors, and the larger community of which they are a part. The last two categories may be the most important. We desperately need, for the sake of our children, a national and global economy in which people act not only as consumers but as citizens, in which workers reassert responsibility for themselves and the success of their companies, and in which our businesses can do well *and* do good.

IN THE PAST, our government has taken steps on its own to improve the lives of working Americans and their families, by legislating and funding programs for families and children, some of which, like the Earned Income Tax Credit, I discuss in other chapters. Government has also mandated business to take certain actions, as with the Family and Medical Leave Act.

There are additional actions we can take, through our government, to preserve our country's promise of opportunity for all. We can raise the minimum wage, which is nearing a forty-year low; two out of five minimum-wage earners are the sole breadwinners in their households, and many recent studies show that a modest increase does not cost jobs. We can give middle-class families a tax deduction for the costs of their own or their children's post–high school education. Congress can pass a "GI Bill" that would give unemployed or underemployed workers vouchers they could use to cover the costs of up to two years of training at their local community colleges. We can increase access to affordable health care and reform insurance laws so that workers cannot be denied insurance when someone in their family has been sick or lose it when they change jobs. We can make it simpler and less costly for small businesses to provide retirement savings plans for their employees, by reducing the administrative burdens and costs of establishing and maintaining those plans.

We can also give business incentives to be better citizens, supporting competitive markets in the process. One example is the urban and rural empowerment zones created under my husband's administration to encourage private investment in distressed areas. The government can also improve its credibility by becoming more efficient and less burdensome on business, as illustrated by the elimination of sixteen thousand pages of unneeded federal regulations that Vice President Gore's Reinventing Government team has undertaken, and by the administration's partnerships with business.

Automobile manufacturers have entered into a partnership with the government to build a "clean car" that uses much less fuel. The Environmental Protection Agency's Project XL has elicited the agreement of companies in many different industries to meet higher environmental standards, in return for government's willingness to scrap the rules telling them how to meet those standards. A number of our most powerful telecommunications and computer companies have joined forces with the government in a project to connect every school in America to the Internet and to see that every classroom has adequate computers, good software, and well-trained teachers. Defense contractors have entered into partnerships to develop commercial products, in an effort to save jobs jeopardized by smaller post–cold war defense budgets.

Community-minded companies are already doing a number of things that citizens should applaud and government should encourage, when possible, with legislative changes to make them more attractive. Some companies tie workers' wages to business performance and to executives' compensation and follow a no-lay-off policy, which means that when business is down, both workers and managers take proportionate reductions in pay. Others offer employees stock options, health and pension benefits, ongoing education and training opportunities, and tuition bonuses or reimbursements for their children. Still others provide child care or at least permit parents to take time from work to become involved with their children's schools.

In 1989, television producer Norman Lear and former Johnson & Johnson CEO James Burke, along with a number of other prominent business leaders, professionals, and educators, launched a national nonprofit organization called the Business Enterprise Trust. The idea was to create a new spirit of enterprise among present and future business leaders that "combines sound management with social conscience." Each year, the trust confers awards on business people and firms whose practices reflect courage, integrity, and social vision. Winners over the years have included individuals and companies that could be models for businesses of all sizes in every American community:

- Finast, a supermarket chain that built and renovated stores in inner-city Cleveland, is proof that business can operate profitably in depressed neighborhoods. The company not only improved its efficiency and profitability, but also spurred economic development in an area shunned by other businesses.

- Fel-Pro, an automotive product manufacturer based in Skokie, Illinois, purchased two hundred acres of land for employees' recreational use and created a summer day camp at the site, which serves hundreds of employees' children each year. Fel-Pro has initiated many other family-friendly policies, including a day care center near the plant, emergency home care for employees' sick dependents, tuition reimbursement for employees, and college scholarships, admissions counseling, and subsidized tutoring for their children.

- Howard Schultz, the CEO of Starbucks Coffee Company, has worked to give his employees a stake in the company's success. All Starbucks workers who work twenty hours a week or more receive health coverage and stock options. The company maintains that the rise in its insurance premiums was offset by a lower turnover rate and a corresponding decrease in training expenses for new workers.

- Rachel Hubka, who founded Rachel's Bus Company in inner-city Chicago in 1989, hired many people who had previously been considered unemployable. She instilled in them a strong sense of pride and entrepreneurial spirit, producing capable school bus drivers and a successful company.

Examples of enlightened business practices are far too numerous for me to mention more than a handful, but there are not yet enough.

Socially minded corporate philosophies are the avenue to future prosperity and social stability. Harvard Business School professors Rosabeth Moss Kanter and Michael Porter argue that the economic future belongs to businesses that invest in their workers and communities. In her book *World Class*, Kanter examines the relationship between globalization and the strengths of local communities. Porter believes that "Companies will understand the need to rebuild the corporation and create a sense of community again. The ones that do that will be the winners in the next stage of the competition." I certainly hope so. It is going to take the contributions of our businesses to give America's children the future they deserve, both to make their living and to build a lasting village.

Children Are Citizens Too

We can succeed only by concert. It is not, "Can any of us
imagine better?" but, "Can we all do better?"

ABRAHAM LINCOLN

In the spring of 1995, Chelsea and I traveled together through
South Asia. As the mother of a teenager, I felt very lucky indeed
that my fifteen-year-old was willing to spend ten days with me. We
toured Mother Teresa's orphanage in New Delhi and talked with
young women who were studying business in Lahore, Pakistan. We
saw a rural bank founded and run by poor women in Ahmadabad,
India, and learned about the place where Mahatma Gandhi lived
while starting the movement for Indian independence. We visited
grassroots efforts in Jessore, Bangladesh, and in Colombo, Sri
Lanka, that are bringing basic health care to pregnant women and
their babies and expanding economic and political opportunities
for women and the poor. Everywhere we went, we were impressed
by the progress people were making, despite overwhelming poverty
and internal political strife. In each country, we met democratically

elected leaders who had endured terrible hardships—imprisonment, torture, exile, the assassinations of husbands, fathers, sons, mothers, daughters—under previous regimes.

We had an unforgettable time and were presented with frequent opportunities to reflect on what it means to be an American. Many of the people we met told us how much they admired our country. Some quoted leaders like Thomas Jefferson, Abraham Lincoln, and Franklin Delano Roosevelt; others expressed appreciation for the educations they had received in our universities, their partnerships with our corporations, and the many forms of assistance provided by our government, churches, and private foundations.

The comment I remember most, however, came from a young Peace Corps volunteer I met in Kathmandu, Nepal. To catch the bus that brought her to meet with me, she had walked ten hours from the remote village where she lived in a house without running water or electricity. She described the work she did at a school where nearly all the students were boys, since most girls were still denied schooling and were often married by the age of twelve or thirteen.

The volunteer loved her experience in Nepal but missed her family and all the blessings of daily life that she had taken for granted in America. She longed for safe drinking water that poured from faucets; meats and vegetables that she could eat without worrying they would make her sick; enough food to eat all year round; free public schools that taught both boys and girls; warm baths and electricity available around the clock; paved roads, and cars to drive on them.

Chelsea listened attentively, and I wished every American teenager could have been there with us. Americans enjoy so many blessings because generations before us paid the price to establish and maintain a stable, democratic government that protects our individual rights and provides public services that benefit us all.

Most of our sons and daughters are lucky enough never to have known a time when millions of Americans didn't have electricity or good roads. Except for the occasional contamination scare, they have no reason to fear the water they drink or the food they eat. They were not alive to witness the origins of many improvements government brought to American life—improvements neither individuals nor the private sector could adequately address. They don't remember that many of the most important advances grew out of controversy and were achieved only after great effort.

Our children may not remember, but older African Americans who could not eat in restaurants or sleep in hotels or vote in elections surely do. Women who were not admitted into certain professions remember; so do those whose reflexes slowed before the federal government passed Title IX and opened up collegiate athletics to their daughters and younger sisters. Asian Americans who were told not even to apply for some jobs and Jewish Americans who were prohibited from buying homes in certain neighborhoods remember. Hispanic Americans who had no legal recourse against exploitative employers remember. Native Americans who lacked access to medical services before the expansion of the Indian Health Service remember.

Men who went off to fight in World War II and were welcomed home by a grateful nation and the GI Bill of Rights remember. They went to college, started businesses, bought homes, received medical care at veterans' hospitals, and built the biggest, most prosperous middle class in the history of the world. No American is alive today who reached retirement before the advent of Social Security, but millions of older citizens depend totally on those checks and remember what their lives were like before Medicare.

Our children may not have witnessed any of these changes, but every noontime, millions of them fill school cafeterias, eating for little or no money thanks to the school lunch program the federal government started in 1946 after the discovery of widespread nutritional deficiencies among World War II draftees. Children breathe cleaner air in cities like Los Angeles, Pittsburgh, and Detroit because of the Clean Air Act. They fish, boat, and swim in once-hazardous bodies of water like Lake Erie and the Cuyahoga River because of the Clean Water Act. One in four of them relies on Medicaid for health care.

When we're reminded of the bounty and protection we enjoy, most of us, like that Peace Corps volunteer, are grateful. Our gratitude has its roots in a view of government that dates back to the Pilgrims and to the successive waves of immigrants who came to this country seeking religious and political freedom and better economic opportunities. In this view, government is an instrument both to promote the common good and to protect individuals' rights to life, liberty, and the pursuit of happiness.

Americans' attitudes about how the instrument of government should be used to achieve these ends have evolved with the nation's circumstances. As we grew from a rural, agricultural society into a more urbanized, industrial one, citizens began to expect government to protect them from economic downturns beyond their control and from corporate unscrupulousness and greed. They expected government to do what it could to encourage economic growth and to create jobs, so that a middle-class standard of living could be within reach of anyone who was willing to work hard. During the 1960s, a majority of our citizens supported government action to guarantee civil rights to all Americans, regardless of race, sex, religion, or national origin; to improve educational opportunities throughout our nation; to take more aggressive action to alleviate the problems of poverty; and to assure senior citizens access to quality health care. In the 1970s, most Americans supported federal action to protect the environment and to assure greater safety in the workplace.

By the 1980s, however, faced with mounting economic and social problems, Americans began to question the ability of government to solve them. Many began to believe government itself was the problem. These feelings, along with the constraints imposed by our mounting national debt, slowed the pace of federal activism. Even those of us who are mindful of the progress we have made through government recognize that there are limits to what it can do. We reject the utopian view that government can or should protect people from the consequences of personal decisions or that it can legislate complete peace, harmony, and brotherhood.

This skepticism, too, has its roots in our history. In part, it has been handed down to us by the colonists who came to America partly to escape the British government's arbitrary and absolute authority. They gave us the Constitution's checks and balances and the Bill of Rights, both strong limits on government. But Americans' wariness about government is also the legacy of the early adventurers, traders, and entrepreneurs who saw America as a land of rich natural resources waiting to be exploited by the fittest and most deserving among them.

Taken to its extreme, this perspective exalts private initiative and regards those who exercise it as deserving to flourish virtually unencumbered by any mandate to share the wealth or apply it toward solving our common problems or creating common opportunities. The role of government, in this view, is limited to functions like national defense and law enforcement. Thus individuals, families, and communities must exercise their own initiative and develop their own resources to maximize both public and private good. Any but the most minimal regulations to protect the rights of individuals and private enterprise and the smallest possible social safety net are seen as burdening us with wasteful taxation and a bureaucracy that saps the resources and entrepreneurial spirit of the citizenry and undermines the values of work and family.

Variations on these competing visions of the role of government and the rights of individuals exist all along the political spectrum. Most of us hold a point of view that exists somewhere between the extremes, even if we do not consciously articulate it that way. We may grumble about paying taxes, but we generally support programs like veterans' benefits, Social Security, and Medicare, along with public education, environmental protection, and some sort of social safety net for the poor, especially children. We are wary of both government interference with private initiative or personal belief and the excessive influence of special interests on the political system. Most of us would describe ourselves as "middle of the road"—liberal in some areas, conservative in others, moderate in most, neither exclusively pro- nor anti-government. We respect the unique power of government to meet certain social needs and acknowledge the need to limit its powers.

In times of profound and overwhelming social change like the present, however, extreme views hold out the appeal of simplicity. By ignoring the complexity of the forces that shape our personal and collective circumstances, they offer us scapegoats. Yet they fail to provide a viable pathway from the cold war to the global village.

At present, the extreme anti-government position is the noisiest one—or at least the one that gets the most attention from the media. There are few voices arguing for more government. Instead, the public debate is primarily between those who argue for much less government, period, and those who advocate a smaller, less bureaucratic, but still active government to meet the demands of the Information Age. Anti-government rhetoric appears to offer a vision of greater efficiency, self-reliance, and personal freedom. (For obvious reasons, it also usually enjoys greater financial backing and better-organized support.) Unfortunately, this rhetoric ignores what has historically been most valuable about our skepticism toward government—the emphasis it places on personal responsibility from all citizens. Instead, it argues against the excesses of government but not against those of the marketplace, where there is great power to disrupt the lives of workers, families, and communities. It even argues against the basic protections government extends to the well-being of individuals, families, and communities, without offering an alternative way of safeguarding them. In fact, its extreme case against government, often including intense personal attacks on government officials and political leaders, is designed not just to restrain government but to advance narrow religious, political, and economic agendas.

We must ask ourselves: Who benefits from the elimination of federal regulations that protect us from outbreaks of contaminated drinking water or cases of tainted meat? Who benefits from a decrease in federal pollution standards, or from the kind of massive deregulation that could allow companies to dump toxins into our nation's oceans, rivers, and lakes? Certainly not our families or our children.

Despite the resurgence of anti-government extremism, it is becoming clear that most Americans do not favor a radical dismantling of government. Instead of rollback, they want real reform. And when a strong case can be made, they still favor government action, as they have demonstrated recently in their support for measures like the Family and Medical Leave Act, the Brady Bill, and the new Direct Student Loan program.

Moreover, our whole history proves that a debate of extremes does little to reform government or to help solve problems that people confront in their daily lives. The clearest example of this is in the public debate over the assistance government should—or should not—provide to children and families. In a 1991 pastoral letter, "Putting Children and Families First," the United States

Catholic Conference cautioned: "There has been an unfortunate, unnecessary, and unreal polarization in discussions of the best way to help families." That polarization has garnered more sound bites than progress, presenting an incomplete and occasionally inaccurate picture of how families and children are affected by government actions. We've had more press coverage, for instance, about welfare benefits that affect nine million American children than about the dramatic expansion of the Earned Income Tax Credit, which is decreasing the taxes of lower-income working parents so that they and the more than twenty-five million children they are raising do not have to live in poverty.

This is but one example of the bottom-line truth about responsibility for the well-being of families and children: it is not an exclusively pro- or anti-government proposition. As the Catholic Conference noted:

> The most important work to help our children is done quietly—in our homes and neighborhoods, our parishes and community organizations. No government can love a child and no policy can substitute for a family's care, but clearly families can be helped or hurt in their irreplaceable roles. Government can either support or undermine families as they cope with the moral, social, and economic stresses of caring for children. . . . Some emphasize the primary role of moral values and personal responsibility, the sacrifices to be made and the personal behaviors to be avoided, but they often ignore or de-emphasize the broader forces which hurt families, e.g., the impact of economics, discrimination, and anti-family policies. Others emphasize the social and economic forces that undermine families and the responsibility of government to meet human needs, but

they often neglect the importance of basic values and personal responsibility. . . . The undeniable fact is that our children's future is shaped both by the values of their parents and the policies of our nation.

For the sake of our children, we ought to call an end to false debates between values and policies. Both personal and mutual responsibility are essential, and we should work to strengthen them at all levels of society. Let us admit that some government programs and personnel are efficient and effective, and others are not. Let us acknowledge that when it comes to the treatment of children, some individuals are evil, neglectful, or incompetent, but others are trying to do the best they can against daunting odds and deserve not our contempt but the help only we—through our government—can provide. Let us stop stereotyping government and individuals as absolute villains or absolute saviors, and recognize that each must be part of the solution. Let us use government, as we have in the past, to further the common good.

Our democracy has survived for more than two hundred years because at critical junctures a majority of the people and their representatives resisted the lure of extremism. Indeed, the founders wrote our Constitution in a way that permits us to be both principled and pragmatic in meeting the challenges of each new era. The willingness to compromise in the interest of maintaining stability enabled our nation to become not only a world power but also a pluralistic society promoting unprecedented tolerance for individual rights and freedoms.

Our strength, in other words, has rested in our determination to reject simplistic absolutes and to redefine and revitalize a productive middle ground, relinquishing outdated solutions and embracing new approaches. As President Lincoln said in his time, "The dogmas of the quiet past are inadequate to the stormy present. The occasion is piled high with difficulty, and we must rise with the occasion. As our case is new, so we must think anew and act anew."

In our time, the revitalization of this middle ground rests in a vision of government as smaller and less bureaucratic, a partner to, rather than a replacement for, personal initiative in tackling many of our deepest problems. The idea is not to weaken government to the point of ineffectuality but to make it leaner and more supple in fulfilling its basic responsibilities: (1) to build a strong, globally competitive economy that grows the middle class and shrinks the underclass; (2) to bring the American people together around the shared values of opportunity for and responsibility from all, to support families at work and at home, and to build communities that fulfill their obligations to families, the environment, and those who need and deserve support; (3) to keep America the world's strongest force for peace, freedom, democracy, and prosperity. The success of this vision can be seen in our recent progress on the economic front and declines in the rates of crime, welfare, poverty, and teen pregnancy, along with a reduction in government to its smallest size in thirty years.

The truth that guides all successful efforts to reinvent government is the recognition that government is not something outside us—something irrelevant or even alien to us—but *is* us. To acknowledge this is to acknowledge that government has a responsibility not only to provide essential services but to bring individuals and communities together. In a democracy, government is not "them" but "us," an endeavor that joins with volunteerism and the efforts of the private sector in sustaining our mutual obligations to our children, families, and communities.

Does this mean that we should overlook flaws and mistakes in government? Of course not. Criticism and public debate are vital to a democracy. They help us to weigh the costs of existing government services against the value of those services, and to consider the practical consequences of budget cuts or reforms to the delivery of those services. Constructive criticism also acknowledges the relationship of one decision to another, rather than lumping them together indiscriminately or viewing each in isolation. But rhetoric that demonizes or dehumanizes individuals or institutions—sometimes baldly, sometimes under the guise of contributing to the public debate—shares none of these characteristics.

If you are confused about the difference, try applying the invective you hear leveled broadly at "government programs" directly to the children who are among their most important beneficiaries. Are the children sustained by government-subsidized day care or fed by government- supported school breakfasts and lunches a "threat to our economic freedom" or guilty of "waste, fraud, and abuse"? Do programs to immunize or educate them "sap their initiative"?

The real problem for families today is the many challenges they face in raising their children according to the values they hold. That is, in part, what this book is about: how we can act together as a village to strengthen families and enable them to obtain from outside institutions the assistance they need to raise strong children and to protect themselves from influences that threaten to undermine parental authority. But many of those who wave the banner of family values seem more intent on promoting an anti-government political agenda than sensibly considering the roles played by all our institutions, including government, business, child care, schools, charities, the media, and religion.

At the beginning of this book, I mentioned that experts on child development know much more today than they did thirty years ago about what children need to develop well, but that their research is not well known to the general public. The research also charts a steady decline in conditions required for healthy development of all our children—not only the poor and minorities—about which the public deserves better information.

Cornell University psychologist Urie Bronfenbrenner evaluates the well-being of children by looking at all the interactions in their lives—at home and at school, in their families and peer groups, in their communities, and also at the hands of larger influences like the health care system, the media, and the economy. This ecological or environmental approach takes research out of the laboratory and into the world by linking the lives of children to the contexts in which they are led. This approach might also be described as the "child in the village" model of human development.

Using this model, Bronfenbrenner has predicted for years that problems we used to think happened only to "disadvantaged" children would confront us all before long. Economic and marital instability, combined with the hectic pace and many other aspects of contemporary American society, led him to conclude, as did other experts, that we face a silent crisis: "The present state of children and families in the United States represents the greatest domestic problem our nation has faced since the founding of the Republic. It is sapping our very roots."

By now, the crisis is painfully apparent to us all. But the solutions that would remedy it are too often ignored, and the means of implementing them are too often withheld. At a time when the well-being of children is under unprecedented threat, the balance of power is weighted heavily against them.

Government has to do its part to reverse the crisis affecting our children, and to do so it cannot retreat from its historic obligations to the poor and vulnerable. Yes, we must work to balance the national budget, but we cannot afford, in the long run—or for much longer in the short run—to balance it on the backs of children. They do not deserve to inherit our debts, but neither should they be denied a fair chance at a standard of living that includes health care, good education, a protected environment, safe streets, and economic opportunity. Children, after all, are citizens too.

Let Us Build a Village
Worthy of Our Children

---

*A civilization flourishes when people plant trees
under whose shade they will never sit.*

GREEK PROVERB

As I finished this book, my husband and I had just come home from a trip to Northern Ireland, where peace had returned after twenty-five years of violent sectarian conflict. For the first time in recent memory, children were able to live in relative safety and comfort as they went about their daily lives. Nine-year-old Catherine Hamill introduced my husband at a Belfast factory where Catholic and Protestant workers still enter through separate doors but work side by side. "My first daddy died in the Troubles," she said. "It was the saddest day of my life. I still think of him. Now it is nice and peaceful. I like having peace and quiet for a change, instead of people shooting and killing. My . . . wish is that peace and love will last in Ireland forever."

During our brief stay, we also met parents—both Catholics and Protestants—who had lost children to bombs and guns. Yet they had overcome their personal anguish to put aside ancient grudges and work to rebuild the larger community. They were determined to pass on to the next generation a legacy of peace rather than of fear, hatred, and mistrust.

The threats to the innocence, promise, and lives of American children are no less severe, and the "troubles" that confront us are no less daunting. As Sylvia Ann Hewlett, founder of the National Parenting Association, has observed, "In the contemporary world it is a hard, lonely struggle, this business of putting children first."

I think we have no choice but to try. Children are like the tiny figures at the center of the nesting dolls for which Russian folk artists are famous. The children are cradled in the family, which is primarily responsible for their passage from infancy to adulthood. But around the family are the larger settings of neighborhood, school, church, workplace, community, culture, economy, society, nation, and world, which affect children directly or through the well-being of their families.

Each of us participates in several of these interlocking layers of the village. Each of us, therefore, has the opportunity and responsibility to protect and nurture children. We owe it to them to do what we can to better their lives every day—as parents and through the myriad choices we make as employers, workers, consumers, volunteers, and citizens. We owe it to them to set higher expectations for ourselves. We must stop making excuses for why we can't give our children what they need at home and beyond to become healthy, well-educated, empathetic, and productive adults.

I'm often asked what I would like to see happen above all else in our country and in our world. There are so many things to pray for, so many things to work for. But certainly my answer would be a world in which all children are loved and cared for—first by the families into which they are born, and then by all of us who are linked to them and to one another.

Nothing is more important to our shared future than the well-being of children. For children are at our core—not only as vulnerable beings in need of love and care but as a moral touchstone amidst the complexity and contentiousness of modern life. Just as it takes a village to raise a child, it takes children to raise up a village to become all it should be. The village we build with them in mind will be a better place for us all.

Notes

31 *Further, the rise in divorce:* Between 1995 and 2000, the number of poor children fell more than 20 percent, from 14.7 million to 11.6 million children. However, in the last five years, child poverty has made up nearly half its 1990s decline. According to the Census Bureau, in 2005, 12.9 million children lived in poverty, that is more than one in six. (U.S. Census Bureau, *Income, Poverty, and Health Insurance Coverage in the United States: 2005,* August 2006.)

37 *A long-term study of children:* In 2002, a group of scientists discovered a gene that provides people with more resilience in the face of trauma, allowing them to better recover from adversity. They found that people who have one "short" segment of this gene called an *allele* are more prone to depression and less likely to bounce back from childhood trauma. (Avshalom Caspi et al., "Role of Genotype in the Cycle of Violence in Maltreated Children," *Science,* August 2, 2002, vol. 297, no. 5582, pp. 851–54.) In 2003, Joan Kaufman, a Yale psychiatry professor, studied the genetic and relationship history of a group of children in Connecticut who were victims of abuse or neglect. She found that kids who had the "short" resilience gene, yet had an adult on whom they could count, had levels of depression as low as those of abused children with the protective gene, and nearly as low as those of children who had not been abused. (Joan Kaufman et al., "Social Supports and Seratonin Transporter Gene Moderate Depression in Maltreated Children, *Proceedings of the National Academy of Sciences,* November 24, 2004.)

39 *The village can take it further:* Many of the ideas from the first edition of this book about how to refocus the foster care system on the best interests of the child were later included in the Adoption and Safe Families Act of 1997, which I worked on with the late Republican Senator John Chafee of Rhode

Island and others. After the passage of that legislation, foster adoptions increased 64 percent nationwide, from 31,030 the year the law passed to 51,000 last year. (Connie Maben, "Foster Adoption Law Brings Success, Challenges," Associated Press, June 28, 2006.) As First Lady, I met many young people aging out of foster care who had little of the emotional, social, and financial support families provide. I worked with Senator Chafee and Democratic Senator Jay Rockefeller of West Virginia on the Foster Care Independence Act of 1999, which provides young people aging out of foster care with support services, including access to health care, educational opportunities, job training, housing assistance, and counseling. In the Senate, we passed a law that provides financial incentives to people who adopt older children and to help reduce the obstacles they face.

47 *The first three years of life*: Experts now believe that the brain is particularly sensitive to new information for the first five years of life, not the first three, and that children learn at an extraordinary rate from zero to five. (Jack P. Shonkoff and Debrah A. Phillips, eds., *From Neurons to Neighborhoods: The Science of Early Childhood Development*, National Academies Press, 2000, p. 5.)

50 *A similar study, best known as the Abecedarian Project*: Federal Reserve economist Rob Grunewald and Nobel laureate economist James Heckman have estimated that every dollar invested in programs like Abecedarian returns between $3 and $17 to society, for total lifetime returns running as much as $276,000 per student. They published these finding in *Zero to Three*, a journal focused on the needs of young children, in July of 2006. (James Heckman, Rob Grunewald, and Arthur Reynolds, "The Dollars and Cents of Investing Early: Cost Benefit Analysis in Early Care and Education," *Zero to Three*, July 2006, vol. 26, no. 6, pp. 10–17.) That is why as senator I have fought to protect programs like Head Start and Early Head Start, which provide high-quality care to low-income children, from attempts to dismantle or undermine them.

60 *If breast-feeding is a problem*: The American Academy of Pediatrics now urges new mothers to breast-feed for as long as they can, ideally twelve months. (American Academy of Pediatrics Work Group on Breastfeeding, "Breastfeeding and the Use of Human Milk," *Pediatrics*, 1997, vol. 100, pp. 1035–39.) Breast-feeding provides a boost to immune systems, helps kids fight off infections, and may even prevent chronic disease later in life. Today, 73 percent of mothers breast-feed their newborns, according to the Centers for Disease Control and Prevention. But that number falls below 50 percent after six months, even though breast-feeding during those later months is still critical to children's health and development. (*New York Times*, "On the Job, Nursing Mothers Are Finding a 2-Class System," September 1, 2006.)

62 *And it is tragic that our country does not do more*: In the last few years, we've seen major breakthroughs in research and effectiveness of contraceptives. For example, Plan B is a new emergency contraceptive that can prevent a pregnancy after another contraceptive has failed or after unprotected sex. I fought for years to get Plan B on the market, so that fewer women will face the choice of abortion. It is now available for over-the-counter use by adult women. I have also proposed Prevention First, a bill that focuses on prevention of unwanted pregnancies through comprehensive education, emphasizing responsible decision-making and expanded access to contraception. With these efforts, it's my hope that the abortion rate will fall further.

74 *Thanks in part to Ruggiero's testimony*: In September of 1996, Congress passed and my husband signed into law the Newborns' and Mothers' Health Protection Act of 1996, commonly known as the drive-by deliveries law, which required plans that offer maternity coverage to pay for at least a forty-eight-hour hospital stay following childbirth (a ninety-six-hour stay in the case of a cesarean section). (U.S. Department of Labor. [2006] *Fact Sheet: Newborns' and Mothers' Health Protection Act*, September 27, 2006.)

87 *The biggest difference among the various households:* We've learned that, beyond talking, having books in the house is also important. A 2005 national study found that minority children were not only less likely to be read to by their parents but also possessed substantially fewer children's books in the household than white children, putting minority children at a distinct disadvantage in reading, language skills, and school achievement. White families had two times the number of books in their home that black families did. (G. Flores, S. C. Tomany-Korman, and L. Olson. "Does Disadvantage Start at Home? Racial and Ethnic Disparities in Health-Related Early Childhood Home Routines and Safety Practices," *Archives of Pediatrics and Adolescent Medicine*, 2005, vol. 159, pp. 158–65.)

92 *Family meals are a time-honored and important ritual*: A study by Diane Beals at Harvard found that mealtime conversations during the preschool years are a strong predictor of literacy development, and are a critical element of children successfully developing early language skills. (David K. Dickinson, Ed.D., and Patton O. Tabors, Ed.D., eds. *Young Children Learning at Home and School*, chap. 4: Diane E. Beals, "Eating and Reading: Links Between Family Conversations with Preschoolers and Later Language and Literacy," 2001.)

101 *In 1993, as part of a larger initiative:* In 1992, just 55 percent of three-year-old children received all the routinely recommended childhood vaccines; in 1996, three years after the Vaccines for Children bill passed, the rate climbed to 78 percent. (CDC, "Status Report on the Childhood Immunization Initiative: National, State, and Urban Area Vaccination Coverage Lev-

els Among Children Aged 19–35 Months—United States, 1996," July 25, 1997, vol. 46, no. 29, pp. 657–64.) In 2004, more than 95 percent of all children received the full, more ambitious schedule of routinely recommended childhood vaccinations. (CDC, "Vaccination Coverage Among Children Entering School—United States, 2003–04 School Year," *Morbidity and Mortality Weekly Report*, November 12, 2004, vol. 53, no. 44, pp. 1041–44.) In 2003, the national Institute of Medicine recommended using the Vaccines for Children program as a model for adult vaccination. (Institute of Medicine, *Financing Vaccines in the 21st Century: Assuring Access and Availability*, National Academies Press, 2003.)

107 *Diet alone does not account for the dramatic increase*: At present, approximately 9 million children over six years of age are considered obese. (Institute of Medicine, "Childhood Obesity in the United States: Facts and Figures," September 2004.) Obesity is on the verge of surpassing smoking as the single highest preventable cause of death for all Americans (CDC, "Actual Causes of Death in the United States, 2000," March 9, 2004); and an Emory University study found that it accounted for a 27 percent increase in health care costs between 1987 and 2001 (Kenneth E. Thorpe et al., "Trends: The Impact of Obesity on Rising Medical Spending," *Health Affairs*, October 20, 2004).

111 *Today there are more than ten million children*: As First Lady, I worked with members of Congress in creating the State Children's Health Insurance Program (SCHIP) in the summer of 1997. It made a tremendous investment in the expansion of children's health insurance, and it has had tremendous results. Today, because of SCHIP the number of children who lack health insurance coverage has dropped from over 10 million in 1995 to some 8.3 million kids in 2005. However, the numbers of uninsured have grown in the general population over the last ten years. In 1996, 41.7 million Americans did not have health insurance; today 46.6 million Americans do not have coverage. (National Center for Health Statistics, June 2006; Carmen DeNavas-Walt, Bernadette D. Proctor, and Cheryl Hill Lee, U.S. Census Bureau, Current Population Reports, P60–231, *Income, Poverty, and Health Insurance Coverage in the United States: 2005*, U.S. Government Printing Office, Washington, D.C., 2006.)

121 *Three times as many children die each year*: Nontraffic automobile accidents, most frequently involving a vehicle backing up, account for one hundred deaths per year. The average age of victims is one year, and in 70 percent of cases, a parent, relative, or close friend is behind the wheel. (Kids and Cars, Child Safety Advocates Join Victims on Capitol Hill to Push for Passage of Tougher Laws to Keep Children Safe in and Around Cars, www.kidsandcars.org, March 9, 2006.) In 2005, I proposed the Cameron Gulbransen Kids and Cars Safety Act, which would prevent child deaths in backing

incidents by requiring a warning system to ensure that drivers can detect the presence of a person or object behind the vehicle. It would also require that power windows automatically reverse direction when they detect an obstruction, to prevent children from being trapped, injured, or killed.

126 *Twenty-five thousand new police officers are being trained:* By the end of my husband's term, the Community Oriented Policing Services (COPS) program had funded over 100,000 police officers. (U.S. Department of Justice, Office of Community Oriented Policing Services, *Attorney General's Report to Congress*, Washington, D.C., 2006.) However, over the last five years, the program has been cut from $8.8 billion to $3 billion, and only 25,000 police officers were hired between 2001 and 2005. (Democratic Policy Committee, *Bush Republicans Cut Law Enforcement Funding, Crime Rate Increases at the Fastest Rate in Fifteen Years*; U.S. Department of Justice, Community Oriented Policing Services, "COPS Count Data Surveys 2001–2005," Washington, D.C., 2006.) Federal statistics show that between 2004 and 2005 violent crime increased by 2.3 percent. This was the first increase since 2001. A preliminary FBI report in June 2006 on crimes reported to police showed a 4.8 percent increase in the number of murders and 4.5 percent increase in the number of robberies in 2005. (Michael J. Sniffen, "Nation's Crime Rate Hits 32-Year Low," Associated Press, September 11, 2006.)

130 *Whatever the reasons for the apparent increase:* Over the last several years, there has been a dramatic increase in media stories of abducted and abused children. While there has not been an increase in the overall numbers of such cases, many families, and children, are more fearful. I have pushed for legislation that would appoint a national coordinator for AMBER alerts, an alert system for missing children; provide additional protections for children; and establish stricter punishments for sex offenders. That legislation passed the Congress in 2003.

160 *The anthropologist Margaret Mead felt that exposure to religion:* A 2004 study of the effects the sexual messages on television have on children found that raising children with religious belief lowers the probability that they will engage in early sexual experimentation, as does having committed and involved parents. (Rebecca L. Collins et al., "Watching Sex on Television Predicts Adolescent Initiation of Sexual Behavior," *Pediatrics*, 2004, vol. 114, pp. 280–89.)

185 *Creating a framework for service:* In the last five years, we have seen an upsurge in volunteerism. Applications to Teach for America, which recruits graduates for underserved urban and rural areas, hit almost 19,000 this year, nearly triple the number in 2000; in 2006, the Peace Corps took 7,810 volunteers—the largest number in thirty years—from more than 11,500 applicants in 2005, up more than 20 percent over the year 2000; and AmeriCorps*VISTA (Volunteers in Service to America), which pairs young

people with nonprofit organizations, has had a 50 percent jump in applicants since 2004. (Beth Walton, "Volunteer Rates Hit Record Numbers," *USA Today*, July 7, 2006, nat. ed., p. 1a.) This year, I introduced legislation to create and fund a U.S. Public Service Academy modeled after the nation's military service academies. The school would provide an education to 5,000 undergraduates, and graduates would be required to work five years in public service.

198 *It may be that women will achieve*: A Radcliffe survey conducted in 2000 found that more than 70 percent of men under forty said they would give up pay to spend more time with their families, and 82 percent said family comes first. (Radcliffe Public Policy Center, *Life's Work: Generational Attitudes Toward Work and Life Integration*, 2000.) According to new research by Professor Suzanne Bianchi for the Russell Sage Foundation, the time married fathers spend on child care had more than doubled since 1965, from 2.6 hours a week to 6.5 hours. (Robert Pear, "Married and Single Parents Spending More Time With Children, Study Finds," *New York Times*, October 17, 2006.)

212 *Child care facilities for infants and toddlers:* A 2006 study of Quebec's universal child-care system found that children under five in full-time center-based care showed greater rates of aggression, anxiety, and developmental delay. (Michael Baker, Jonathan Gruber, and Kevin Milligan, "Universal Childcare, Maternal Labor Supply, and Family Well-Being," National Bureau of Economic Research, Working Paper No. 11832, June 2006). However, studies of Abecedarian and other high-quality, intensive early learning programs have demonstrated dramatic positive results for low-income children.(See Heckman et al. above, in note for p. 50.) Unfortunately, high-quality day care isn't available to everyone—nationally known pediatric specialists T. Berry Brazelton and Stanley Greenspan estimate that only 10 percent of American children had access to truly high-quality day care—and many parents can't afford to stay home to take care of their children. (T. Berry Brazelton and Stanley I. Greenspan, *The Irreducible Needs of Children*, 2000, p. xiii, from a 1995 University of Colorado study.) I proposed the Choices in Childcare Act to allow lower-income parents who receive government support for child care to use the subsidies to defray the cost of caring for their young children themselves.

240 *Education is fundamental to our country's future*: The standards and accountability movement has grown dramatically over the last decade. The No Child Left Behind Act became law, and it has laid bare the problems in many of our poorest, worst-performing schools. We can no longer say that we didn't know that these schools were failing some of our most vulnerable kids. To improve the quality of education, we need to improve instruction in the classroom. Nationwide, two million teachers will leave teaching over the next decade. New York City already loses 30 percent more math

teachers and 22 percent more science teachers than it certifies every year. In 2001, I proposed the National Teacher Corps, which brings teachers into the classroom, and a new initiative that would provide more schools with strong principals. Both became law.

252 *Children themselves report:* A 2004 study for the National Institute of Child Health and Human Development found that teens who watch a lot of television with sexual content are more likely to initiate intercourse in the following year. This was true for girls and boys, regardless of race. Overexposure to highly sexed television made kids act older—twelve-year-olds behaved like fourteen-year-olds. (Rebecca L. Collins et al., "Watching Sex on Television Predicts Adolescent Initiation of Sexual Behavior," *Pediatrics, vol.* 114 (2004)pp. 280–89.) Another study published in the journal *Pediatrics* showed that boys and girls, across all races and economic groups, who listened to sexually degrading lyrics were more likely to start sexual experimentation sooner. (Steven C. Martino et al., "Exposure to Degrading Versus Nondegrading Music Lyrics and Sexual Behavior," *Pediatrics,* vol. 118 (2006), pp. 430–41.) While this research is critical, there are still more questions about the effects of media on our children, especially young children. I've introduced CAMRA—the Children and Media Research Advancement Act. The bill, which recently passed the Senate, coordinates and funds new federal research on the effects of viewing and using electronic media, including television, computers, video games, and the Internet, on children's cognitive, social, physical, and psychological development.

252 *Whether, and under what circumstances, the violence people see on television:* A 2005 study by researchers at Indiana University School of Medicine showed that playing violent video games triggers unusual brain activity among kids who are most vulnerable to aggression and misbehavior. (Vincent P. Matthews et al., "Media Violence Exposure and Frontal Lobe Activation Measured by Functional Magnetic Resonance Imaging in Aggressive and Nonaggressive Adolescents," *Journal of Computer Assisted Tomography,* vol. 29, no.9 (2005), pp. 287–92.) Violent video games are getting into the hands of our kids at younger and younger ages. The National Institute on Media and the Family's 2003 study found that 50 percent of boys between the ages of seven and fourteen successfully purchased M-rated video games (games appropriate only for people aged seventeen or older), and an astonishing 87 percent of boys play M-rated games. Furthermore, nearly a quarter of retailers in the study don't even understand the ratings they are supposed to enforce, and only half of the stores train employees in the use of the ratings. (David Walsh, et al., "Eighth Annual MediaWise Video Game Report Card," *National Institute on Media and the Family,* vol. 8 [December 2003].) Yet, video game makers continue to push the envelope. A year ago, the makers of Grand Theft Auto: San Andreas, sold a game con-

taining graphic pornography that anyone could unlock with instructions widely available on the Internet. I called attention to these games, and because of the public outrage that followed, they were pulled off store shelves.

268 *But spurred on by cultural messages:* James McNeal, the nation's most influential estimator of the size of the children's market, believes that the amount of advertising and marketing dollars directed at children rose more than one hundred times between 1983 and 2004. (Juliet Schor, *Born to Buy: The Commercialized Child and the New Consumer Culture,* 2005 [paperback], p. 21). Too many kids are getting the message that our worth is measured by what we can buy. A recent national survey found that more than a third of all children aged nine to fourteen would rather spend time buying things than doing almost anything else, more than a third "really like kids that have special games or clothes," more than half agree that "when you grow up, the more money you have, the happier you are," and 62 percent say that "the only kind of job I want when I grow up is one that gets me a lot of money." (Marvin E. Goldberg et al., "Understanding Materialism Among Youth," *Journal of Consumer Psychology,* vol. 13, no. 3, pp. 278–88.)

272 *Even workers' jobs may be sacrificed:* Today, our globalized economy has seen an increase in the number of jobs outsourced to other countries. Goldman Sachs has estimated that 400,000 to 600,000 professional services jobs (or about 2–3 percent of employment in that sector) were offshored in the first years of the decade. (Andrew Tilton, "The 'Giant Sucking Sound' Is Fading," *Goldman Sachs US Economics Analyst,* March 19, 2004.) Goldman estimates that another 6 million jobs could be lost over the following ten years. (Andrew Tilton, "Offshoring: Where Have All the Jobs Gone?," *Goldman Sachs US Economics Analyst,* September 19, 2003.) Former Vice Chairman of the Federal Reserve Alan Blinder projects that 42 million jobs, or 25–35 percent of all services could be outsourced in the next several decades. (Alan S. Blinder, "Offshoring: The Next Industrial Revolution," *Foreign Affairs,* March-April 2006.)

276 *There are additional actions we can take*: The last minimum-wage increase was in 1996, when Congress and the president raised it to $5.15 an hour. However, the impact of the 1996–97 increase has been eroded by inflation. (Economic Policy Institute, *Minimum Wage: EPI Issue Guide,* August 2006.) Adjusting for inflation, the minimum wage is at its lowest point in fifty years. (Center for Economic and Policy Research, *Federal Minimum Wage at Lowest Point in 50 Years,* June 19, 2006.) While minimum-wage workers have not had a single raise, Congress has given itself $31,600 in pay raises. In the Senate, I've proposed blocking Congress from giving itself another pay raise until it lifts wages for workers.

292 *Government has to do its part*: After this book was written, my husband and

the Congress not only balanced the budget for the first time in a decade, but began to run federal budget surpluses. In 2000, the Congressional Budget Office projected federal budget surpluses for the foreseeable future. However, after 2000, our federal budget went from record surpluses to record deficits again. In 1996, our national debt was $5.2 trillion; as of September 2006, our national debt has reached $8.4 trillion. (1996 U.S. Treasury, "Historical Debt Outstanding," 2006, *http://www.publicdebt.treas .gov/opd/opd.htm*; U.S. Treasury, "The Debt to the Penny and Who Holds It," 2006, *http://www.publicdebt.treas.gov/opd/opd.htm*.) Today, every baby born in America starts life with $28,000 of our national debt—a birth tax that is higher than it has ever been in our nation's history. (House Budget Committee, "Your Share of the National Debt, 2006," extrapolated from the number of households in: Carmen DeNavas-Walt, Bernadette D. Proctor, and Cheryl Hill Lee, U.S. Census Bureau, Current Population Reports, P60–231, *Income, Poverty, and Health Insurance Coverage in the United States: 2005*, U.S. Government Printing Office, Washington, D.C., 2006; U.S. Treasury, "The Debt to the Penny and Who Holds It.")

ACKNOWLEDGMENTS

———————

IT TAKES A village to bring a book into the world, as anyone who has written one knows. Many people have helped me to complete this one, sometimes without even knowing it. They are so numerous that I will not even attempt to acknowledge them individually, for fear that I might leave someone out. Instead, I would like to thank those who encouraged and advised, read and reacted; those who typed and retyped, edited, copyedited, proofread, designed, set type, and printed; and those who kept the engines of daily life humming the whole time. The opinions expressed in this book are my own, as is the responsibility for any errors it may contain. Yet I am indebted for my ideas—and for any contribution they make to public and private debates and agendas—to a long line of family and friends, teachers and classmates, colleagues and mentors; to the many tireless and often unheralded experts and advocates whose work I have been privileged to know; and most of all, to the millions of families and children who are building tomorrow's villages.

Index

Page numbers beginning with 299 refer to Notes.

Picture Credits